A Long Home

To Molly with best wishes
Norma

By
Norma Mudd

MAPLE
PUBLISHERS

A Long Way Home

Author: Norma Mudd

Copyright © Norma Mudd (2022)

The right of Norma Mudd to be identified as author of this work has been asserted by the author in accordance with section 77 and 78 of the Copyright, Designs and Patents Act 1988.

First Published in 2022

ISBN 978-1-915492-84-5 (Paperback)

Book Cover Design and Layout by:
    White Magic Studios
    www.whitemagicstudios.co.uk

Published by:
    Maple Publishers
    1 Brunel Way,
    Slough,
    SL1 1FQ, UK
    www.maplepublishers.com

A CIP catalogue record for this title is available from the British Library.

All rights reserved. No part of this book may be reproduced or translated by any form or by any means, electronic or mechanical, including photocopying, recording or by any information storage and retrieval system without written permission from the author.

The book is a mixture of fact and fiction. Some names, characters, and incidents are either the product of the author's imagination or used in a fictitious manner. Any resemblance to actual people living or dead, events or locales is entirely coincidental, and the Publisher hereby disclaims any responsibility for them.

ACKNOWLEDGEMENTS

My very special thanks are given to my daughter, Cathy. Without her encouragement this book would never have been written. She has given me advice and her valuable time throughout the writing and the editing process.

Thanks are also due to my granddaughter, Marianne who designed and painted the cover of the book.

Contents

Chapter 1 – A Problem for Pat 7
Chapter 2 – The Famine. (Cartron, County Sligo, 1845) 10
Chapter 3 – Aftermath 13
Chapter 4 – The Tooey Family 16
Chapter 5 – Kitty in School 20
Chapter 6 – The Rising of the Moon (May 1846) 24
Chapter 7 – We Want Food (Sligo, May 1846) 29
Chapter 8 – Harvest Time (August 1870) 35
Chapter 9 – Return to Ireland 40
Chapter 10 – Changes (1874) 44
Chapter 11 – Kitty in Riverstown (March 1877) 50
Chapter 12 – Blackberry Picking (August, 1877) 56
Chapter 13 – Pat and Kitty 63
Chapter 14 – Fate's Cruel Trick 71
Chapter 15 – Trials 76
Chapter 16 – St Joseph's (December 1877) 79
Chapter 17 – Griddle Cakes (1878) 84
Chapter 18 – Decisions 89
Chapter 19 – The Secret is 'Out' 92
Chapter 20 – Cards On the Table 99
Chapter 21 – More Decisions 104
Chapter 22 – Anne Calls the Shots 108
Chapter 23 – The Sting 115

Chapter 24 – Crossing the Irish Sea 120

Chapter 25 – Enter Mrs Rourke 126

Chapter 26 – Looking for Work... 131

Chapter 27 – Sunday in Wigan 137

Chapter 28 – 'The Packet' 143

Chapter 29 – The Night Shift.. 147

Chapter 30 – Sad News and New Friends... 151

Chapter 31 – Letters and a Tram Ride 155

Chapter 32 – Robert.. 160

Chapter 33 – Kitty is Confused... 166

Chapter 34 – Kitty Decides 170

Chapter 35 – Married Life 175

Chapter 36 – Aftermath... 183

Chapter 37 – The Move.. 188

Chapter 38 – Lizzie.. 192

Chapter 39 – News from Ireland 197

Chapter 40 – Mary Catherine... 201

Chapter 41 – Mrs Rourke Takes Charge 205

Chapter 42 – Bad Days for Robert 209

Chapter 43 – Mrs Rourke is Hatless.. 212

Chapter 44 – A Wake 217

Chapter 45 – Desperate Times 221

Chapter 46 – Lizzie (1885) 226

Chapter 47 – A Special Letter 231

Chapter 48 – A Time of Changes... 235

Chapter 49 – Suffragettes 240

Chapter 50 – Llandudno 243

Chapter 51 – Romance for Anne 246

Chapter 52 – Anne and Catherine (1910) 250

Chapter 53 – Bolton Market 255

Chapter 54 – Events up to 1914 258

Chapter 55 – Anne and Harry 264

Chapter 56 – 1914 270

Chapter 57 – War Years (1915) 274

Chapter 58 – A Tragic Fall (1916) 278

Chapter 59 – Robert's Wake 284

Chapter 60 – Kitty In Bolton (1916-17) 288

Chapter 61 – Kitty in Bolton (1917 – 1918) 293

Chapter 62 – The War's End – 'Spanish' Flu (1918) 298

Chapter 63 – Post-War Developments (1919) 304

Chapter 64 – Time to Leave 308

Chapter 65 – Bottling Wood 313

Chapter 66 – Riverstown 317

Chapter 67 – World events. Kathleen's New 'Friend' 327

Chapter 68 – Visitors for Kitty 335

Chapter 69 – Surprising News From Anne 340

Chapter 70 – Kitty's Final Journey 346

Chapter 1

A Problem for Pat

Early March 1878

Pat arrived at the landlord's estate just as the sun rose, and quickly resumed his work of preparing the ground ready for planting the potatoes which, according to tradition, all had to be done by St Patrick's day on the 17th. He worked the manure well into the ground, though his strong and usually regular thrusts had become increasingly violent and haphazard. Pondering still on the news he'd had from his wife, Anne, he exclaimed, "Jesus, Mary and Joseph, what will I be doin' now? Workin' every hour God sends to feed three children, and now I'm told there's another on the way!"

With another frenzied thrust of the spade, he continued his tirade, "And, more importantly, what in God's name am I goin' to tell my lovely Kitty now?"

No sooner had he said her name, than forty-eight year old Pat's thoughts turned to his life before Kitty's arrival in Riverstown some eight months earlier. A life before everything had been turned completely topsy-turvy.

True, it had been a hard but regularly patterned life. Most of the day he'd worked on the 120 acres of land belonging to Landlord 'Miser' Murray. Sometimes he was asked to transport cereal crops and vegetables to a nearby pub and guest house, the 'Coaching House.' Spare time was spent in growing vegetables on his own small plot of land (gairdeen). However, 'Miser Murray' charged such a high rent - like many other landlords - that he had to sell most of his best vegetables to help complement his meagre wages. Luckily, he usually managed to smuggle a few of these on the cart along with Murray's stuff, and was then paid a fair price for them by Mr Laverty, proprietor of the pub.

Indeed, Pat's only relief from seemingly endless work came on Saturday nights when men from the village got together for a few 'jars' of porter and he entertained them with jigs played on his penny whistle.

However, in June last year, seated on Murray's cart pulled by the donkey, Molly, he'd driven up to the Coaching House's rear entrance when suddenly, he'd had to bring her to a halt. Out of the door ran four-year-old Thomas, son of the proprietor, Mr Laverty. On his heels came a striking young woman, auburn curls peeping from beneath her white cap as she ran out and bent to catch him firmly by the hand, saying sternly, "Now Master Thomas, ye know full well that ye shouldn't be running out into the yard! Whatever would your father say if he knew?"

The young boy stopped, turned to face her, flung his arms round her neck and planted a kiss on her cheek saying, "Oh Miss Kitty, I'm sorry, please don't tell Daddy and I'll be your friend. forever."

The recipient of the kiss looked somewhat surprised, replying, "Well Master Thomas, just ye make sure it never happens again! Also, I'll have less of that blarney!"

With that, firmly taking his hand again, she began to return with him to the kitchen, seemingly unaware of Pat looking at her in undisguised admiration. It was only when she was about to go inside that she looked round and saw Pat on his cart.

Smiling, Pat addressed her. "Good day, Miss Kitty. Now I'm wonderin' what it would take for *me* to be allowed to put me arms round that charmin' neck of yours?"

Bright green eyes looked back at him scornfully. "Well now, I can tell ye, it'd take a far better man than the likes of you! Now get on with your business here - and then get back to your wife and children."

With that, Kitty marched Thomas swiftly indoors.

Pat sat there - nonplussed and silent.

Tallish, bearded and still ruggedly handsome, though now with greying hair, Pat usually found his harmless banter was appreciated by the ladies, so this put-down was totally unexpected. After a few minutes of thought, he gave a shrug and drove on through the large yard to make his delivery.

That night though, Pat's usual sound sleep was disturbed by a pair of green eyes looking out at him mockingly from a mass of red hair.

Chapter 2

The Famine. (Cartron, County Sligo, 1845)

Fourteen-year old Pat and Dad, Francis, yawned as they ate their oatmeal porridge. It was already daybreak and the two would soon be out bringing in the pratie crop from landlord Paisley's extensive land. Pat glanced enviously at eight-year old sister, Anne, who was still sleeping on her straw mattress by the kitchen fire. She'd fallen and sprained her wrist whilst helping Mam carry water from the well the previous day and so had been allowed to sleep on a bit longer.

"Never mind" Pat thought to himself, "it's been a good summer and all our crops have done well this year so me and Dad should be able to get in enough praties to be able to keep a load for ourselves to sell at the Saturday fair".

Nevertheless, Pat couldn't resist going over to Anne once he'd downed his porridge, bowing dramatically, and saying, "Good mornin' m'lady. I'm hopin' ye'll be strong enough to help with the pittin' once the praties are brought back by those not too *lazy* to work!" Mam, now giving a final stir to the pan of food she'd been preparing for the livestock, turned to him, putting a finger of 'sh' to her lips.

But at her brother's voice, Anne stirred, sat up, and pulled out her tongue, her injured wrist now resting on the sheet which covered it. Pat feigned giving the wrist a slap, but then followed the action immediately by fondly tousling her hair. Dad was waiting none too patiently for him at the kitchen door, so he turned and left her with a quick wave of the hand.

The two, armed with forks and their usual morning light meal of buttermilk, oatmeal water and soda bread, set off. Already, the sun was feeling warm on their backs. In fact, Pat, looking up, noted the swooping graceful flight of a swallow.

"That's right," he called to it, "make the most of this good summer before ye go south."

Father and son worked steadily until nine o'clock when they sat down thankfully in the shade of the hawthorn hedge. Pat immediately grabbed the jug of oatmeal water, gulping it down thirstily. Francis watched only for a moment before giving his greedy son a clip round the ear, exclaiming, "Don't you be drinking it all - sure yer still only a gasureen!" Feeling more hurt by the implication that he was only a young lad, Pat turned to reply, but Dad was now looking up at the sky and said warningly, "Jaysus, Pat, would ye look over to your right! I'm not likin' those great black clouds - and they seem to be comin' nearer!"

Pat did as instructed. Dad was right! Within minutes the clouds were overhead and drops of rain were falling ominously. Both decided to carry on working, hoping that the rain clouds would pass quickly. A vain hope as thunder, lightning and heavy rain followed quickly, drenching both them and the pratie crops.

Back in their cottage, Mam and Anne (her wrist now bandaged in a rag soaked in a comfrey decoction) helped them to store the day's produce in their storage pit. Mam, ever a worrier, said, "We should be prayin' that this storm isn't goin' to ruin the rest of the pratie crop!"

"Now don't ye be worrying yourself about that, Mam, this is the best crop we've had fer years, and the weather tomorrow's goin' to be just fine." was Pat's reassuring reply.

A little later that evening, Pat noticed that Anne still didn't seem as full of energy as usual and before long she was lying down on her mattress by the dying fire. Wanting to cheer up his baby sister - as well as Mam- he took out his whistle and began playing a jig he'd heard when with Dad and the locals.

"Come on Annie, let's see you dance." he urged. But Anne, shook her head, replying, "I'll let my fingers dance for ye."

And, with her 'good' hand, she began tapping out the fast rhythm in perfect time. Mam, happy to see her daughter joining in, was soon clapping along as well, and smiling indulgently at her son. Dad just sat smoking his clay pipe, still dwelling on the recent, unexpected storm.

But next day, sure enough, Pat's forecast had been correct. In fact, he and Dad worked during most of the month on crops which promised to be abundant. And it was still fine weather on a Tuesday morning near the end of August when the two Dowds set out to work in quite good spirits. They'd been working for about half-an-hour when Francis stopped abruptly as he noticed small black spots on one of the potato leaves. Alarmed, he found the same spots visible on a couple more of the crops and called urgently to his son working a little distance away. "Pat! Would ye take a good look at some of the leaves on the spuds and tell me what ye see." A puzzled Pat did as he was told, and soon he too was looking at small black spots on some of the potato leaves. After a few moments of consideration, he declared, "Well now Dad, I can see what ye mean all right but the spuds are fine, sure they'll still be the best tasting ones we've had for years!"

Francis wasn't as optimistic; he'd been a child in the terrible famine of 1817 and was dreading the same thing happening again. Nevertheless, he called to his son, "Aye ye might be right lad, so let's just get on with the job!"

But within three days, Mam, who was checking the newly dug potatoes boiling on their peat fire, let out a cry of horror. "Frankie, can ye not whiff the stink from these spuds? And would ye look at the mush at the bottom of the pot!"

Immediately, Francis put down the fork he'd been cleaning and, grim-faced, dashed into the house. The smell alone told him all he'd feared since seeing the black spots - he hardly needed to look at the disgusting pulp in the pan. For sure, this meant another famine. And with it, starvation for many.

Chapter 3

Aftermath

September 1845 - Ballinafad

Things got no better as the days went by. At first, Pat tried to boost family morale with comments such as, "Now Mam, away with the face - ye know full well the Dowds are made of strong stuff. Don't they always come out on top in the end!" Here, he gave a quick wink in Dad's direction. "I'm, tellin' ye, the pratie crop will be fine again before the end of the month!" Mam gave her son an uncertain smile whilst Dad just took another puff on his pipe and continued gazing silently into the fire

Only Anne seemed to have faith in his words. She smiled up at her big brother, saying "I think so too, you *always* seem to know these things. Isn't that right Pat?" He returned her smile, though in his heart, he was far from sure about his predictions. Also, he was concerned about Anne. She'd recovered from her sprained wrist quite quickly, but seemed to have lost some of her former high spirits and energy.

Indeed, by October, the situation was much worse. In fact, when Dad returned from a meeting with the local men, he said there was news that Ireland's potato crops were beginning to show signs of the blight nearly everywhere and, worst of all, there were no signs of any improvement. Angrily, he declared, "And that damned government of Peel are doin' nothin' but talk even though we've been askin' for help since September! Sure we all know that empty bellies need food not fine words!"

Mam, Pat and Anne listened in thoughtful silence.

The Dowds, however, had been luckier than many people since Mam had always been careful with both food and money. Neither were ever wasted, so they had managed on her 'put by' stores during the early days of the famine. But recently, stocks were more or less finished and, like others, they'd started to look for any new praties which, seemed fairly sound (apart from the black-spotted tubers). These they would quickly dig up and get them boiled. The hope being that they could then be eaten *before* they turned black and emitted the dreadful stench of disease. Though if truth be told, this didn't happen very often.

At the end of October, desperate hunger forced father and son into the fields again to have one more attempt to find some apparently sound potatoes. They'd searched for an hour or so, when Francis threw down his fork in frustration. Looking over to his son, he called out, "Leave it Pat, leave it. We're wastin' time here, we'd be more use at home wi' Mam and Annie."

For once, there was no optimistic reply from his son. Without a word, Pat, fork over his shoulder, followed Dad in striding out towards their cottage in the damp, chilly October weather.

As they went into the kitchen, they were shocked to see Mam, tears streaming down her face, bending over a listless Anne. The young girl's face was pale, contrasting with her flushed cheeks. Under her thin blanket, her once small belly, now distended, was protruding. Gently stroking her brow, Mam whispered words of love and comfort to her daughter. "Mam's here luveen, Mam's here."

Father and son stood there, shaking their heads and exchanging knowing glances. Both recognised those signs - it was the dreaded typhus which had taken the life of the Dowd's second child, Michael, only two years before.

By mid- December, Anne had joined her brother in the graveyard.

Mam, inconsolable after the death of a second child, was now a mere shell of her former self, and privations wrought by the famine did nothing to improve her condition. Both father and son were sure she was merely existing until the Lord reunited her with Michael and Anne.

To add to the family's problems was the worry that their landlord, 'Miser Murray' might decide, as some other landlords had done, to return to his property in Scotland. This would occur if people could no longer afford to pay their rents, and if it did occur, there would no longer be money to buy grain.

Soon, however, that problem was no longer uppermost in Francis and Pat's minds as by May that year, Mam had her wish and joined her two beloved children.

After tears and words of farewell at the graveside, "Codladh Samn Luveens" (Sleep well, my darlings), Francis, turned to his son, now as tall as him, saying, "Well now Pat, they're all together, at peace."

A moment's pause and he continued, "But we'll not be letting this curse of Ireland get the better of *us,* will we son? There's got to be a better life than this - and together we'll find it."

Surprised but pleased at such positive words from a father who, so often had had a pessimistic outlook on life, Pat gave an immediate reply of, "Aye, we will Dad! For sure we will!"

Together they turned and strode purposefully in the direction of their cottage with its gairdeen, now little more than a slimy, smelly mesh of weeds and rotted praties.

They had plans to make, things to do. For Pat, a better, and successful life loomed large in his thoughts.

Chapter 4

The Tooey Family

Cloonacool, County Sligo, September 1863

After some early morning rain, the sun managed to break through by eleven o'clock and Margaret Tooey, having finished most of her morning's work, decided to take a walk in the direction of the River Moy with her two younger children, Sarah and Kitty. It was an opportunity not to be missed whilst her three elder ones were at school. Also, the days would soon be turning much cooler as October arrived, for though Cloonacool was a beautiful place in the summer, winters could be very harsh. On being given news of the outing, the two girls, aged five and four years, ran to the door of their rented RIC house (Royal Irish Constabulary, their father being a constable), and stood waiting impatiently for Mam to join them.

Days out with her were precious since they didn't occur often due to the seemingly never-ending work Mam did each day. This included cooking for the family and the animals, fetching water, washing, ironing, knitting sewing, and so on. They were also precious because, once Mam was away from work and out in the countryside, she became a different person. Her severe expression would seem to melt away, giving place to one which reflected the sheer enjoyment of being alive. She would tell them how to recognise the animals, birds, trees and flowers which they came across on their walks. Often, information was accompanied by stories based on old Norse legends or superstitions.

Best of all, had been last spring when Mam had taken them to see the newly born lambs in the fields about two miles away. Whilst walking, she'd pointed out the dark granite rock of the Ox Mountains in the far distance. Eventually, they reached the field where sheep grazed with their high-spirited lambs. As they'd sat to watch them, she'd given the names of her five children to some of the lambs, and then made up amusing little tales about the adventures they were having.

On returning from watching the lambs, they passed a copse of hazel trees. Here, mam signalled for the trio to sit down and wait in silence. At last, a red squirrel appeared on the branch of a tree. A head, with long pointed ears, and bright, cautious eyes emerged first. Then, thinking itself safe, it climbed quickly down. Mam had already told them to look at its feet which made it an excellent climber. The larger back feet with five toes, all with long, curved, sharp claws, enabled it to grip the trunk securely. Once on the ground, it began quickly gathering hazel nuts which it opened with sharp incisor teeth and proceeded to bury them in holes which it dug and covered, ready to eat during the days of winter. Sarah and Kitty were fascinated by this 'squirrel drama' and were sorry when 'Sammy squirrel'- a name given to it by Mam - had finished its work and scampered quickly back up to its nest in the tree. On the way back home, Mam made them laugh by telling them that, after all the work of hiding future food, squirrels often forgot were they'd left their winter store when cold days arrived.

"Aye, they're interesting little devils, right enough, but a bit like your brother, Edward, they can sometimes be eejits!"

Once home, it wasn't long before the three elder children returned from their schools, all ready for the meal of bacon and boiled potatoes.

By 1864, all five children were old enough to attend school. Both parents were great believers in the value of education. Margaret Tooey, a Presbyterian, had been born in Ayr, Scotland, and when her parents moved to Ireland, her father, Alex Wyllie, had been relatively wealthy with a large house and lands in Toomour, so naturally a good education was a 'must' for their daughter. Similarly, her husband, Edward, a staunch Irish Catholic, being a constable in the RIC, had had a good education, this being mandatory for all members of the RIC. ([1])

On a cold, rainy day in February the same year, Mrs Margaret Tooey was feeling tired and sickly. She'd recently discovered that another child would be joining the Tooey clan some time in September. Luckily, it was a Saturday, so there was no school that day, and the two elder children,

Mary Anne and Edward, had been helping her with the daily chores - unlike Margery, Sarah and Kitty. They'd done nothing but pick quarrels all morning and so had been ordered to stand silently in different parts of the kitchen.

Suddenly, just before noon, the rain stopped. Mrs Tooey was relieved to send the three squabblers out to play saying, "Och, away out with ye, and make your stramash there!" Needing no second telling, Margery now seven, Sarah, six and Kitty, five, ran eagerly out of their kitchen into the fresh air. Margery, who had brought out her skipping rope, looked at her siblings and announced, "Now listen, you two, I'm going to be letting ye both play with me - but ye've to be good, mind, cos it's *my* rope. Ye can both be turners and I'll be first jumper."

"How many jumps before it's our turn?" queried Sarah.

"I'll be telling ye *that* when I've had enough!" was the sharp reply. "Now, will ye get turning?"

So the 'game' commenced, but after what seemed ages, the 'boss' showed no signs of having had enough - though the turners certainly had. So much so, that their tired arms could now scarcely keep the rope high enough for their sister to jump properly. She glared at them, saying, "What's the matter with you two eejits? Are ye trying to *hit* me with the rope?"

Near tears, Sarah responded, "We're not eejits, it's cos our arms are aching." Kitty chipped in as well. "Ach, it isn't fair, and we're not eejits. Anyway, it should be our turn to jump by now!"

That was enough for Margery. "Your turn? Ye don't deserve a turn! You're nothing but a couple of babies who can't turn a rope."

She paused, as though pondering what to do next. Mind made up, she declared, "Right, that's it. I'll be going in now to Mam - and I'll be taking my rope with me!" With those words, she snatched it from her sisters.

However, she hadn't noticed the uniformed figure standing behind her who'd silently witnessed the latter part of the 'game'. It was their Dad, who had, as usual, 'cadged' a lift home on the pony and trap of a retired RIC man. He did this most weekends when work at the RIC barracks in Ballinafad was finished.

His first words were to the 'boss'. "Margery! Is that any way to treat your young sisters? Now get inside and give me that rope! Ye can come out again, but only when you're ready to say 'sorry' to us all. Do ye understand?"

A shame-faced Margery quietly said, "Yes, Dad" and returned to the house.

The other two immediately ran up to their Dad who bent down to kiss each in turn. To Sarah he said, "Sure I'm glad you managed to stop yourself from crying just now. Good girl." To Kitty, whose auburn hair caught the morning sun, he asked, "And how's my little ray of sunshine then?"

Kitty just gave him one of her lovely smiles. Indeed, it was this fourth daughter that held a special place in Edward Tooey's heart because of her feisty nature, winning smile and also sharp little brain.

Margery then reappeared and, under her father's stern gaze, she apologised to her siblings. Immediately, he bent down to her saying, "Sure 'tis good to have the real Margery back."

The four of them then went inside their home where Constable Tooey greeted his wife and two elder children.

Footnote[1]

Margaret Wyllie's friendship with an Irish Catholic certainly wasn't what the Wyllie's had hoped for their daughter. However, being a strong-willed young woman, Margaret had her way and, in 1853 in a Presbyterian Meeting House in Ballymote, she and Edward were married. The Wyllie family had hoped that any children would be baptised as Presbyterians. However, the Catholic church was even firmer about 'rules' in mixed marriages, especially for boys. In fact, only the two eldest daughters were baptised in the Presbyterian Meeting House - which had added another problem for the family since it meant that the elder two daughters attended the Presbyterian school, whilst Edward went to the Catholic one.

Chapter 5

Kitty in School

Cloonacool, County Sligo, 1870

It was seven o'clock on a cloudy, though warm, July morning. Eleven-year old Kitty had been up for some time. She made her way to where their hens were kept, her auburn hair in a single, long plait. Over her long dark-green linen dress was a white apron. She was carrying a bucket of the boiled up potato peelings and egg-shells which Sarah had prepared the night before. There was impatient clucking as the hens ran towards her, crowding unhelpfully round her feet as they awaited their feed.

"Kitty! What's taking ye so long with the hens?" It was Mam's voice from the kitchen door, "I need ye *now* to look after the bairn and Alexander while Margery helps me fetch the water from the well."

Kitty sighed as she knelt down and tipped out the contents of the bucket for the hungry birds. "It never ends, does it?" She addressed her question to the hens - who were otherwise occupied. But still she continued, glad of her 'captive' audience. "It's, 'Kitty would ye help me with the washing,' 'Kitty would ye feed baby David?'" She paused, adding "I'm just hopin' there isn't another babe on the way this year!" One hen looked up and fixed a beady eye on her - -but never ventured its opinion on the subject. So, aloud, she called, "Coming Mam, I've nearly finished."

Since Kitty's birth, Mam had given birth to four more children: Anne, Margaret (often known as Madge), Alexander and David. The almost yearly arrival of another sibling had meant that all the elder children had to help Mam with the many jobs to be done for such a large family. And although Mary Anne, the eldest child, had recently commenced work as a 'live in' assistant in a large 'Drapery and Dressmaking' shop in Sligo Town, and Edward was hoping to find work on a cargo ship there, it still meant there were seven children to feed and clothe. So from the age of six, Kitty had been helping Mam with some of the daily household chores.

She ran back to the house where Mam was walking round, patting David's back as he cried lustily.

"The bairn needs to get some wind up, he's never settled since I gave him the breast." Kitty's mother then quickly thrust the distressed little fellow into Kitty's arms and joined Margery who was waiting for her outside.

Alexander, who'd been sitting dejectedly in a corner of the kitchen, moved over to her and asked pleadingly, "Big man, Kitty, big man." Kitty sighed but knew exactly what her little brother wanted, it was the story of the giant who walked across from Scotland to Giant's Causeway in Northern Ireland to fight the Irish giant who lived there. He loved that story told by Dad when he was home from work. So, ever the one to improvise, she began the story but told it quietly in rhythmic style whilst patting David's back as she rocked him. The baby ceased crying and his eyes gradually closed. Alexander, now seated on a small wooden stool, had Kitty's full attention. The idyllic scene was suddenly interrupted by laughter from the kitchen door. It was Sarah, who exclaimed, "Well that's the first time I've heard the story of the giants' big fight sung as a lullaby."

When the two water carriers, Mam and Margery, arrived back, the former was pleased to see a sleeping baby in the well-used, Tooey cradle, and Alexander quietly playing with his bricks. "That's my good lassie!" she said, looking at her contented boys."Now it's time that ye were off to school, the other three are already waiting for ye in the lane."

Soon, four of the Tooey girls were making their way to the local National Catholic school, a distance of just over a mile. Madge, the youngest, had only recently started attending and was still unsure about the different regime there. Anne, a mere eleven months older, had adjusted herself to going to school. For Sarah, now aged twelve, it was her last year and she was hoping that she might find paid work outside the home as Mary Anne had. In fact, it was Kitty who loved school the most. She had a quick, inquiring mind and was eager to learn. This was recognised by her teachers who had indicated to her that, like other very able pupils, she was likely to be kept on as a 'pupil-teacher' instead of leaving at the age of twelve. ([1]).

They reached school just in time to hear the large school-bell being rung by one of the nuns who taught there and so were able to get into line for entry into the building. Like many other schools, it was under-resourced, and so it was damp, cold, poorly lit and with a perpetual musty smell. Once inside, the pupils went to different parts of the building according to their age groups, though all rooms catered for more than one age-group, such as five to six year-olds, seven to nine year-olds and ten to twelve year-olds. 'Pupil-teachers' usually worked alongside teachers of the younger children.

Kitty sat with a dark-haired girl who was a year older than her called Mary. Like Kitty, she wore her hair in one long plait which hung down her back. She had always greeted Kitty with a smile rather than the hostility shown by some of the other children and adults in Cloonacool. Indeed, the whole of Constable Tooey's family was often viewed with distrust and dislike on account of the nature of his job, which sometimes meant he had to attend local petty sessions and courts. So Kitty greatly valued the friendship which had developed between her and Mary.

The latter's home was a two-roomed, thatched cottage about half a mile away from the Tooey's RIC house. Money was short, and Mary was often absent from school due to having to help her mother with all kinds of work which included taking in the washing and ironing for some of the wealthier people of the village. She'd once told Kitty that her mother would have liked her to have full-time schooling. But when she put forward this suggestion to her husband, saying that education gave children knowledge and taught them to think, Dad's reply was, "Damnit woman, she can get all the bloody knowledge she needs by workin' in the home and on the land. And as fer thinkin', well, ye can't *think* food on the table!"

When the children's 'playtime came that day, Mary had a question for Kitty.

"I've asked about ye bein' able to help me on Landlord Holt's land when school closes for harvest at the end of July. Ye should really be twelve to help the women who bind the sheaves, but they're short-handed this year, and have agreed ye can work alongside me. The work can be hard but the pay's not too bad. So what are ye sayin' to that?

Kitty looked delighted, "Well, though I'm hearing it's hard work, it would be a fine chance to get to know some of the women and other girls of the village. Certainly a change from looking after my two little brothers and doing all the jobs Mam will be sure to find for me in the holidays! Also, it'll be a bit more money for Mam -she's having to be watching the pennies even more now, both to pay the rent and buy the food to fill the bellies of our big family."

"Ach, yer right there Kitty. It's the same for us too. But it'll be great to spend time with each other durin' the holiday. Make sure ye ask Mam about it tonight!"

As Kitty had thought, Mam was pleased at the thought of a bit more money coming into the house especially since Edward still hadn't been taken on by the owner of one of the cargo boats in Sligo Town. To be fair, her brother worked hard by helping some of the local men to scraw (strip) the turf of its top layer of grass, ready for cutting into sods. And though that gave the family free fuel, it didn't bring in any money.

Footnote[1]

As with all National Schools, the focus was on reading, writing, arithmetic, with certain hours allocated to religious teaching. Yet the text books of National Schools revealed they were definitely 'schools of the state' in their promotion of: social deference, respect for one's 'betters', and loyalty/obedience to the State and officialdom.

Chapter 6

The Rising of the Moon (May 1846)

Soon after Pat and his Dad had said their 'goodbyes' to Mam and Anne, they went to a meeting held by the local Drumfin men. It took place in the nearby tavern. Every man there was enraged by the latest news from the Government in London who were considering passing a so-called 'Coercion' bill.

First to address the men was Michael Flynn. He'd three children under ten years old and his wife had recently given birth to a still-born babe. Both blamed her under-nourishment for their loss. He was tall with broad shoulders, thick black hair and penetrating dark eyes. Thumping his fist on a wooden table for silence, he glared round at everyone. You certainly wouldn't want to knock over *his* porter! He had the full attention of everyone - except his dog, which had settled down for a sleep.

"Well now men, ye know full well why we're here, those bloody English are kickin' us up the backside again. First, they make promises to send cheaper Indian corn to the starving' people of Ireland. Ach, such generous folk!" This remark was accompanied by him spitting savagely on the floor.

"But not one morsel of food has been sent - we still have to *buy* the bloody corn!! Then that's held back fer two months. It's no fuckin' wonder that when it does come, families who are nothin' but skin and bone, are fightin' to get it! Now that damn government's talkin' of curfews and transportation.

"So I ask ye lads, are ye ready to do somethin' fer yerselves and yer families before they think up another way of puttin' the boot in?"

There were cries of "Aye, that we are, Michael" and "Down with the bloody English!" All accompanied by the stamping of feet and banging of tables.

Michael held up his hand for silence, then continued, "I say we head for Sligo Town until we come to an estate where the landlord's not run off back to his homeland once no rent's comin' in. Then we take his sheep and whatever we can lay our hands on. And I say we do it *now* - before that damned new bill gets passed! Agreed lads?"

There was a roar of agreement from most of the men but one or two seemed uncertain. One of these being Francis Dowd who stood up. Catching Michael's eye, he spoke clearly and with deliberation.

"Michael, I'm thinkin' yer right in sayin' we act now and make for Sligo.

But to be stealin' sheep along the way is the quickest way to get ourselves a long sea trip with 'a 'holiday' of fifteen years or more in Australia!" He paused, "God knows I'm no landlord lover, especially those who've just left us, and scuttled back to their homeland. But to be stealing livestock from the landlords who've stayed - well, it makes no sense."

Michael was scowling at these words, but Francis went on, "Just ye think, every landlord will have his enforcers keepin' watch day and night. And when they catch us, and mark my words they will, there'll be no mercy for any of us! Especially if the English government get their damned bill passed quickly."

There was muttering from the men, some now looking uncertain. Michael sat glaring both at the speaker and the 'mutterers'. Francis then asked the question."So tell me lads, how will *that* be of any use to ourselves or our families?" Letting that sink in for a moment, he continued,"So what I'm thinkin' is that we go along with Michael's idea of making fer Sligo. We take with us some food and drink. But we also take our shovels or spades, showing we're ready to do the work that's there in Sligo. They have money to pay us - provided by Peel's government. I know wages won't be much, but at least Peel has also got the price of corn reduced." Another pause. "And if necessary, we'll not be afraid to *demand* the work!"

He looked around the room, asking, "So what do ye think lads?"

During the option put forward by Francis, many of the men had, one by one, started nodding in agreement. So along with the latter's final words an excited chatter broke out as the men, now in small groups, decided where their support lay. It wasn't long before one of them, Joseph, a small but muscular man thumped his table and stood up, calling, "Aye Frankie, yer talkin' plain, good sense. I'm thinkin' most of us would rather do some honest work for a small wage that'll help us buy corn fer our families than find ourselves at the mercy of some landlord's bully boys, or, worse still, end up in Australia and a living death!"

These words were followed by cries of 'Yer right there' and a thumping of tables. Even Michael seemed less hostile to the suggested changes to his proposals. However, it was clear that he wasn't happy with this undermining of his leadership.

At these reactions, Joseph spoke again, "Why don't we have a show of hands now? Then we can act quickly and follow one of the plans ye've just heard?"

There soon followed a show of hands, with the counting done by Joseph. The votes showed a clear majority for Francis' plan. With some hesitation, Michael and a couple of dissenters nodded their acceptance of the result.

Pat clapped his Dad on the back saying, "Sure, I'm proud of ye Dad and the way ye spoke tonight."

Cheers rang out and tankards were refilled. The dog at the back, slowly opened one eye, gave a yap of indifference, and padded out of the tavern.

"Clearly *not* one of yer supporters, Dad!" observed Pat in amusement.

Although those at the meeting managed to rise early the following day, it was eight o'clock by the time everyone was ready to move. It had rained steadily all night, and was still pouring down when Francis, Pat, and twenty other men began making their way north towards Sligo Town. Despite the weather, they trudged on through bogs and fields, shovels over shoulders, from time to time breaking into song. Their favourite being 'The Rising of the Moon' which told of the Irish rebellion at the end of the previous century.

Just before one o'clock that afternoon, the rain-soaked and weary band of men came across several deserted cottages. Francis Dowd, having been voted as unofficial leader of the 'marchers', took stock of the situation, then spoke.

"We're near Drumfin, and it looks as if the landlord here had his tenants evicted only a few days ago. The poor hoors must have been desperate, tryin' to save what they could from their homes, then runnin' to God knows where for shelter. I reckon they must have cleared off before the bailiffs came to loot, then pull down the cottages. I say we rest here for a break and some food lads. Though a lot of the thatch has gone, the insides of the cottages should be fairly dry."

There was ready agreement to Francis' suggestion. And, finding turf left in some of the cottages, the men were able to get a fire going and were soon sharing out their food and drink.

Aware that they were now much nearer to their destination, Francis chatted with Michael (there now being an uneasy truce between them) and both agreed it would make sense not to rest too long in the cottages - tempting though it was. With a bit of luck, they hoped to reach Sligo Town by six or seven o'clock, spend the night there, and be ready to find work early next day. Reluctantly, the group stirred themselves, accompanied by grunts and farts, and were soon on their way again before two o'clock.

Again, their journey was mainly through bogs and fields, though luckily the rain had stopped. On nearing their final destination, the men's spirits were raised, now they were sharing dubious jokes and singing bawdy songs.

Francis and Michael felt the men would benefit from a brief break before completing the final few miles to Sligo Town. So, having spotted a clump of trees at the base of a hillock, they beckoned to the rest of the group to head for the trees. This seemed an ideal spot for a rest and a drink, especially since the sun had come out.

Sensing the very positive mood of the men, Michael decided to give the group something to laugh at. He suddenly got up, and began a comical impersonation of the hated Trevelyan, Head of the Treasury. He was the man who kept trying to curb Peel's attempts to provide relief for the Irish.

Strutting round pompously at a little distance from the others, he placed his thumbs under an imaginary lapel. Then he stopped, gazed slowly round at the men, and declared in an exaggerated imitation of an English, upper-class accent, "I think you will all agree, gentlemen, that this government has been very generous in giving help to our lazy and ignorant Irish neighbours."

Of course, this was met with jeers, cat-calls and crude gestures from the listeners.

Meanwhile, Pat had speedily been making a 'crown' from the twigs of overhead sycamore trees. He now moved in small mincing steps to the side of 'Trevelyan' with the 'crown' on his head. Here, in a falsetto voice, he opined, "One is pleased that one's government has been so charitable towards those poor Irish people."

'Victoria's' words were greeted with loud cheers and howls of laughter. Joseph snatched the crown from 'her' head and threw it over by the trees, whereupon, the men, one by one, proceeded to urinate on it.

Not long after, the men were moving again towards Sligo, the leaders hoping that, if they kept going, they could reach their goal before seven o'clock.

Chapter 7

We Want Food (Sligo, May 1846)

In fact, it was just before seven o'clock when the group reached the outskirts of Sligo Town. Since most of the food and drink they'd managed to 'salvage' for their journey had been consumed, everyone thought it might be a good idea to make for the work house. Though Francis knew that normally it was the rule of workhouses not to allow relief to be given to those who were not inmates, he hoped rules might be 'stretched' in these dire times. Perhaps a bowl of soup might be available to them.

This hope was soon to be dashed.

Outside the workhouse were crowds of men, women and children, many in ragged clothes which exposed painfully thin limbs. Hollow hopeless eyes stared at the group as they approached, but nobody spoke to them. One woman was sitting down on the ground, cradling a young motionless child in her shawl. It was hard to know if it were sleeping or dead. Though not one person had addressed the group, the noise was deafening and pitiful to hear. Men and boys hurled curses at the closed doors, many women were stretching out their hands towards the indifferent, stark building, They called out, "We need food! Give us food! We're starving!"

Helplessly, the men took in the pitiful scene. Times had been bad in Ballinafad but they'd witnessed nothing like this spectacle of misery. Francis was the first to speak, "We can't do anything for them lads, better just to tighten our belts and move on to get some sort of shelter for the night. In the morning we can find out where the nearest public work's depot is."

And so the group walked on, considerably sobered by all they'd seen and heard. Fairly soon, they came across an open stretch of ground on which stood ramshackle wooden buildings, probably having served as stables before the famine. Though still hungry, the men were glad to get some rest there for the night, and since temperatures were still quite high for a May evening, they slept tolerably well.

By five o'clock next morning, the men, roused by their leaders, were awake and on the move again. After about a mile, seeing a group of seven men with shovels making their way purposefully along the road ahead of them, they decided that was the route to take. Young Pat suddenly spoke up with a suggestion. "I'm thinkin' it might be a good idea if we joined them so that when we get to the depot, we're with the front runners."

Everyone looked in surprise at young Dowd voicing his opinions. His father fixed him with a look - wondering whether he should give him a clip round the ear for speaking out of turn. At last he said, "I can't think they'll be too happy at the idea of us pushin' in with them. That lot look as though they're handy with their fists!"

"Aye Dad, but if we start up our singin' again, full voice, it might just make 'em take notice of us, and maybe they'll gradually join in, not even noticin' we've caught up with 'em."

It seemed worth a try and it worked. Before long the two groups were singing lustily together until they reached the depot. It was a large, dark, stone building with a notice on its wooden door which read

'PUBLIC RELIEF WORKS'

At six o'clock, a burly, sour-faced official opened the door. Looking round the already growing crowd of men, he produced a large, black book and pen, saying, "We're wantin' fit, strong men for road buildin', the younger the better - ye can be sure there'll be no pay fer any shiftless spalpeens" (itinerant workers).

Stepping outside, and ostentatiously putting on a rimless pair of spectacles, he scrutinised the men crowding in front of him, "Now let's be lookin' at ye and if I put a hand on yer shoulder, tell me yer age, yer name, and where ye've come from."

Despite a great deal of jostling, pushing and shoving, the group from Ballinafad and their 'brothers in song' managed to hold positions near the front. The official's eyes quickly fell on Michael, his height and bulk making him stand out from the crowd. Soon a hand was placed on his shoulder, and gradually the surly official did the same with about twenty others from the crowd, including Pat and his father. Unfortunately, Joseph and three others from Ballinafad were rejected, though 'sour-face' told them there might be work available the next day for 'pot-hole fillers'.

By seven o'clock, the selected men, shovels over shoulders, were following their overseer, a grim-faced man in his late twenties.

"A cheerful lot these Town men" whispered Pat to his Dad. Francis gave his son a warning look.

After about a mile, they reached a long wooden shed. Here, the overseer was greeted by a well-dressed, middle-aged woman wearing a fashionable green hat.

"Good morning to you, Edward, so this is the latest band of workers for the road, is it? I've no doubts they'll all welcome a bit of breakfast before they start work."

At this unexpected mention of food, the men's faces brightened.

Edward's erstwhile grim face changed to one of deference as he doffed his cap and said, "Aye, Mrs O'Donnell, this is the latest band, and I'm sure they'll be grateful for a bite to eat." Looking at the men, grim-faced again, he added, "Even though they've done naught to deserve it yet."

Like a few other philanthropic middle-class women in parts of Ireland, Mrs O'Donnell, wife of a wealthy land owner in Sligo, had been moved by the plight of the poor and starving. She now provided food for families on their land, even extending her generosity to any outsiders who came seeking work.

The men were then beckoned inside the wooden building where a long table was set out with three bowls, one containing hard-boiled eggs, a second containing chunks of bread, and a smaller one which held smallish pieces of cheese. In front of each bowl stood a young girl, each wearing a pinafore over her long skirt and blouse. Mrs O'Donnell was standing by a large pitcher of buttermilk, ready to pour it into mugs for the men. At the back of the men remained Francis, he'd decided to keep there until he knew the food and drink was shared equitably.

Whilst the men were eating and drinking, Edward banged on a table for silence and informed the men, "Ye should think yerselves lucky. Mrs

O'Connell, fine lady that she is, has provided ye not only with food but also with beds and breakfasts in the nearby pub - that is provided ye work well! And that will last only until ye get yer first wages. Then, ye find and pay fer yer own food and sleeping place."

A glare around, and then he began leading the men, shovels over shoulders, towards the place where a new road would eventually be built.

To their surprise, the first job was to break up the existing road. Back-breaking work which seemed unnecessary since the original road would have lasted for some while. Indeed, one West country gentleman had written that such work appeared as, '...an anomalous mode of meeting a calamity...'

It wasn't until four weeks had passed that they received their first wages. And a great and bitter disappointment it was to them. Apart from it being well below their expectations, they now had to pay for their accommodation and victuals. Luckily Francis and Pat, having no family back in Ballinafad, were able to afford to stay on at the pub quite cheaply, provided they shared a room with others.

The two Dowds realised before the end of 1846 that their original plan of saving money from their combined wages to buy a small plot of land of their own, was doomed to failure. Pay packets continued to be delayed quite frequently, and sometimes even reduced in amount. However, they were managing to survive, despite the soul-destroying daily work. Also there was some respite for them during evenings in the pub. Those workers who could afford the odd mug of porter would gather together at night and try to forget the trials of the day. It was here that Pat came into his own. By October, he was already taller and considerably broader than his father. And though not handsome in the traditional sense, he had a smile and natural humour which made him popular to both men and women. All this, together with his skill at playing his tin whistle, meant he was often the centre of attention amongst any gathering.

Not the easiest of lives, but Francis and Pat just about managed to get through the terrible winter that year, even when wages remained low and irregular. However, life seemed slightly better when the government allocated extra funds for soup kitchens. So, in addition to the soup, other basic rations were doled out from enormous barrel-like containers. As they queued for their first, more substantial food portions, Francis commented, "At last, that bloody lot at Westminster have realised we need something more than a teaspoonful of watery soup to keep us going!"

But little did the Dowds realise that fate had another 'present' in store for them.

In 1847, a dreadful fever affected the whole of Ireland.([1]) And it wasn't long before, along with others, Francis and Pat decided to cut their losses and leave their homeland to seek work in Scotland. Word had got round that in Ayrshire, potato - pickers were needed urgently in its large farmlands. So they sailed from Sligo northwards then eastwards via the Firth of Clyde, and eventually landed in Ayr.

Men who had made this journey were generally welcome as far as work was concerned, but the Scots, especially Scottish Presbyterians, were no lovers of the Irish. They hated the 'popery' of the Roman Catholics. Nevertheless, Francis and Pat considered their options in Scotland held more promise than remaining in Ireland and were relieved that it took only a couple of days before they were employed as labourers on a farm several miles north of Troon.

Living quarters, however, were no more than sheds or huts - called bothies by the Scots - and the men had to sleep crammed close together in these windowless 'cells'. As Pat remarked to his Dad after a first night of fitful, cramped sleep, "I'll tell ye what Dad, these Jocks know how to make a man feel welcome - and that's for sure!"

Their wages, however, though not much higher than in Sligo, were at least paid regularly, so they were able to afford to eat regularly each day, despite the food being very basic and very plain. As February 1848 moved to a close, the weather became slightly milder, ideal for 'feeding' the ground ready for planting the potatoes in March. It was whilst working on this job that Pat suddenly became aware that his Dad, who usually worked quickly and expertly, was breathing heavily, his digging slowing down. He watched closely for a minute, but on seeing Dad leaning on his shovel, head down, he rushed over to him. As he reached his father, the latter fell to the ground, face down on the newly-dug earth. Alarmed, Pat quickly bent down to turn him over, "Dad, Dad." he shouted," Look at me, Dad!" But Francis' eyes remained closed, his lips blue. Tearfully Pat looked for any signs of breathing, but soon realised that his brave, feisty, and much loved Dad had breathed his last.

The famine, the back-breaking work, the rough sleeping and eventually the cruel winter weather had all taken their toll on Francis Dowd. This time it was Pat's turn to bid, "Codladh sámn" to the last remaining member of his family.

Footnote[1]

Throughout 1847 fever raged and soon affected the whole country. It became commonly known as 'Road Fever' since it was spread by starving, sick people fleeing from the more stricken counties in the west. Moreover, in one part of County Mayo, during a period of eighteen days, only four days' rations had been given out. Enough was enough for some people. They decided on the big step of emigration, mainly to the USA, especially New York, often via Sligo and Liverpool. Yet for many passengers, there was more misery ahead, conditions were often horrific and large numbers died at sea or were found dead on arrival.

Chapter 8

Harvest Time (August 1870)

School had finished for the summer two weeks ago and it was time for oats and barley to be harvested. Kitty was up early as she would be meeting Mary that morning to start her first day of paid work. She was excited and just a little nervous at the prospect of joining the village women and girls. She'd already seen a bleary-eyed Edward set off to join the reapers on Landlord Holt's land. He too, on Mary's recommendation, had been given harvest work there. Mam was busily stirring pans of food for the pigs and hens. It would though be her job to go out and feed them as David would soon be crying to be fed.

By six o'clock, all her jobs done, it was time to set off to call for Mary since her cottage was nearer to Landlord Holt's fields than her house. As Kitty stood at the door, she could see ahead the women who would be binding the cut sheaves. There was chatting and some laughter as they walked hurriedly along the dusty road. She knew they were the experts. Mary, herself and a few other girls would carry the bound sheaves to the field where they would be stacked (stooked).

With baby David in her arms, Mam waved Kitty off with the reminder, "See ye work hard and don't be giving any cheek to the women there!"

It wasn't long before she saw Mary standing by her cottage door, and soon the two were walking arm-in-arm along the dusty lane towards the field of reaped barley. The air was sweet and pungent with the blending odours of cattle and crops.

"On the whole, they're not a bad lot, the binders" said Mary, but sure they can get really angry and impatient if they think anyone's slowing down their work - and ye wouldn't believe what they talk about! The one to watch is Edna, she's the best binder of the lot, she throws the sheaf over her shoulder and when it's bound she can quickly pull out the exact number of straws needed for the next sheaf almost before the first one falls on the ground! But the Lord have mercy on ye if you don't get it away quickly for stacking!"

Kitty made a mental note to try to work some distance from Edna if possible.

It took about thirty minutes to get to the barley field where the reapers, stripped to the waist, had been working earlier that month. About ten women binders were there and three other young girls besides Kitty and Mary. One of the women immediately stepped forward on seeing them arrive, still arm-in-arm. She was small and wiry, dark hair tied severely back - and a face that would have stopped a clock.

"Reckon this must be Edna" thought Kitty. Mary confirmed this by immediately unlinking their arms and quietly clearing her throat.

"Right now, Mary Mahon, ye know me, and what I expect from you girls, so be sure to pass this on to your new friend! "Turning to Kitty, she demanded, "And what might *your* name be? And move away from Mary Mahon. I'll be separating you two - I want hard, quick work, not blather from ye!"

Kitty moved away a couple of steps, gave her full name clearly whilst, at the same time, meeting Edna's gaze steadily - seemingly not in awe of the other's stern expression. Inwardly, she was somewhat taken aback by this unexpected start to her day.

"Well, Kitty Tooey" went on Edna, "ye'll be comin' with me first and I'll show you how it *should* be done. So look sharp!"

Soon followed a skilful and precise demonstration of a stacker's job. It was repeated only once and then Edna observed a somewhat nervous Kitty taking a deftly bound sheaf from her, carrying it over her shoulder, then carefully stacking it.

"Ye'll do," said Edna with what Kitty thought - or hoped - was a half smile. "Now shift yerself and get started!" Anything resembling a smile had disappeared.

The work was certainly hard and the sheaves heavy. Moreover, as the day wore on, the sun came out and the increasing heat made the work seem even harder. So it was a great relief when a loud whistle was blown at eleven o'clock marking time for the first break. Quickly, everyone was heading for the shade of the enormous horse-chest-nut tree over by the hedges, it was already revealing small, green 'conkers', its autumn fruit. Mary sought out Kitty since they'd been told to work in different parts of the field, and the two ran together to the shadiest part of the tree and flung themselves thankfully, face down, on the ground. The three other girls similarly kept together, and settled some distance away.

Respite for Kitty and Mary was, however, brief. Both soon felt sharp kicks on their backsides and a strident voice saying, "Ye've another think comin' if ye think yer settled there in the best spot. Now shift yourselves! And make room for yer elders and betters."

It was Sarah, one of the binders. Startled, Mary jumped up immediately. Kitty however, took a moment to consider her options. But on seeing the unsmiling face of Edna next to Sarah, she got up and joined Mary.

It wasn't long though before all the workers were settled comfortably - the binders keeping a little distance from the five girls. Then everyone was tucking into whatever food and drink they'd managed to bring along with them. In truth, there was little variation amongst the refreshments which consisted, in the main, of soda bread, potato cakes, oatcakes and buttermilk. As they ate and drank, Mary and Kitty chatted about work as stackers and also about Edna and Sarah. Suddenly, loud laughter came from the binders' 'camp'; they appeared to be sharing some dubious joke. Kitty looked over in their direction, wishing they were nearer and able to hear what was so funny. As the laughter faded, Sarah noticed Kitty apparently looking at her Again came her strident voice.

"Well now, ye'll know me when ye see me again! Have ye asked yer friend how the hoor and her bastard is?"

An uneasy silence fell on the group as they waited for Kitty's reply, some of them looking over towards Mary who had gone bright red. Edna, however, was shaking her head in strong disapproval at Sarah's question.

Puzzled, but noting Edna's silent disapproval of Sarah's words, Kitty replied somewhat defiantly, "Sure I don't think ye should be asking *me* that question! I'm thinking it's none of *your* business anyway!" Before a furious Sarah could reply, Edna said sharply, "There'll be no more of this talk!"

Turning to Kitty she said, "The girl Sarah spoke about committed a sin but we should be praying that the Lord will forgive her - not abusing her. Now everyone! Back to work!"

As she returned to her work, Kitty was still bewildered by the conversation, and also surprised but glad that Edna had put Sarah in her place regarding the sinner. She was also wondering how Mary knew the girl referred to so crudely.

When work finally finished for the day, the two girls walked along together through the fields, but this time Mary didn't take Kitty's arm. Once they were out of earshot of most of the other workers, Kitty lost no time in saying, "Mary, ye seemed upset by Sarah's question to me, and I'm sorry about that. But I'm thinkin' ye must know *something'* about the matter. Are ye able to talk about it?"

There was a slight pause, then Mary replied, a bitter tone in her voice. "Sure I'm able to tell ye something all right, but I doubt if ye'll be wantin' to walk with me again. Ye see, I'm the sister of the hoor." Mary waited for some shocked reaction. But Kitty merely nodded, saying, "I'm sure there's more to tell. So, go on, I'm listening."

Mary continued, "Well, my sister, Margaret, is eighteen now but when she was fourteen, she found work as a 'live-in' servant at one of the big houses in Sligo Town. Sure, wages were poor but she was hopin' to get to be a cook or housekeeper by workin' hard. For a while, things weren't too bad." A pause.

"But wouldn't ye know it? It wasn't long till the Master had his eyes on her! Ye can guess what happened. Of course, as soon as the babe was showin', Mistress sent her packing. And home she comes - disgraced and broken-hearted with the shame. And all because of that man!" The word 'man' was virtually spat out by Mary.

"I'm truly sorry for your sister. But tell me now, did Mam forgive Margaret? And did she take the poor, wee babe into the family?"

"Holy Mother of God, sure ye must be livin' in a dream world, Kitty! As soon as word of her pregnancy got round Cloonacool, round goes Father Kelly to our Mam and Dad, reminding them that anyone who has a child out of wedlock has committed an abomination before God. Doesn't he then go on to tell them they must send Margaret away from the village to one of the places in Sligo where 'the good Catholic nuns' look after sinful girls.'"

Another pause then "So that's where she was sent."

"Oh that poor girl!" exclaimed Kitty in amazement. "I remember hearing Mam once talking about homes for unmarried mothers and babies to a friend. But I'm thinking' they didn't seem the places you'd want to go to have your babe. Mam said the nuns weren't always too kind."

"Kind? Kind?" Asked Mary incredulously. "Not one of those nuns knew what kindness meant - their job was to make life hell for the girls there. Every one of them was reminded of their sin from morning till night - and especially when it was their time to give birth. Margaret's baby came out the wrong way, his little backside first. She told me she was screamin' with the pain of it all and the *kind* nun just smiled, saying, "Well now Margaret, that's what happens to those who go against the teachings of our Lord. So ye can stop all that noise!"

Tears came to Mary's eyes as she thought of her sister's ordeal. Kitty placed an arm gently round her shoulders. And Mary, continued, "After the birth, didn't they keep her working there in the laundry for two years until she'd repaid all their so-called care and expense? Also, she was never allowed to see her little son, *my* nephew, after his birth. Anyway, Kitty, now ye know I'm from a disgraced family and that some people are *still* mindful of what happened there four years ago. So ye don't need to be calling on me tomorrow."

Two arms were immediately placed firmly on her shoulders, and Mary found Kitty facing her. "Now hold your whisht Mary Mahon, I'll have ye know that as far as most decent people are concerned, what befell your poor sister is in the past. Think on how Edna put that spiteful and ignorant Sarah in her place in front of everyone! As for yourself, *you've* committed no sin but ye *have* proved a good, caring friend to me." Kitty then smiled, adding, "So I'll be calling for ye tomorrow, will I not?"

A vigorous nod and a look of relief swept over Mary's face. The two linked arms once again, bound for home.

That evening, Kitty thought about the events of the day. The work, Edna, spiteful Sarah, and also Mary and Margaret. Kitty's eyes had certainly been opened to some of the less desirable aspects of life. And she felt saddened.

Chapter 9

Return to Ireland

The situation back in Ireland continued to be dire. In fact the potato harvest of 1848 was another disastrous one and so Pat continued his work as a labourer on various farms in Ayrshire. By 1849, Ireland was more convinced than ever that the government in Westminster was neither just nor humane in its rule over Ireland. The only answer being that the Irish should run its own affairs.

Working in Scotland had brought Pat nothing which could be classed as happiness, but after his experiences during and after the famine, he found life bearable. After all, he was able to eat reasonably well, and occasionally, he was able to afford the odd mug of porter. Another bonus was that farmers often employed young women, and he usually had no problems in finding solace in some of their beds. Indeed, one 'guy, bonnie lassie' (as Scotsmen called attractive girls), had even turned his thoughts to considering marriage.

It was 1851 when he met her. Pat was twenty, and red-haired Jean McGregor, a servant in the house of a largish farm near Ayr, was twenty-three. They'd been attracted to each other right from the start, she was allowed to have her own small bedroom in the farm-house, whereas, Pat was given an outdoor shed to sleep in. It was next to one where the farm's horses were stabled; not ideal, but far more comfortable than the bothies he'd been used to.

It only took a week before Pat's charms had persuaded her to leave her own room during the night, and creep into the shed. On their first night together, the two had been kissing whilst he fondled her breasts. Both were soon breathlessly ready to move to the 'next stage.' Pat, whispering words of love, began to mount her, "Oh, Jeannie, Jeannie, my beautiful Jeannie - I feel ..."

But Jean McGregor never found out what he felt since, at that moment, one of the horses began to fart. It went on for what seemed ages. Then it stopped. Then followed a cascade of urine.

Of course the amorous atmosphere was shattered. But after a moment's frustrated pause, Pat simply threw back his head in a burst of laughter as he declared, "Jesus, Mary and Joseph. I've heard of couples having their love-makin' interrupted before, but never by a fartin', pissin' horse!"

Far from being angry at the incident or Pat's words, Jeannie joined him in the laughter. It seemed somehow to increase the pair's 'togetherness', and desire for each other.

As their affection increased, the forthright and more experienced Jeannie, gradually taught Pat that a woman needed more satisfaction in this area and that mutual pleasure was not necessarily attained by speed. Moreover, she explained that it was often beneficial to both if the woman was sometimes 'in the riding saddle.' An eager and willing learner, Pat soon discovered that Jeannie's advice was well worth the taking.

However, after a couple of months, Pat became aware that some of the other farm workers seemed to be becoming aware of their 'trysts'. He knew it wouldn't be long before they were reported to the farmer by one of them, and that probably both would lose their jobs. It was this thought, together with his genuine fondness for Jeannie, and also his longing to return to his homeland that prompted him to ask her to leave Scotland and travel to Ireland with him. Here they could put together their savings and get married.

As they lay together after Pat's suggestion, Jeannie put her arms around him, saying softly, "Och, Pat yer a braw lad right enough, but though I love ye dearly, what ye ask is impossible. Neither of us has much money. Anyway, I know I could *never* live anywhere but Scotland."

This reply was certainly not expected. Pat now felt the only thing to do was to return to Ireland alone to the place of his birth. The two parted sadly, but at least it was amicable - in his heart, he knew Jeannie was right.

❧ ❧ ❧

On his return to Ireland and Ballinafad a month later, Pat was shocked to find so few of the people and friends he'd known there. Some, he was told, had managed to scrape together, or more likely borrow, the fare of between two and five pounds in order to find a better life by emigrating to America, Canada or even New Zealand. Pat wondered if those who'd taken that enormous gamble would survive perilous sea- journeys of twenty days or more, and then be able to settle in countries so far away. They must indeed have been desperate.

It was even more shocking to hear of the great number of people from Ballinafad and surrounding areas who'd simply died of starvation. And worse still, was seeing the many mounds where bodies had simply lain on the ground until covered by relatives or the elements.

However, as with many tragedies, something positive emerged for people like Pat. The resulting greatly reduced population in most parts of Ireland meant that most of those seeking work, and especially labourers, found it easier not only to find work, but also to receive higher wages. Being September, Pat soon found work near Ballinafad since crops of potatoes were still being harvested. A couple, who'd lived near the Dowds, having lost all three of their young children, were glad to supply bed and board to Pat for a small payment.

And so, for several years, Pat continued life travelling between the villages and towns nearby to find work. Sometimes, during winter months, when work was scarcer, he'd again make the sea journey from Sligo to Scotland where he could always find farmers needing strong men, able to turn their hand to a variety of jobs and at a reasonable wage.

Yet, deep down, he wanted a more settled life with a wife who wouldn't make too many demands on him, and give him healthy children.

However, it was 1865 and he in his thirties before fate led him to Riverstown to work. It was here he met twenty year old Anne O'Conner (nee Benson), a pretty, pleasant young Catholic who'd been widowed for two years. The fact that she'd already been married didn't worry Pat; indeed her husband had left her with a cottage and small plot of land which was rented from the local landlord. And, in truth, meeting someone with Anne's assets after the itinerant life he'd led, seemed to be well-suited to Pat's 'requirements'.

They'd met at a local market where Anne was selling eggs and Pat was buying some to take back to the family he lodged with. He teased her about the high price she was charging, asking why a lovely woman like her couldn't find it in her heart to drop the price for a hard-working but penniless fellow like him. True to form, Pat ended up being given an extra couple for free.

They were soon meeting on a regular basis at markets, and before long were seeing each other as a 'couple'. It was just a few months later that Anne informed Pat she was having his child. There was no hesitation in him asking her to marry him, likewise, Anne was content to share her rented property with an attractive, strong husband with a sense of humour.

Within a month the two were married. Sadly, their first child was stillborn but others followed quite quickly and by 1876, they had three fine sons: Francis, Michael and John.

So apart from the on-going political unrest in Ireland, Pat was quite content with life.

That was until one day in 1877 when, whilst calling at the 'Coaching House' with his pony and cart, a young girl ran out of the kitchen door, chasing a small boy.

Chapter 10

Changes (1874)

A year passed in which Kitty's life went on with its fair share of hard work tempered by some happy evenings spent at Mary's home. Here, by candlelight, the two young girls would dance, sing, laugh, and hold whispered conversations involving their growing breasts and the cheeky remarks of local lads.

However, whilst at home one evening, Kitty was surprised when Mam gathered together the older members of her family, saying she needed a word with them all. She stood to address them, a stern-faced, smallish, bespectacled woman in her late forties, auburn hair now sprinkled with grey.

"Now ye all know that Dad will be retiring from the constabulary in July this year. And he'll be getting a police pension. But it won't be enough to support our family of ten children with only three bringing in a wage. That's for sure! So what he plans to do is move from here and rent a house in Sligo Town."

At this there was a murmur of shock and strong disapproval from some of the family, in particular, Sarah and Kitty. They hated the thought of moving to busy town-life.

Mam raised a warning hand, "Och, it's no use ye blathering on about the move. We need more money, and there's money to be earned in the town. And that's all there is to say! It's May now, so what Sarah and Kitty need to be doing is thinking about what paid work they might be able to get, and then going to try to get it!"

By the time July arrived, the Tooey family were living in a rented house in Sligo, but Kitty still hadn't found a suitable job. However, that same month, she spoke to her mother excitedly, "Mam, Mary told me that their Margaret, who's been working in Sligo for some time now in a big drapery shop, says the business is growing, and so another 'live-in' assistant is needed. And would ye believe it? Margaret's going to put in a good word for me! She's a supervisor there now."

Kitty's mother was pleased with this possibility, especially since it meant Kitty would be a 'live-in' employee. Within the month, Kitty was working at a shop whose sign read:

DOOLEY'S DRAPERY AND HIGH-CLASS DRESSMAKING

Edna Dooley was the owner of the shop, a wealthy widow originally from Lancashire, who had developed a good head for business since her husband's death. She had given Margaret Molloy the task of showing Kitty round on her first day and explaining what her work would entail. Margaret greeted her sister's friend with a smile of welcome saying, "Ye've been a good friend to Mary and to all our family, so I hope ye will be happy here at Dooley's. But I warn ye that the work is hard with long hours. That is why I'm thinking it will be a good idea to firstly show ye the type of garment which our dressmakers are capable of making. Dressmakers whom you will be helping."

Kitty was then shown to the front of the shop where Margaret held up a long turquoise dress. It had been taken in at the waist, but the skirt was slightly flared at the hem-line and a wide collar of white delicate Irish lace set off the neckline. She said proudly, "This dress is based on the latest style. Notice that its skirt is much narrower than those in fashion last year. And everything is stitched by hand, none of those new ugly sewing machines here!" Mary then explained what the job involved for Kitty.

Firstly, she would have to carry heavy rolls of material from the store room to the front of the shop where customers could make their choice. Of course, this would also involve Kitty in knowing how to recognise the wide variety of materials available. Moreover, she would have to sort through all pieces of material from the work tables and floor, and decide which larger pieces could be used again. At the front of the shop, she would be required to pass pins to the dressmakers as they fitted clothes on models or clients, and she was expected to do this quickly and accurately. And of course, there was always ironing to be done.

"Holy Mother," Kitty thought, "I wonder what I'll do with all my *spare* time?"

Indeed it was as Margaret had foretold: hard work with very long hours and little time to oneself. However, as time passed and Kitty was able to work more quickly, she found time in the evening to enjoy walks along the banks of the nearby River Garavogue. Here she could admire the lovely trees which grew there, especially the willows with their graceful, trailing branches. A welcome change from the bustle and noise of Sligo Town's centre.

Kitty had to wait three months before she was allowed to spend a day with Mam and the family. Though her assistant's pay was poor, she had been able to save most of it and couldn't wait to see Mam's face when she proudly handed over money to her.

Of course, Mam was delighted to see her daughter again. "Welcome home, lassie. Your favourite bacon and potatoes will be ready soon."

Dad was home too, having returned from his work as a night-watchman and time-keeper with a firm in Sligo Town. Not a job he liked doing, but necessary in view of the family's finances. He greeted his daughter cheerily with his usual, "Ach 'tis good to have my ray of sunshine home again - and a wage-earner now!"

During the family meal, Kitty asked, "How's our Sarah liking her work as a housemaid? I know she works in Sligo Town, but I haven't seen her around. I'm thinking she's like me, and has little free time."

"Och, ye have that right, Kitty!" was Mam's reply. "She hasn't a good word to say about her work or her employers. Now she's talking about emigrating to New Zealand. I ask ye! It's the other side of the world!"

"Don't be worrying yourself about that, Mam, she'll soon find a better family to work for, and forget all about emigrating."

Two years passed, and a seventeen year old Kitty was still working at Dooley's. The hours were still long and the pay only minimally better than when she had first started, and though she was now used to all the jobs required of her, and on fairly friendly terms with the staff, she found no satisfaction in remaining a general 'dogsbody.' Many were the evenings after work when Kitty would ask, "Holy Mother of God! Surely there must be a better life for me than this?"

Her words must have been heard, as she was to find out on her next visit home.

It was still early morning when Kitty and her mother were alone in the kitchen boiling up potato skins for the pigs. Anne was out feeding the hens and collecting eggs. Mam said conspiratorially, "Well now, I've been hearin' some news which may be of interest to a clever girl like you. I was at the market the other day when I got chatting with some women from Riverstown. It seems they have a new owner at the 'Coaching House' pub called Thomas Laverty. His wife's expecting another bairn soon, and she has a four-year old son as well. The word is that she seems a bit of a feckless lassie, and finds it hard to keep him in order. A lively child by all accounts! So they need domestic help as soon as possible. *And* Mr Laverty is willing to pay extra money if the successful person is also able to teach his son some reading and writing."

She looked pointedly at her daughter, continuing, "Now I'm thinking that could be *you*, my girl."

An amazed Kitty said nothing at first. It seemed the Holy Mother had listened to her plea. But she had her doubts about the idea. "Mam, I'm not qualified to be a teacher! Also, how would I go about applying for the job? I'm due back at work tomorrow."

Her mother's reply was immediate, and obviously planned. "Of course, you're able to teach a four-year old! And as for applying for the job, one of the women said old Seamus Kelly will be glad to meet ye at Ballymote Station with his donkey and cart *today*. Ye just need to catch the first afternoon train from here. He's taking two crates of week-old chicks to Mr Laverty, and can easily take you as well - for a penny or two."

Seeing Kitty was about to make some protest, her mother continued quickly,

"So, all ye've to do is have something to eat, and be on that train. And soon ye'll be making yourself known to Mr Laverty. Then ye 'll be telling him all about your pupil-teaching."

"Ach, Mam, ye dark horse! Ye've had all this worked out! But what if I don't get the job?" Kitty paused. "And what if I *do?* What will I be sayin' to Mrs Dooley? It would be grand if I got the job - but Mam, ... Her mother jumped in quickly, "Hold yer whist, girl! Aren't ye just made for the job? For sure Mr Laverty and his wife will welcome ye with open arms. As for Mrs Dooley, I'm sure Margaret will help you there. And don't be thinkin' too long. It's the early bird that gets the worm!"

In fact, her daughter had made up her mind before the sentence ended.

It wasn't long before Kitty set off to catch the train from Sligo Station. She was quite excited at the prospect ahead and also this first journey by rail. It was lucky that prices had recently been reduced, allowing poorer people to afford third class tickets. As she reached the station platform, she was surprised to find it already quite crowded. Most were farmers, returning from the Saturday Market. Before long, the train came roaring and steaming into the station, the air filled with specks of soot.

As passengers climbed on board, Kitty found herself being pushed and shoved as third-class passengers tried to find seats on one of the few wooden benches. She had enviously glimpsed the first-class carriages with their comfortable seating, arm-rests between passengers, and overhead shelves for luggage.

But she just found herself standing, squashed between two very portly farmers. They talked non-stop above her head about the merits of their respective cows. The strong smell of whiskey was on their breath.

After only two stops, Kitty was relieved to hear the cry of a station employee,

"Ballymote, Ballymote!"

Alighting from the train, Kitty left the station and heard a voice call,

"Miss Kitty Tooey, would that be yerself, now?"

Turning, she spotted an elderly man sitting on a cart, waving with one hand and holding the reins of a brown and white pony with the other. He was wiry with a wrinkled, weathered face, but he still had the thick hair of a much younger man, albeit now totally white. He was still sprightly too, and in no time at all, he'd brought his cart and pony to where she was standing, carefully placed his crates at the front, and thrown a tattered piece of material on the back for Kitty so sit on. Then he jumped on himself, and reins in hand, flicked the pony into movement, saying, "Here we go Miss Kitty, 'tis a grand afternoon to be travellin' to Riverstown, 'the town by the river.'" And off went the cart, the pony keeping up a steady trot, and Seamus tunelessly whistling some old Irish song.

"Yes" thought Kitty to herself, "'Tis a grand morning' indeed, and 'tis grand companions I have! A pony, an old man and two crates of crowded, young chicks! But sure that's of little matter if I'm now on my way to a better life."

Chapter 11

Kitty in Riverstown (March 1877)

Seamus stopped the cart at a large solid two-storey slated building. There was a swinging sign at the side of the front entrance. On it was painted a shiny black coach pulled by four powerful black horses. The driver, also in black, sat resolutely and unsmiling as he held the reins.

"Right ye are Miss Kitty, this is where ye get off. 'Twill be better if ye make yer way round to the back entrance where the cook, a *fine* figure of a woman if ever there was one, will let ye in. I'll be waitin' here fer ye when I've finished my business."

Jumping down from the cart, pausing only to wave and shout a 'thank you,' Kitty walked purposefully round to the back of the house in the direction indicated by Seamus. However, her racing heart belied her outward demeanour, 'What if they don't like me? Or think I'm not good enough for the job?' were some of her inner thoughts. Reaching a wooden door, newly painted in white, she knocked firmly - but not so hard that it sounded like a 'demanding' knock, and took a deep breath.

A white-capped, pleasant looking woman in her thirties opened the door. Wiping her hands on her apron, she smiled and asked "Will it be Miss Kitty Tooey that's calling?"

On the caller's identity being confirmed, she held out her hand and continued.

"Pleased to meet you, I'm the cook here, and my name's Miss Keating. Mistress Laverty is waiting for you in the parlour with her husband, so if you'd like to follow me, I'll be introducin' you to them."

Kitty shook hands, instinctively taking a liking to her, and followed her out of the kitchen, through a darkish passage. Here, Miss Keating tapped twice on a brown door, then, followed by Kitty, entered a room with heavy maroon curtains at its large window.

She was introduced to a pale-faced, heavily pregnant woman seated in an armchair. Kitty noticed the dark shadows under her eyes. The woman greeted her with a weary smile. Then her husband nodded to Kitty, and indicated she should sit down on the wooden, high-backed chair opposite to him. Older than his wife, he stood at her side, a tall man with receding hair and a moustache tinged with grey.

Firstly, he asked Kitty to verify that her age was eighteen and also that she was of the Catholic faith. He then told her his family attended nearby St Joseph's Church. Next came a string of questions aimed at ascertaining that she could read and write well, and was also capable of teaching those skills to Master Thomas. He added that she would, of course, be expected to help Miss Keating in the kitchen, and also his wife in her household duties.

It seemed to Kitty that Mr Laverty gave priority to his son's education above her general help in the house. However, she simply replied she was ready and willing to undertake all her responsibilities, and give of her best. The quick response was,

"Well then, Miss Kitty, we'll give you two weeks' trial. If we are satisfied, the job will be yours. I've been informed that you are already employed, but I'm hoping you can start work at the week-end. So I trust you will make arrangements accordingly."

Kitty nodded, saying she would do so as soon as possible.

At this response, Mr Laverty took out a gold watch from his waist-coat pocket, said he had business to see to, and would now send in his son to meet her. Then after patting his wife's hand, he strode out through a door at the other end of the room.

During the 'interview' Mrs Laverty had looked on anxiously, saying nothing. She gave a relieved sigh when her husband left the room. Within a minute, there were two taps on the door and Miss Keating appeared, holding the hand of a struggling child.

"Thank you, Miss Keating, that will be all," said Mrs Laverty. Addressing Thomas, she spoke coaxingly, saying, "Come in now, Thomas, and meet Miss Kitty, she will be helping you with your reading."

A boy with fair hair and large, defiant brown eyes reluctantly entered the room, saying in a petulant tone, "I want to play with my bricks!"

Then seeing Kitty, who'd risen from her chair, he went up to her and scowled.

His mother, shook her head, sighing "Thomas, you know that's naughty. Now say you're sorry to Miss Kitty or I will have to send you to bed."

At this the child shouted, "No! I want my bricks." This was accompanied by a tattoo of angry stamps on the floor.

To herself, Kitty thought, "He wouldn't get away with that if he'd been brought up by Mam."

To Thomas, she smilingly observed, "Well now, Master Thomas, I didn't know you could dance Irish jigs. My brother, Alex, is ten and for sure you're nearly as good as he is. Would ye like me to teach you how to do a jig?" And Kitty then expertly danced one of the jigs she used to do with Margaret.

Surprised at this unexpected reaction to his temper, and also impressed by Kitty's intricate footwork, the boy, nodded.

Kitty moved to his side and showed him some jig patterns. Thomas proved to be a quick learner and was soon attempting one of the easier routines. Left stamp - right stamp moving forward, left stamp moving forward, right stamp at its side. The pattern was then repeated, but this time, moving backwards. Gradually, they built up quite a speed. Kitty hummed a catchy melody as they jigged happily along together. Finally, both pupil and teacher stopped to rest. Thomas looked eagerly at his dance partner asking, "I like you. Please will you stay and play with me?"

On hearing these words, Mrs Laverty smiled at both of the 'dancers' saying, "And I like Miss Kitty too. So now, I'm sure if you tell her you're sorry for that nasty face you pulled, she'll come back here in a day or two, and will be doing all kinds of interesting things with you." The apology was given immediately.

When it was time for Kitty to take her leave of Mistress Laverty and young Master Thomas, she found Seamus was already waiting for her with his pony and cart. They jogged back to Ballymote with Kitty reflecting on the events of the morning. Certainly there was plenty of varied work involved in her new job, but more importantly, she felt she had 'the measure' of Thomas and would enjoy teaching him.

Indeed, Kitty was soon quite settled and happy at the 'Coaching House' and had established a good relationship with Miss Keating and Mrs Laverty. The following month, the latter, after an anxious time during the birth, presented her delighted husband with a second son, Joseph. He was a good baby, and slept well which gave his mother time to rest and recover her strength. So it wasn't long before she had colour in her cheeks and had lost her previous look of weariness. She was also glad of Kitty's help with him, especially during the night.

As for Thomas, he enjoyed being with his new friend and teacher who had the knack of making learning fun. So, combined with the boy's natural curiosity and desire for knowledge, Kitty's role as a teacher never threatened their steadily growing affection for each other.

Mr Laverty instructed Kitty to keep his son away from the public house part of their home and also never to let Thomas play in the large yard outside the kitchen. This was where frequent and varied deliveries were made. However, to Kitty's great delight, he was keen that his son should take regular exercise by walking in the surrounding countryside.

And so, when Kitty's morning tasks in the house were completed, the two would set out to explore Riverstown in its rural setting between the two rivers, Arrow and Douglas.

On a sunny morning in June, Kitty and Thomas visited one of their favourite spots which was reached by walking along to the end of the main street in nearby Ardkeeran, then going through the fields to the woods. Thomas was fascinated by the glossy black rooks with their white faces and grey-black tails, and he would try to imitate their harsh calls of 'Kaaa' as they flew up to their untidy nests of twigs at the tops of trees. Often the two would make up stories about what they were 'saying' to each other.

Many ash trees grew in the wood and Kitty explained to Thomas that Norse people regarded the ash as 'The Tree of the World' since its roots reached down into the pits of hell, whilst its crown touched heaven, the trunk joining the two together. The young boy soon firmly believed that the largest ash tree in 'Caw Wood' was the actual tree the Norse people had revered long ago. (Thomas had given the wood its name: Caw.)

It was in this way that Kitty helped to widen Thomas' education. He was given information and also encouraged to ask questions about it, so letting his child's imagination and curiosity have 'full flow.'

On returning home, and before Miss Keating called to say that lunch was ready, Kitty and Master Thomas would go to the room which held playthings, as well as his desk, chair and shelf containing books and writing materials. Here, seated on the wooden chair, Thomas, with some guidance from his teacher, would write the names of the day, month, then date in his notebook. Below this heading, he would draw his impression of whatever had interested him that morning. Kitty would ask Thomas what he would like her to write about each illustration. So, with him watching, she would print the gist of what he had suggested in about two sentences. Finally, Kitty read the sentences to Thomas which he, in turn, attempted to read back to his teacher.

Both parents were delighted with their son's early progress in literacy, and also his increased knowledge of the surrounding countryside. Their own early education had been mainly restricted to reading and writing out parts of the Bible or learning poems of an 'uplifting' or moral nature.

And, of course, Kitty considered that, after her work in Sligo Town, she was very lucky to have found contentment in Riverstown.

One afternoon later that month, all housework and teaching having been completed, Kitty had a little time to spend building a brick-castle with her charge. The task being completed, Thomas had an idea. "Miss Kitty, let's play 'hide the brick'. Can I go first please?"

Kitty didn't mind the variation and readily agreed to him being the first to do the hiding. As usual, she went to the far end of his room, closed her eyes, faced the wall, and began to count to twenty slowly.

The young boy was smiling to himself as he picked up a small brick. If he hid the brick outside in the yard, Miss Kitty would never find it and he'd be the winner. On tiptoe, he quietly opened the door of his room and began making his way to the kitchen's open door. He was almost there when Kitty's sixth sense made her aware that something was not as it should be. Accordingly, she made her way quickly through the open door in time to see Thomas about to go into the yard. Immediately, she began to run, shouting, "Stop, Master Thomas! Don't go out!" With a squeal of laughter, the young Master dashed outside - and almost under the feet and wheels of a pony and cart which had entered the yard.

Kitty, both alarmed at the near-accident and also cross that Thomas had disobeyed his father's wishes, managed to catch hold of his hand, and remonstrated with the young boy. She was taken by surprise when the four-year old planted a kiss on her cheek whilst begging her not to tell his father he'd been in the yard.

That night, in the small bedroom she shared with Miss Keating, Kitty reflected on what might have been a terrible accident in the yard, possibly leading to her dismissal. Next she recalled the arrogant driver with the pony and trap who had tried to flirt with her, and almost aloud, she declared, "What a nerve he had! Behaving like a young lad and hoping for a kiss. If I *never* see him again, it'll be too soon!"

Chapter 12

Blackberry Picking (August, 1877)

It was a warm sunny day in August and, once again, Thomas and Kitty were out on one of their morning walks. This time the boy asked if they could take the road which led to the property owned by Landlord Murray. They'd been there the previous month and Thomas remembered seeing some rowan trees with their bright, red berries. He'd attempted to draw them in his 'diary' but hadn't been satisfied with the result, so this time he'd brought a special book for sketching. It had been given to him by his father who had been impressed with his young son's artistic attempts. He too had enjoyed sketching in his younger days.

Soon they reached the line of rowan trees, distinctive with their bright, red berries and branches of feather-like leaves, dappled in the morning sunlight. Kitty asked,"Now tell me where you'd like to be sitting and I'll put down this blanket for ye whilst working."

It took him about five minutes before he found a suitable spot for his art work and, after studying one tree carefully, he began to draw. Kitty stood nearby, watching her charge with pride and taking in the warmth of the sun and the unmistakeable smell of the nearby ripened corn.

While lost in her daydreaming, there came the sound of a pony and trap coming down the nearby lane. Kitty turned to see who the 'intruder' was.

"Holy Mary," she thought, "not him again!" Deliberately, she turned away to watch the young artist.

Indeed, it was none other than Pat O'Dowd on some errand for 'Miser Murray.' He'd recognised Kitty before she'd been aware of him, and the sight of her again roused disturbing feelings within him. Here was the striking young girl who'd kept him awake during the past months. Automatically, he brought his pony to a halt, hoping she'd turn round again.

Aware that the pony had stopped its steady trot, Kitty quickly began talking to Thomas, "I forgot to tell you that the rowan is a special tree, but in a different way from the oak tree. It's believed to have special charms which can keep away witches and bad spirits. A lot are planted in churchyards. Can you remember seeing the one in Ardkeeran's churchyard when we went to 'Caw Wood'?

There was a nod from Thomas and he said excitedly, "That means they are magic trees, so I'll take care with how I draw *this* one."

A voice from behind them broke in, "Magic is it, young sir? Then I'm thinkin' ye'll be correct in taking care how you draw yours, as it *will* have some magic in it too."

Two heads quickly turned in the direction of the speaker. Thomas beamed, clearly delighted at the idea of creating a magical drawing. Kitty gave Pat a distinctly frosty look and seemed about to say something disparaging. But before she could speak, the latter cut in with, "Miss Kitty, I believe? I'm hopin' ye'll accept an apology from me for my rudeness and ignorance the last time we met. Sure, I didn't wish to offend ye. In truth, I was just so taken with yer fair self that I spoke quite out of turn." He paused a moment. "So could ye possibly forgive a stupid, old man by the name of Pat Dowd?"

There was a long silence before Kitty answered. She was quite impressed by the change in this man's demeanour since their first meeting. His arrogance was all gone - though she still felt some of his words had a touch of the 'blarney' about them.

Finally she replied, "Very well then, Mr Dowd, we'll say no more about it. Now if you don't mind, I'd like to get on with supervising Master Thomas' work."

Pat would have liked to speak further with this young woman who reminded him a little of Jeannie in Scotland due to her lovely auburn hair. But whilst Kitty was not beautiful in the accepted sense, she was more than that. She had a youthful, lively spirit. And then there were those bright green eyes. Eyes which both attracted and fascinated him. However, there was no doubting the dismissal he'd been given. But at least it seemed he'd been forgiven. So it was with mixed feelings that he moved on with his pony and trap.

Meanwhile, Thomas was taking special care with his 'magical' drawing whilst Kitty observed him. When he was satisfied with his artwork, he and Kitty made their way back home. The former, eager to show his parents his achievement, the latter pleased with the success of the morning's outing. Little thought being given to that second encounter with Pat Dowd.

Life for Kitty at the Coaching House was good. In addition to the great relationship which had been established with Master Thomas, she and Miss Keating were becoming quite good friends. Indeed, for some time now, she had been invited by the latter to use her Christian name, Margaret. She still found Mrs Laverty to be a somewhat shy person but, as time went on, she regained health and strength and became more confident. Moreover, she always showed her gratitude when Kitty got up during the night to help nurse and comfort young Master Joseph when cutting his first teeth.

Of course, Kitty always looked forward to her monthly visits home. Here she caught up with all the family news. Dad, had been retired for three years now and was working as a part-time security guard in Sligo to help supplement his pension. Though remaining active, and retaining his sense of humour, Kitty had noticed he was looking slightly thinner than on her visit in August. As usual, Mum was perpetually busy having four children to care for.

Anne though, who had turned thirteen and had left school, was able to help Mam in the home. William, at five years old, was the youngest, and twenty-three year old Mary was the eldest. She was already married with twin daughters, a baby boy, and now living in Drumfin, about two miles from Rivertown. The other three, Edward, Margery and Sarah, had found work in Sligo Town. The two girls worked in shops, whilst Edward worked on one of the cargo ships which sailed regularly from Rosses Point to Scotland or Liverpool. None of their pay was good, so Kitty's money was extra welcome. And Mum was always interested to hear of her daughter's progress with Thomas Laverty's education.

As September arrived, a time when blackberries were usually at their ripest, Margaret Keating asked Kitty if she and Master Thomas would make their next morning walk a 'blackberry pick' so that she could make blackberry jelly jam for the family and also blackberry and apple pies.

Naturally, this request met with eager approval from the two concerned, and the next morning they set off armed with three baskets. On earlier walks, when the blackberries were still red, they had noted that the greatest number of bushes were to be found near 'Miser Murray's' land. So once again they headed in that direction.

It took only twenty minutes or so to reach the bushes which stretched for about a mile down the lane. The purple-black berries looked at their best, and in no time the two were at work - but not before Kitty had passed on all the advice given by her Mam. "Mind ye pick berries that are firm, not ones which are too ripe! They're nice to eat, but they make jam runny. And ye should pick a few that are still red to help the jam set better."

In quite a short time, they had filled two of their baskets. But suddenly dark clouds appeared, and it seemed that rain might follow soon. So Kitty warned Thomas that they should stay no longer than two minutes if they were to get back ahead of a downpour. Disappointed at this change of plan, he pleaded, "But Miss Kitty, I've seen such a lot of ripe berries on that high branch, just near us! I think *you* might be able to reach them all very quickly. I could hold a basket underneath so you could just drop them in." Noticing her look of doubt, he added, "Oh please say yes Miss Kitty! Then we'll stop all our picking, and walk quickly before the rain catches us."

She hesitated a moment, but couldn't resist the eager, young eyes fixed upon her.

"Well, I think I can reach that branch, but we'll both start counting. And when we reach one hundred, we stop! And you must be ready to walk back quickly. Is that agreed?" Thomas nodded eagerly, and when they reached one hundred, he was ready to set off with Kitty and their harvest of berries.

Thomas went on ahead with a half- full basket; Kitty was behind him, carrying the two full ones. All at once he turned round, calling proudly, "Miss Kitty, I think Miss Keaton and Mummy will be very pleased with all these blackberries."

Without waiting for a reply, he turned again, about to recommence his fast walking. It was then he found his foot caught in a straggly length of bramble, but in trying to regain his balance, his leg had twisted awkwardly, and he fell to the ground.

Kitty ran forward immediately. Thomas gave a cry of pain as he tried to get up. The contents of his basket, scattered around him. He looked up at her, stammering between sobs, "My leg - won't l- let me stand up - it hurts - a lot - ."

Kneeling beside him, Kitty spoke soothingly and examined his ankle. "Shh now, Master Thomas, don't ye try to move, I'm going to say magic words over your ankle, I think ye may have sprained it. The magic will stop the pain."

Moving her right hand in a slow circling movement over the injured part, Kitty began to chant in a low, rhythmic voice. They were the words her Mother had used whenever one of her children hurt themselves.

"Tirromy, torromy diddle-de-die! Ev-ery bit of hurt must fly!

Tirromy torromy diddle -de-doh! Ev-ery bit of hurt must go!"

The 'spell' ended, she asked, "There now, can ye feel the pain flying away?"

Her question was never answered. Unnoticed by both of them, Pat Dowd, on his way to Murray's house, had been standing a little distance away, listening with interest to the strange 'performance.' As Kitty's chant finished, he moved closer, then spoke before Thomas could say a word.

"Ach, it seems to me that ye've had a tumble, Master Thomas. Is it yer ankle that's givin' ye such pain?" Thomas nodded.

Pat then said, turning his attention to Kitty, "Would ye allow me to look at his ankle, Miss Kitty? Sure I've had plenty of dealings with all kinds of injuries." He hesitated a moment before adding, "Though I'm certain your magic has already begun to work on the lad."

Although aware that this man, Pat Dowd, was again using his blarney on her, Kitty felt glad of his offer since she wasn't sure if the ankle was broken or not. So her reply was, "Yes, thank ye, I'd be pleased if you'd examine it."

A polite but brief reply, but it satisfied Pat as he looked again into her green eyes. Bending down on one knee, he gently began to feel around the inflamed and swollen ankle. As he put some slight pressure on the area, he saw Thomas flinch.

"Well, Master Thomas, ye've not broken any bones, but ye must have given yer ankle a nasty twist when ye fell. It's a sprained ankle ye have."

"That means ye shouldn't try to walk on it. Now I've got work to do for Landlord Murray, but I can get ye back to yer home if ye don't mind me carryin' ye on my shoulders. Sure, it'll be like riding on a horse!"

The youngster nodded eagerly at the idea. And Kitty thankfully gave Pat her permission to carry Thomas back home though she'd first asked if the extra journeys would cause trouble between him and Landlord Murray.

"Don't ye be worryin' about me and the 'Miser' now. When I arrive late, I'll just explain how I saw two of those Roscommon sheep-stealers in the village last night, and how I saw them lurkin' near these bushes just now."

And, winking at Kitty, he lifted Thomas up on to his shoulders.

"So I ask ye, what could honest, brave Patrick Dowd do, but watch them for a while, then have a 'gentle' word with them? Helpin' them understand that men and dogs will be waitin' if they come near again."

Despite herself, Kitty couldn't help but smile at Pat's audacity, imagination and blatant lie.

"Sure it was the devil himself who gave you that tongue! May the Lord forgive ye for such lies, Pat Dowd!" But another smile accompanied these words.

They walked in silence for several minutes, Thomas, happily imagining he was riding a real horse. The 'wurching' in his ankle seeming less painful now. And Pat, hardly able to believe that he was walking with, and speaking to, this bewitching young woman. The actual content of her words were of no consequence - she'd smiled at him twice, that was all that mattered.

"Do you think sheep-stealers are all from Roscommon then?" Kitty asked, hastening her step to catch up with Pat's strides. He looked taken aback at the question, replying hastily, "Oh Holy Mary, Miss Kitty. I'm so sorry. Do I take it you come from there? I thought you came from Sligo Town. I wasn't trying to insult yer place of birth, I was ..."

The sentence was never finished as Kitty's manner changed instantly.

"Mr Dowd, I don't come from Roscommon and I certainly don't come from Sligo Town. Though my family now live in Sligo Town, I was born in Cloonacool. A country girl is what I am!"

There was a loud and greatly relieved roar of laughter as Pat exclaimed, "Well, it seems we have similar opinions on Sligo Town. But I know Ballinafad well, Miss Kitty. Wasn't I born in Cartron, only a few miles away? Two of the loveliest villages ye could wish fer."

"I don't know Cartron well, but you're certainly correct about Ballinafad." Another smile from Kitty. And Pat was again walking on air. By now they were almost at the 'Coaching House' where Pat was thanked for his concern and help. Kitty also mentioned that Thomas would be fine now, and that she'd be bandaging his ankle in boiled comfrey leaves as soon as soon as possible.

Pat smiled and nodded, saying, "Yer a country girl for sure. Comfrey will have the young Master walking about in no time. Goodbye, Miss Kitty, it's been a pleasure to have yer company."

However, the mention of comfrey had brought back Pat's memories of his Mam using it to bandage Anne's sprained wrist all those years ago, shortly followed by her death during the famine years. Then followed his recollections of Mam's death only months later, and also memories of those horrific days of the famine and all the unburied, unnamed bodies that still remained in Cartron. Now with only boulders and earth as their 'headstones'.

His face darkened as he recalled friends and family, so cruelly lost during the years of famine and starvation. Then he turned, and started to walk back in the direction of Murray's land.

But it was a change in mood which didn't go unnoticed by Kitty. She wondered why her mention of comfrey had caused that change. She'd said nothing, but along with Thomas had waved a cheerful 'Goodbye' to their rescuer. Then she'd helped the former to 'hop' round to the back door of the 'Coaching House'.

But that night was a restless one for Kitty.

She kept going over the events of the day. Wondering why this man, Pat Dowd, whom she had disliked on their first meeting, had now, for the third time, come into her life. A man who too loved the countryside. She felt certain he had a wife and probably children. A man she should keep at arm's length. Yet thoughts kept coming.

Chapter 13

Pat and Kitty

That night, after the meeting with the two 'blackberry pickers,' Pat was once more awake and reflecting on the fact that fate had stepped in and allowed him the chance to engage in conversation with the young woman who, unbidden, kept occupying his thoughts. During the short time he'd walked and talked with Kitty, he'd felt so happy, and indeed much younger than his forty-six years. The fact they shared the same views on Sligo Town and had the same rural backgrounds, seemed to give them a special link.

The latter thought led him to consider what he and Anne had in common apart from the fact that, when they'd met, he just wanted someone 'suitable' to settle down with and have a family. And she, a young widow, was just on the lookout for a strong, healthy man to help manage her land. For sure, she was a good mother to their three young children, Francis who was six, Michael aged four, and fifteen months old John. She saw that they were well-fed and clothed. She could have a sharp tongue at times yet she always kept him warm in bed.

"But isn't it every wife's duty to do these things?" he asked himself.

At that moment, young Michael awoke crying. After listening for a moment or two, Anne turned to Pat, saying sleepily, "I think our Michael's had a bad dream again, I'll go and see to him before he wakes up John." The next thing he heard was Anne talking soothingly to Michael.

As he listened to her, Pat's train of thoughts changed quickly and he heard an inner voice speaking. "Ye bastard, Pat Dowd! Anne's a kind, caring wife. And doesn't deserve a husband who spends nights thinking of another woman!"

There and then, Pat decided to face the realities and blessings of his life and put Kitty Tooey out of his mind.

❦ ❦ ❦

September came to an end. Pat still made several deliveries to the 'Coaching House' for Landlord Murray, but on each occasion he lost no time in getting his business done quickly so there was little chance of catching sight of Kitty in the yard. However, one day, when returning from a delivery at the new pub in Ballymote, unimaginatively named 'The Station', he unexpectedly came face to face with Seamus and Kitty. They were travelling in the opposite direction, making their monthly visit to Ballymote Station. At this sudden sight of her, he felt his stomach turning over, but somehow managed to hide the tangle of emotions he was feeling. So there was merely a nod to old Seamus, a touch on his cap, and a curt, "Mornin'" to Kitty.

Yet Pat's journey back to Riverstown was dominated once more by thoughts of Kitty. He'd seen the smile and wave she'd started to give him which quickly changed to surprise on receiving his decidedly chilly greeting.

And it was a very puzzled Kitty who left Seamus to buy a ticket to Riverstown. On boarding the train, she managed to find a carriage with a free seat, and there spent the short journey reflecting on Pat's unsmiling, cold greeting. She wondered why this man who had, on three occasions, gone out of his way to speak to her, so suddenly changed in his attitude towards her.

She tried to recall the conversation at their last meeting, and remembered that when she had mentioned using comfrey on Thomas' sprain, his reaction had been strange. Was comfrey connected in some way to a very sad event in his life?

However, having almost reached her destination, Kitty began looking through the train window, eager to alight and be with her family again.

As usual, Mam was waiting for her at the door, young William at her side, the latter put his arms around Kitty's waist, squeezing it tightly. Mam gave her a smile saying, "And how's my teacher-daughter then?"

Before she could reply, sister Madge appeared, a large, wooden spoon in her hand, remarking, "So my big sister's joining us for the day, is she? Well, I'm hoping ye've brought your appetite with ye, Mam's put aside a mountain of spuds, vegetables and bacon for me to cook today - all in Lady Kitty's honour."

Kitty gave her sister a hug, saying, "I'd forgotten ye'd just left school now you're twelve. Mam will be glad of your help round the house for a while until ye get a job."

Mum nodded emphatically, adding, "Aye, but away with ye now Madge, we need dinner ready for when Alex and David get home from school."

Once she had left them, Kitty's mother asked, "And how's the wee laddie progressing with his learning,?"

In reply, Kitty told her that Thomas was now reading and writing quite well. She also included a description of their blackberry expedition and Thomas' sprained ankle. Casually, she also mentioned the kindness of the man called Pat Dowd who helped by carrying the boy back home.

It wasn't long before Kitty's Dad returned from his night-shift as a security guard - not a job he liked much. He looked thin and weary as he came through the door, but his face brightened on seeing his daughter, and he patted her cheek asking,

"How's my Kitty? 'Tis a breath of sunshine ye are."

She smiled back at him as she said, "Sure I'm fine Dad, it's grand to see ye."

Yet, she noticed how slowly he walked to 'his' chair, closed his eyes, and was asleep almost immediately.

The rest of the day passed quickly and happily. It was a pity that her Dad slept most of the day, though he did rouse himself when it was time for her to leave, and waved her a fond farewell with the rest of the family.

Being now the beginning of October, it was already dusk as she alighted from the train at Ballymote where Seamus was already waiting for her. After the first greeting between Kitty and her driver, there was no further conversation, just the latter's cheery whistling in time with the pony's trotting.

Thoughts were mixed for Kitty. Firstly, she dwelt on her father's deteriorating health having noticed how concerned Mum had seemed when he refused any dinner, asserting he'd prefer to remain napping and eat later.

As the pony and cart drew nearer to Seamus' cottage where the two always parted, Pat Dowd's cold greeting that morning flashed across her mind's eye. Her woman's mind wanted to discover the reason for it - particularly since she was just getting to like this once 'annoying' man.

However, these thoughts were interrupted by the arrival at their destination. Kitty paid Seamus the small, agreed sum of money, and jumped from the cart. The coins were spat upon for good luck, then man, pony and cart made their way to the side of his cottage to be stabled. In the dusk, Kitty set off for the 'Coaching House.'

On returning from Ballymote that morning, Pat stabled his pony and continued work on 'Miser' Murray's land, namely harvesting potatoes. Traditionally, these must all be dug up before the feast of All Saints on November 1st. He remained uneasy and confused for the whole of the day. Despite himself, he kept picturing Kitty looking at him in bewilderment. Then he would picture Anne, busy at home cooking, seeing to the chickens and pigs, breast-feeding young John, and generally keeping everything in order, ready for his return from work. Also, he kept reminding himself of the promise he'd made to himself some weeks ago - to dismiss Kitty Tooey from his thoughts.

When work was finished and he returned home, he made a point of praising Anne for the tasty meal she'd prepared - something he rarely ever did. She gave him a surprised smile remarking, "'Twas nothing special Pat but 'tis grand to have praise from ye."

Yet, shortly after playing his tin whistle for sons, Francis and Michael, before they went to bed, another glimpse of Kitty's hurt look pushed its way into Pat's head. He rationalised his inner conflict, "I *will* keep the promise I made to Anne, but surely Kitty needs some explanation about this morning. I owe her that much! So I'll try to catch her briefly tonight when she returns from Sligo Town. I'll explain that it's been grand knowin' her but that I have a good wife and three fine boys and I should never have tried to get so friendly with her. There was a long pause before he concluded with, "Then I'll be able to get on with my life as it was before Kitty's arrival."

Having made that decision, Pat began putting on his boots and working jacket, announcing, "I'm off to check that all's as it should be near 'Miser's' land. That lot from Roscommon have been hangin' around his fields for a day too and I'm thinkin' they're up to no good. Be back soon."

Busy with boiling up the animal's food for next day, Anne merely replied, "Well just ye take care and don't be getting into a fight with that lot."

But once he'd set out on his mission, Pat began to wonder if Kitty might have caught an earlier train and was already back at the 'Coaching House.' He decided he'd have to chance that possibility, and walked to the 'Coaching House.' From there, he took the pathway to Seamus' cottage - hoping to meet Kitty at some point.

He was soon at his first destination and had only been walking for five minutes when, in the distance, he saw a figure stepping out briskly towards him. Even in the semi-darkness, he sensed it was Kitty. Pat's stomach began to churn and he stood quite still, waiting apprehensively for the figure's approach.

As she neared, Kitty became aware of someone standing ahead of her. Cautiously, she slowed her step and then realised with a start that here was the man who'd been occupying her thoughts most of that day.

"Pat Dowd!" She exclaimed. Then her surprised expression turned to a smile. "Now I don't know what you're doing here, but whatever the reason, I'm glad to see ye - and that's for sure!"

Having been prepared for a cold greeting, or indeed no greeting at all, Pat was perplexed. His prepared 'Goodbye' speech went totally out of his mind. All he managed to say was, "Hello, Kitty, I'm also glad to have met ye. I guessed you might be returnin' about this time after visitin' yer family."

"So this isn't a chance meeting, Pat? But never mind, it's one I'd hoped for. Ye see, when you ignored me this morning, I realised I must have been the cause of whatever 'black' place ye went to when I mentioned comfrey last month." Then placing a hand gently on his, Kitty said, "All I can do is apologise."

These words, and Kitty's action left Pat even more bewildered. It was quite a chilly night, but the touch of her hand on his was warm, a warmth which increased and spread quickly like a raging fire to his entire body. Meanwhile, his mind was trying to make sense of her words and apology. It seemed she thought his actions that morning had been caused by *her* at their last meeting. Then he recalled how the word 'comfrey' had brought back memories of Anne, his Mum and all the devastation and deaths caused by the famine.

Still waiting for some response to her apology, Kitty slowly removed her hand from Pat's, and stood looking at him expectantly. After what must, in fact, have been only a few seconds, Pat began to laugh.

Kitty regarded him quizzically saying, "Well, I was expecting *some* reply to my apology, but certainly not laughter! Maybe ye'll share the joke?"

"Ach, I'm sorry for that, Miss Kitty. But what a pair of eejits we are! You wantin' to apologise fer mentioning somethin' that looks like a weed, and me wantin' to apologise fer seemin' to ignore ye this mornin'!"

He continued, "Let me explain exactly why the mention of comfrey could take me to a 'dark place' as ye called it. But shall we start walkin' back to the 'Coachin' House' as I talk? I wouldn't want to be the cause of ye bein' late back."

There was a nod of agreement from Kitty, and the two walked slowly together as Pat related what had happened to his mother and sister during the first year of the famine and its increasingly devastating effects. He went on at some length to tell how he and his Dad had eventually gone to Scotland in search of work. At this point, Kitty interrupted him.

"So ye've spent time in Scotland Pat? I'm wondering if ye ever travelled to Ayrshire for work, that's where my Mam was born, though she's never mentioned exactly where in Ayrshire it was. Of course, her family left there at some point and she, a Presbyterian, married my Irish Catholic Dad over here."

Surprised at this information, Pat was also pleased at her mother's Scottish origins. This meant he and Kitty had something else in common, so his reply was, "Would ye believe it? That's where Dad and I worked, Ayr! The wages were better than in Ireland, but those bothies which we were packed into at night were nothing but hell holes. Didn't a group of men in one die from suffocation?

He paused a moment and shook his head. "Ach now, I shouldn't be talkin' to ye about that. Ye've heard enough misery from me already! Sure the Spring in Scotland was lovely, and there was some fine countryside round Ayrshire. Maybe your Mam lived in one of those places?"

"I think she probably did, as she was always telling us children legends about the flowers and trees and healing properties of certain plants."

Pat smiled, then asked, "How many children did yer Mam and Dad have?"

Kitty's reply of, "Ten. I have five sisters and four brothers," brought a long whistle of surprise from Pat who then exclaimed, "Ten children! And all from a Catholic and Presbyterian union? Bejaysus, they must have found *something* in common then!"

Immediately, realising his last remark might have seemed offensive, he added, "Now, there I go again, opening my big stupid mouth before thinkin'"

But he needn't have worried since Kitty was already nodding her head and laughing, "Sure you're right there Pat! I remember only too well how we girls would notice another swelling in Mam's belly and say 'Holy Mother! Here we go again!'"

Relieved, Pat joined in her laughter. With pleasure, he'd noted too that this young and feisty woman had started referring to him as 'Pat'.

"How often do you get to visit yer family then, Miss Kitty?"

Before replying, she noticed how close to the 'Coaching House' they were. Not wanting anyone from there to see them talking, she suggested, "Would ye mind us standing by the entrance of St Joseph's church to finish our conversation? I don't want Mr Laverty seeing me chatting to anyone."

Pat nodded, realising this would be prudent for both of them.

At the church gate, Kitty replied to Pat's question.

"Well now, I'm allowed to have the first Monday in every month 'free'. So I go home then as it's one of the 'quiet' days in the pub. Of course, with darkness coming earlier now, I'll have less time with my family."

Both were silent for a few moments, busy with their own thoughts.

Kitty was first to speak. She looked up with a serious face and said,

"Perhaps 'tis better if we say 'Goodnight' now Pat. We've cleared up our misunderstandings and I'm thinking ye have a wife and children to get home to."

Guiltily he relied "Yes, I do have a good wife and three sons. They'll be expectin' me soon."

Inwardly, he challenged himself, "Ye bastard, gutless coward! Isn't that only a part of what ye were supposed to say when you met Kitty?"

In as matter-of-fact a voice as she could manage, Kitty spoke again. "Well goodbye to ye Pat, I'm glad ye took the trouble to walk to meet me. And I wish ye 'Beannaht!" (Good night!)

"For sure, meetin' ye and walkin' with ye was no trouble at all. Good night, Miss Kitty, Beannaht."

The two, just for a moment, stood without speaking. Then they met each other's eyes. The look and silence which followed before they went their separate ways spoke more loudly than any tirade of speeches.

Chapter 14

Fate's Cruel Trick

As October moved on, the weather became distinctly colder and wind brought leaves fluttering to the ground. Morning walks were now spent in games of identifying the various leaves and fruits which carpeted the earth in the woods. Young Thomas was delighted to show off his knowledge to his teacher and ran on happily ahead to find items named by her. On these occasions, and indeed for most of her busy days, she was fairly contented with life. It was the times when her mind was allowed to wander that she became unsettled, and this occurred mostly at bed-time.

As soon as they were both settled, Margaret would chat about the events of the day and she'd share snippets of conversation overheard when serving food to the pub's visitors. Also, she'd always want to know what Kitty and Thomas had seen and done on their walks. Of course, Kitty was quite happy to engage in these chats for a little while, but since the last unexpected meeting with Pat, she was relieved when the two had settled for the night and she was able to ponder over recent events.

She could see her mother shaking her head warningly, saying "Yon man's nae to be trusted! Away with these foolish thoughts, lassie!"

But that was something Kitty couldn't do, she kept reliving over and over again every moment of their last short walk from Seamus' cottage to St Joseph's Church. It would begin with her pleasure as she saw him, and end with the 'electricity' which passed between their eyes before parting.

Just before the month ended, young Thomas asked if their morning walk could again be in the direction of 'Miser' Murray's land where, earlier that month, they'd spotted red squirrels near two large horse-chest-nut trees. These creatures had been busy scampering around picking up fallen chestnuts which had come out of their spiny, split cases, and hurrying away to bury them. Thomas had been attracted by them with their long, plume-like tails and tufted ears and he wanted to draw them as accurately as he could. Accordingly, they set off, armed with a blanket and the necessary art equipment.

Luckily, one red squirrel was actually burying a chestnut as they arrived, so work began quickly. As usual Kitty stood watching the young artist, yet part of her mind was recalling that this wasn't far from the spot where she'd seen Pat for the second time. A time when she'd been somewhat annoyed at his appearance. Now she kept wondering if he might just pass by at any moment. And if he *did* appear, how would she feel then? She knew she ought to forget this man with his 'fine wife and three sons.' Instead, she kept imagining she'd heard footsteps and a voice bidding her, "Good morning' to ye Miss Kitty."

On that same morning, Pat was making a delivery of eggs, potatoes, cabbage and a side of pork to 'The Seven Stars' near Ballymote Station. His thoughts too were wandering. Since last seeing Kitty, he had made an effort to concentrate on giving more time to his family, especially his two elder boys. But despite good intentions, he found himself becoming unfairly impatient with Anne and his sons.

Now, nearing the station, he was reminded of Kitty looking at him in bewilderment as they'd passed each other earlier in the month. He then went on to recall every detail of their walk to St. Joseph's church. Once again, he could feel her hand placed over his, their shared laughter, and their parting when her eyes met his."Oh God," he thought to himself, "please help me! In just a few days it'll be the first Monday of the month. And though I know full well it would be madness to see her again, I don't know if I'll have the strength to resist the temptation!"

But it seemed that God hadn't been listening. The very next day fate played a cruel trick on Pat and Kitty.

Mr Laverty was walking along the passage to have a word with Miss Keating in the kitchen. On passing by his son's room, he saw through the open door that Thomas was putting the finishing touches to his drawing of the red squirrel. Impressed by what he saw, he went in to take a closer look and picked up the sketch book. Whilst his father was admiring the picture, Thomas suddenly exclaimed,

"Daddy, look in the yard! It's the man that gave me a ride when I hurt my ankle."

Putting down his son's book, Mr Laverty replied in surprise, "Oh! So it was Pat Dowd, was it? Well, I think we'd better tell him how well your ankle has healed, and thank him for his kindness."

And so Thomas was ushered into the passage and through to the kitchen where Margaret was busy preparing soup for lunch-time customers. Kitty was taking oatmeal cakes out of the oven over the fire.

"Kitty, leave those cakes to cool, and ask Pat Dowd into the kitchen before he drives on. Hurry now! Thomas and I want to thank him for his recent kindness."Already flustered on hearing a pony trotting into the yard, this unexpected order just added to Kitty's confusion. Would she betray any of her inner feelings to Pat? She'd come to the firm decision that it was up to her to lead the way by behaving politely, but distantly, should they come across each other. So, pushing a stray red curl under her cap, Kitty hurried to the door and called out in an impersonal tone, "Mr Dowd, would ye please stop the pony here, and come into the kitchen? Mr Laverty and Thomas are wanting a word with ye."

On hearing Kitty's words, Pat too was puzzled as he brought his pony to a sudden halt. He jumped from his cart, searching her face for any sign that she was glad to see him. Like her voice, it betrayed nothing.

His inner self was saying, "Well now that's good Pat. That's what ye wanted isn't it? She's forgotten the last meeting. That makes it easier for ye to do the same."

But at the same time, another part of him wasn't so sure his conclusion had been correct.

However, he made his way into kitchen, trying to avoid Kitty's eyes as he bade her, and then Mr Laverty, "Good day."

Kitty merely nodded in reply, turning to busy herself with the cakes again, her face flushed and agitated. Something which Margaret didn't fail to notice. She raised a quizzical eyebrow at Kitty who just shook her head dismissively.

Unaware of these 'exchanges,' Mr Laverty beckoned to Kitty, indicating that she should leave the cakes and join him and Thomas. Trying desperately to behave naturally, she moved to the landlord's side as he began to speak.

"Good morning, Pat. Thomas here tells me that you helped get him home after his accident a little while ago. It's already healed well so we've you to thank for that." Then looking down at his son, he said, "Now, Thomas haven't *you* something to say to Pat?"

Eagerly, Thomas ran forward to Pat, his words tumbling out. "See! I can run now! Oh, and thank you for being my horse."

He was about to return to his father when another thought occurred to him so he turned back, saying, "Can I show you how I can hop on it as well?"

Before he began any demonstration, Pat smiled, advising,"Ach no, Master Thomas. It's too early for ye to be thinkin' of hoppin'. But in a while, ye'll be hoppin' and runnin' faster than a mad March hare! And I promise I'll be watchin' ye then."

Disappointed, Thomas looked at Pat and pleaded, "Well, you will *keep* your promise, won't you? And I want Miss Kitty to watch me too."

This unexpected linking of Pat with Kitty startled both of them. Instinctively, they glanced at each other before assuring Thomas that they would watch him.

But the glance had been unguarded, and revealed far more than each had intended.

Mr Laverty, now wanting to get on with his own business, merely nodded, saying to his son impatiently,"Yes, yes, but only when your leg has healed fully. Now I'll bid you 'Good day' Pat." Looking at Thomas again he said firmly, "Now back to your painting son. I've things to see to."

And he made his way briskly back to the living room whilst his son gave a smile and a wave to Pat, then turned to go to his room.

After first smiling and waving to the young boy, Pat addressed both women, retaining his smile,"Good day, Miss Keating and Miss Kitty."

Margaret returned the smile and greeting. Kitty, unsmiling, politely replied, "Good day, Mr Dowd."

That night, once the two women were alone in their room, Margaret looked questioningly at Kitty,"Now then, young lady, what was all that about in the kitchen this morning? Sure I've never seen ye so tense and uneasy before. It started the minute Mr Laverty mentioned Pat Dowd."

There was a shrug of the shoulders, followed by an exasperated sigh and an almost angry voice saying," I've no idea what you're prattling on about!"

But there was no way Margaret was going to let things end there. And eventually, Kitty, near tears, revealed how, in the short period of time she'd been in Riverstown, there'd been several accidental meetings with Pat. And how, despite herself, her feelings towards Pat had changed gradually from dislike to feelings of attraction. She admitted she'd been aware that he probably had a wife and children and so had been striving to get him completely out of her mind. She added finally, "Yes Margaret, I felt I was managing until his unexpected appearance today. And that knocked me sideways for a time. But I'm over it, and from now on any thoughts of Pat Dowd will be shoved out if they *try* to enter my mind again. Ye can be sure of that!"

An attentive and quite sympathetic listener, Margaret commended Kitty's resolve, saying, "Well, you're right to be forgettin' all about him. Sure he's a nice enough man, always has a cheery word when he comes round, but I have the feeling he's also a one for the ladies. So ye'd do well to remember that too. Now let's get some sleep!"

That same night, Pat was also reflecting on the events of the morning. Finding himself once more in close proximity to Kitty had caused him to ignore all his recent, noble resolutions. All he'd wanted to do was take Kitty in his arms and tell her how he felt. These thoughts kept him awake most of the night. At last, sheer exhaustion brought some uneasy sleep in the early hours of the morning.

Luckily, the morning brought renewed self-will. Anne was already up preparing breakfast and young John was holding on to his mother's apron as though, any moment some wicked sprite or beast might suddenly snatch him away. It was a habit which Pat had frowned on in the past. Now it made him realise how all his children loved and depended upon her. It reminded him too of *his* dependency on her. All that was truly meaningful to him was here. Not with Kitty Tooey. With that thought in mind he got up to start the new day.

Chapter 15

Trials

Two days after the unexpected 'kitchen incident' was the first Monday of November, and so Kitty was up early on a frosty but sunny morning to get ready to visit her Mam and family. As usual, Margaret had baked an assortment of pies and oatcakes for her to take to Sligo Town, while Mrs Laverty had provided eggs and a ham joint for the Tooey basket. Thomas waved to her from the kitchen door as she walked round to the front of the pub and from there to Seamus' cottage. The old man was already waiting for her, cheerfully whistling. A quick exchange of greetings followed. Kitty climbed carefully on the cart with her loaded basket and soon they were en route to the railway station, the fields on either side still 'white -over' with frost in the morning sunshine.

She couldn't help remembering seeing Pat a month ago, travelling that road in the opposite direction. But that thought was quickly dismissed as she returned to thoughts of her father, wondering if she'd find any improvement in her Dad's health. Yet some deep, inner foreboding was warning her against any such expectations.

As she reached their home in Sligo Town, she saw Mam and William waiting at the door, but though smiling, Mam looked older and paler. It seemed Kitty's instincts were going to be proved correct. Young William gave Kitty his usual hug but, speaking quietly so her son didn't hear, Mam's 'greeting' was, "Better be prepared ma lassie. Dad's already home, he's ill and had to give up his job, but wants to keep it from ye. So just ye mind that!"

Nodding agreement, Kitty went into the kitchen where Dad was sitting in his chair, trying to raise a smile as he saw her. "Ach, 'tis grand to see my ray of sunshine. Didn't I finish early today so I'd be waitin' for ye?" Kitty gave him one of her brightest smiles, but hidden behind it was the shock she had when she saw the pale face, watery eyes, and increased loss of weight from his once fine, strong body. Aloud she replied, "Sure isn't that a grand surprise for me! And I've brought ye all a basket full of good stuff from the Laverty's. So ye'll be eating like gentry for some while." The sick and sunken man managed, "Ach, so we will, so we will, Kitty." This was followed by a bout of coughing which left him exhausted. Mam motioned that they should leave him, allowing him the sleep he so clearly needed.

As on her last visit, Madge had prepared a tasty meal for Kitty, the boys, Mam and, of course herself. Dad, on Mam's instructions was left to sleep. For her opinion was that rest was more important than food at times like these. But unlike last time, there was no cheery chat and banter. On this occasion the main topic was Dad's failing health and also the hard fact that the family must now cope without Dad's wages. Though the pay for his part-time job hadn't been great, together with his policeman's pension, Mam had just about been able to pay the rent and keep everyone fed.

Looking at Kitty, she declared, "Aye lassie, 'tis a blessing I can count on the good money and food that ye bring to the house." So saying she lightly touched her daughter's cheek. The latter smiled, unused to any show of affection from her loving but undemonstrative mother. She replied, "Sure ye can count on me, Mam, and we'll be fine, just ye see."

"Of course we'll be fine Mam" joined in Madge, "I'll soon be able to find a job in the town and when I do, these two idle beggars," pointing at her brothers, "can start to do their share of work." The two beggars made comical but derisory faces at her - whilst making sure Mam wasn't watching them.

Later that afternoon, Kitty had been heartened to see Dad awake from his sleep and eat the thick onion soup and soda-milk bread which Mam had prepared specially for him. According to her mother, onions contained effective medicinal powers. Moreover, just before it was time to leave to catch her train, Dad was able to make it to the door to see her off with the rest of her family.

The day's light had almost gone as she and Seamus drove back to Ballymote, and a cold wind which brought some of the remaining leaves scuttering down from the wayside trees, emphasised the approach of winter.

Since leaving home, Kitty's thoughts had been solely on Dad, his deterioration in health and also the possible future affects on the family in terms of coping financially. All the while, the old man kept up his whistling and humming.

On reaching his cottage, the usual small payment was made, 'farewells' were bidden, and Kitty set off on the last part of her journey, still deep in thought. It was only when she came in sight of the 'Coaching House' and the nearby church of St. Joseph that she was reminded of the last occasion when Pat had accompanied her, and their last brief moments inside the porch there. Once again, there came that gnawing feeling in the pit of her stomach and she almost said aloud, "Aye, it's no wonder people talk of 'love sickness' - it's certainly that for sure. And it's a sickness I could well be doing without!"

On that same day, though fully aware that it was the first Monday of the month and Kitty would be making the journey back from her family that evening, Pat was determined to keep his thoughts on his work. Being November and almost the end of the agricultural year, his jobs now included making sure that potatoes were pitted and then seeing to the digging of ditches and drains. And so he put all his energy into carrying out these tasks keeping his mind determinedly off those lovely eyes - though as day gave way to evening, he couldn't help thinking that Kitty would be arriving in Riverstown any time now.

He wavered only a moment or two before picking up his work tools and making his way back home to Anne and his sons.

Chapter 16

St Joseph's (December 1877)

After Kitty's visit to her family at the beginning of December, she was glad to see Seamus waiting as she arrived at Ballymote. She still felt cold on the dark winter afternoon despite the two layers of warm clothing under her grey-green woollen shawl. Her basket, once filled with food for her family, was now empty. Greetings were exchanged and, as usual, the driver began his whistling.

As on the short train journey, Kitty continued reflecting on the situation at home. She'd been relieved to see her Dad actually no worse than on her last visit. Yet, she realised that the winter months to come would prove the hardest for him to endure. Also, the family's financial situation was beginning to be a big worry and Alexander had confidentially said to her, "Would ye believe Mam could only afford to give us turnip soup last week?" He'd made an 'oinking' noise, then continued, "For sure, we only ever used that stuff as pig-food before we came to damn Sligo Town!"

Seamus' voice broke into Kitty thoughts. "Here we are, Miss Kitty, will ye be wantin' me to take ye to the station on Christmas Day?"

"Christmas! Holy Mother, what will things be like at home by then?" She asked herself. Aloud she replied, "No thank ye, Seamus. The trains don't run on that day. But I'll be seeing my family in early January."

She jumped down from the cart, and made the last part of her journey to the 'Coaching House.'

Now thoughts of Christmas day itself, a time to be with family and those we love, filled her mind. Again Kitty began an inner conversation with herself, "Be with the ones we love. But where will Pat Dowd be then? Sure he'll be with his wife and sons. And quite right too. So what's the problem, Kitty Tooey? Everything's as it should be. Now away with the nonsense!"

But another voice inside her was having quite a different conversation as she walked on in the darkness.

Pat, having completed his work on digging ditches and drains in the early days of November now turned to the job of thoroughly cleaning all agricultural implements on the landlord's land. Unfortunately, it was work which allowed much more thinking time than harder manual work. Despite trying to occupy himself with singing songs from the days when he'd 'marched' with the men to seek work, something kept reminding him that this day was the first Monday in December. And with that was the knowledge that Kitty Tooey would be making her way back from Seamus' cottage at dusk that day. He'd resisted the temptation to meet her on the November visit. But on this frosty December day, he was also aware that Christmas was near. And another inner reasoning process began. "Pat, me lad, could ye really miss this last chance to wish Kitty happiness at Christmas? Along with what must be a *final* 'God be with ye'? After all, Christmas is the time to wish loved ones well." He paused in this inner 'debate' saying fervently, "And by all that's Holy, right or wrong, I love that girl!"

Having thus come to a conclusion which appeared both logical and honourable, Pat worked until the afternoon's light told him it was time to set off for Seamus' cottage if he were to see Kitty for one last time.

A chill wind caused Kitty to wrap her shawl more tightly round her shoulders as she walked. Whilst doing so, she became aware of a familiar figure in the distance, striding towards her. "Ach! No!" were her anguished thoughts, "It can't be him. It mustn't be him!"

Rooted to the spot, she waited for Pat's approach. She had no idea of what she would actually say to him. Yet when he was still a few yards away, quite suddenly and involuntarily, she found herself running towards him. Stopping directly in front of him, eyes filled with tears, she exclaimed, "Ach Pat, Pat! Why have ye come? Is it after tormenting me ye are? Haven't I put ye out of my mind, knowing ye belong with your family?"

Gently brushing away tears from the sorrowful eyes which looked up at him, Pat felt a mixture of emotions. Although sorry to see his dear

Kitty so upset, her words had told him what he'd been afraid to hope for - that she too had been feeling the same way as him. Then his words came tumbling out: "Kitty darlin' shame on ye to think I could ever torment ye. A young woman I had no right to fall in love with - but fall in love I did! Ye spoke of putting me out of yer mind -which tells me I've been *in* yer mind. And, so help me, I'm glad of that. But also my Kitty, I know that nothing can or should be done about what we both feel".

"I came here tonight *only* to give ye my best Christmas wishes. 'Tis for sure we'll not be together on Christmas day, nor on those to follow. But I'll be honest with ye Kitty, I'm also asking for permission to kiss ye - just the once! In that way, we both have a treasured memory to keep for the years we'll be apart."

There was no immediate reply from Kitty. She stood there in thought. At last, she looked at him with the faintest glimmer of a twinkle in her eye, took hold of his hand, and said, "Now then Pat Dowd, every bone in my body tells me to send ye on your way. But on seeing ye - well I just don't know whether I'm coming or going!" Kitty looked away for a minute then continued, "So what I'm thinking now is - we'll walk back together to St Joseph's. And maybe then, I'll have an answer for ye."

With her hand still on his, Pat felt reasonably optimistic about his request, yet knew it would be foolish to interpret her words as a 'yes'.

And so the two walked slowly, hand in hand, to their destination. It seemed that both were savouring the moments of just being close to each other. Neither spoke, but the grips on their closed hands were becoming ever tighter. And the tightening was now accompanied by a strong, stirring sensation passing between and through each of them.

When they reached the path leading to the church's porch, Pat halted and, taking both of Kitty's hands in his he asked quietly, "Well my darling, have ye an answer yet?"

Her response was a nod and "Yes, Pat. I think we deserve to remember each other with love. And then we must move on with our lives without regret or bitterness."

Without further words, Pat gently led Kitty along the path and into the dark church porch.

There, Kitty was immediately enveloped by his arms, her raised lips eagerly responding to his kiss. Breathing grew faster, more kisses followed, now there was an urgency in them. Pat removed his warm outer coat and placed it on one of the long stone seats at either side of the porch, at the same time guiding Kitty to sit down on it with him. Now he was instinctively searching under layers of clothing to find his darling's breasts. Just for a moment, it seemed that Kitty was about to remove his hand - but then she took his hand in hers, and helped it to find its goal. The clear, close awareness of Pat's manhood and desire had awakened in her an overwhelming passion. And she was also exquisitely aware of the increased firmness of her nipples and the moistness between her thighs.

As Pat caressed her breasts, he and Kitty found themselves now lying on the coat. Soon his tongue was moving around her erect nipples whilst his hand moved under her long clothing, exploring the inner, 'secret' part of her body.

The two were gradually joined together in the act of love. Pat somehow had the will power to move steadily as his body thrust inside her. Softly saying, "Slowly, slowly, my Kitty. Ye must be the one to tell me when to run."

It wasn't long before Kitty was thrusting impatiently upwards, saying repeatedly, "Oh, Pat, Pat, my love!"

They remained joined in their union for some minutes - both breathing heavily. As their breathing slowed, they looked at each other, both wanting to remain in those moments as long as possible.

It was Kitty who broke the moment. She had suddenly become painfully aware of where they were and the significance of what had passed between them. Instinctively, she moved to a sitting position and crossed herself, praying, "Forgive me Holy Mary. I was weak and have sinned." Then she looked at Pat, saying, "Sure ye must know that wasn't how I intended our first kiss to end, Pat. But it was something so beautiful that I'll treasure it for the rest of my life." Then standing up, her tone became brisk and determined, "Now, we both need to move and go our separate ways. And may the Good Lord, forgive us for using His House in this way!"

A feeling of emptiness filled Pat as he realised that this wonderful experience was over. *This* was the moment of truth. His response was, "My darling, darling Kitty, I swear to ye that I never intended it to be more than one kiss. I also swear I never experienced such wonderful moments in my whole life. Not one moment do I regret I..."

Too emotional to speak for a while, Pat finally put his hand lightly on Kitty's shoulder, adding, "I'm sure the Lord will forgive us since we're both about to relinquish this love we have found. And so my darling, I wish ye happiness throughout life. Just know there'll always be a treasured memory of ye in my heart."

Slowly, they made their way back down the church path. Here, Kitty turned to Pat saying, "I wish ye well, Pat Dowd. Now go please."

Feeling there was no more he could say, Pat turned and set off in the opposite direction. Grim-faced he told himself firmly, "Well Pat, now you must settle back into the routine of life with Anne."

He quickened his pace towards home.

Arriving at the back door of the 'Coaching House,' Kitty knocked once, and then entered the kitchen where Margaret was busily preparing a piece of pork for next day's meal. Looking up, she noted the high colour in Kitty's cheeks and her distracted manner. Worried, she inquired, "Are ye alright? Your Dad's not worse is he?"

"No! Ach no, Margaret. Dad's about the same, but thank ye for asking. It's just that I'm feeling a bit tired after the travelling, so I'm thinking it's best for me to go to bed and rest awhile." There was a nod and a smile of agreement from Margaret.

"Aye, close yer eyes fer a bit and ye should soon be fine." However, she felt sure something had upset Kitty that night.

Chapter 17

Griddle Cakes (1878)

January brought with it biting cold winds followed by many falls of deep snow, so preventing Kitty's visit to her home. Similarly, the usual walks with Master Thomas were very much curtailed. Though a big disappointment to the young lad, there was one advantage as far as Kitty was concerned. Namely that the temporary 'confinement' meant there would be no chance of coming across Pat. For Kitty had to confess to herself that, despite her 'vows', she couldn't in all honesty say whether she could have ignored him were that to happen.

Lessons were now based largely on two books given as presents on Christmas Day. The one from Kitty gave descriptions of all types of wildlife to be found in North-West Ireland, and was beautifully illustrated. The second, from Mr Laverty, was a text book for improving the mathematical knowledge of young scholars. Though impressed by his son's progress in reading and writing, he now wanted Thomas' literacy to be balanced by an early knowledge of handling money. Both teacher and pupil found mathematics less interesting than literacy, but it did help to keep Kitty's mind from straying elsewhere.

February brought a lot of rain which cleared the snow. So on the first Monday in the month, Kitty and Seamus were again able to make the journey to Ballymote Station. The train was fairly packed with people going to Sligo Town. Many were farmers, off to do business in their corduroy knee-breeches and long grey stockings. Others, in their bowlers or caps, worked there. However, still being early in the year, with no new produce to be harvested, there were fewer women 'regulars' with their pannier-type baskets of vegetables to be sold at the market. So luckily, Kitty was able to find a seat. For this she was thankful, as she'd been feeling slightly queasy during her cart-ride to the station.

Once home again, she was relieved to see that Dad hadn't lost any more weight since December. And, as usual he gave her his 'My ray of sunshine greeting'. But she soon noticed his bouts of coughing seemed more frequent.

At meal time, Kitty was concerned to hear that brother Edward had been 'laid off' from his work as a seaman since January. This was due both to the snow that month, and also the greatly reduced amount of cargo being sent to Scotland at that time of year. The loss of his wages was something the family could well do without.

Later, when outside helping her Mam to feed the livestock, her mother had given Kitty a penetrating look and asked, "Now, ma lassie, perhaps ye'll tell me what ails ye? Ye don't seem your usual self. And I'd like to know what's causing those circles under the eyes."

Kitty ought to have known her hawk-eyed mother missed nothing. She forced a smile and replied, "Ach Mam, haven't ye enough to be worrying about? I'm grand, just a wee bit tired after all the January snow. But I'll be here in March, bringing my usual basket full of good things to eat. There'll be some money too. And our Eddie 'll be back at work by then. 'Twill be fine Mam, ye 'll see!"

Mam was not convinced by this evasive answer. She was concerned, and she also had her suspicions.

As Kitty entered the 'Coaching House' by the kitchen door, she found Margaret busy dropping a mixture on to a hot pan over the fire. Pausing, she gave a warm smile of greeting to Kitty, asking, "And how was Dad today? I'm hopin' he was no worse."

"About the same thanks," was Kitty's reply. "At any rate, he's not lost any more weight. Our Eddie's been laid off since January, but we're hoping he'll be back at sea by March."

"Ach, I'm glad about yer Dad and, as ye say, Eddie should soon be bringing in money again." Then, pointing to the pan emitting sizzling sounds, Margaret added, "I'm makin' your favourite griddle cakes, so sit down and I'll put a few out for ye. Sure ye hardly touched your porridge this morning."

Glad to be sitting by the warm fire, Kitty ate three of the cakes while listening to Margaret's news of the day. When the two went up to bed, she was quickly in a deep sleep.

It was just before dawn when Kitty awoke. She jumped out of bed, and began vomiting into the chamber pot. As she finally lifted her head, she was aware of her friend sitting up in bed, looking at her in dismay.

"Now Kitty Tooey, I know ye had a fair bit of my cookin' last night, but I'm thinkin' there's more than griddle cakes in that belly of yours! Did something happen last December when ye came back late from Sligo Town?"

There was no immediate answer so Margaret added, "Remember ye'll be needin' a good friend if I'm right."

A flood of tears was Kitty's response. Gradually, the tears subsided to sobs. Between these, Kitty stammered out, "Oh M-Margaret - I've been…. sinful….and … so stupid!" A brief silence as she gulped for breath. Then, as though trying to mitigate her stupid sinfulness, she declared, "But I swear it was only the once."

Trying to hide a slight smile at the naivety of the remark, Margaret responded, "Well, Kitty, luveen, I'm thinkin' that sometimes it only takes the once!"

Before long, Kitty was giving an account of how, over a short period of time, she had changed from disliking Pat to finding him a very interesting man. A man she had found increasingly attractive. She deliberately avoided using the word 'love' to Margaret. Then she told of how their last, unexpected meeting was definitely their final one. Omitting any intimate details of their union, she ended with,"And there ye have it."

Putting her arms round her friend, Margaret whispered, "Now, now, luveen, for sure that Dowd bastard certainly played ye like a fiddle!" Then, anger rising in her, she said vehemently, "Ye can bet he had that final, 'unexpected' meeting all planned!"

Seeing tears once again begin to well in Kitty's eyes, she carried on with, "Well at least he's away to his wife now, the poor hoor. And when we know for sure it's not just my griddle cakes that caused this morning's shindig, I'll help ye plan what's to be done."

Kitty managed a half-smile of thanks. She was certainly glad of Margaret's support, and thankful it hadn't been accompanied by condemnations of her behaviour. However, she felt her friend's opinion of Pat as nothing but a bastard out to seduce her was both unfair and untrue.

"Margaret, ye've been very kind, and I'm so grateful for the offer of help. Yet I want ye to know that Pat's no bastard. I was as much to blame as him for the events of our last meeting."

The other's reply was brief, "Mm. If ye say so."

In the Dowd's home, Pat's moods fluctuated daily. Sometimes he made great efforts to treat Anne more kindly and with more consideration. On other days, he was irritable for no particular reason or, worse still for Anne, there were long silences in which he seemed far away.

Which indeed he *was* most of the time.

However, the days of Christmas-tide passed tolerably well for him. He'd noticed that his eldest son, six year-old Francis, had managed to pick out tunes on a crude, wooden whistle he'd carved a year earlier. So as a Christmas treat, he'd taken him to Sligo Town and bought him the best quality tin-whistle they could find. When playing together in the evenings, he derived pleasure from knowing his son had inherited some of his own musical talent.

As usual, the family attended Christmas Mass in their local church of St John's - a service during which Pat was filled with guilt. However, afterwards, the family was soon sitting down to a meal of roast chicken with a delicious herb stuffing and an assortment of vegetables. Pat gave high and due praise to his wife for the spread. The latter responded with, "Thank ye, 'tis grand to see a return of the old Pat. The Pat I like - though ye can be a bit of a rogue at times."

But by the end of January, snow and bleak days brought him unrest and thoughts of Kitty. Again, Pat began comparing Anne with the lovely and feisty woman who'd recently been his lover. Sure his wife was loyal to him, a good wife and mother, but he recalled that in her praise of him on Christmas day she'd described him as, 'The Pat I like', *not* the Pat she loved. He concluded that that was what they were - a married couple who liked each other.

Having reached this conclusion, he then went on to consider how, by March his sons would be aged seven, five and two years. So John would no longer be a baby requiring the attention of a young infant. Also, young Michael would then be able to attend school along with brother Francis. In fact all three sons were becoming far less dependent on Anne. This logic brought about Pat's second conclusion - that, as time went on, life would gradually be getting much easier for his wife in terms of looking after the children.

This line of thought was daily in Pat's mind and, near the end of February, he'd reached a third conclusion. This was that Anne would soon be needing him less, and that he and Kitty *could* be together eventually. Of course this wouldn't be for some time yet. But he could begin to plan things carefully *now*, making sure that Anne and his boys would live comfortably without him.

Pat also felt he needed to share his ideas for the future with Kitty as soon as possible. And so he planned to meet her after her journey home on the first Monday in March. By then he'd have worked out the details of how the two of them could soon find a life together, far away from Riverstown.

Chapter 18

Decisions

It didn't take long before morning vomiting was a regular occurrence, so confirming Kitty's fears. An additional confirmation was the 'springeing' feeling in her breasts. This, according to her mother, was always the sure sign of a babe on the way. Kitty's first worry now was how to tell Mr Laverty her sorry news. Her second was how Mam would cope without her wages when she was inevitably dismissed.

That night she confided her worries to Margaret, who quickly reassured her regarding Mr Laverty. "Think I can help ye there, Kitty, I've known the missus since she and Mr Laverty took over the pub. It's probably best if I prepare *her* for the news first - it will give her time to think about what to tell her husband. Don't forget what a grand opinion she and the Master have of ye as a teacher. And Mrs Laverty speaks highly of your work in the house, as well as the many times ye've been up in the night, helpin' her nurse baby Joseph." Margaret thought a moment, then asked,

"Would ye let me speak to the Missus tomorrow? I could do it whilst you and Master Thomas are takin' your morning walk? 'Tis well that it's done soon, I'm thinkin'."

"I suppose you're right. But I'm wondering how long that high opinion will last once they know how I've disgraced myself?"

"No more of that! Now get to sleep. We've both a busy day ahead."

The next day was the last day of February and already there was a touch of spring in the air. Perfect weather for Kitty and Thomas's walk through 'Caw Wood'. As the two entered the woods, he was delighted to be the first to spot clumps of early coltsfoot plants with their bright yellow

flowers. Kitty explained to him how her Mam used to boil up its leaves to ease sore throats. Hearing this, Thomas gave a series of forced coughs, saying they could pick some to boil at home, and make his throat better. An amused Kitty advised her pupil, "Look carefully, Master Thomas, no leaves yet. They only appear when the flower has died - so we can come back then, and try to cure that dreadful cough of yours!"

Though she'd managed to raise a smile for the 'cough', Kitty was inwardly pondering on some of her present problems. There was Dad's worsening cough, her Mam's reaction to her news, and also that of her employers. Would she still have a job when she returned from the walk? Then there was Pat? What if he should appear in the woods as he had in the past? Would she tell him she was carrying his baby? Or would she keep the babe her secret?

Meanwhile, Pat had continued with his future plans for his family and Kitty. He'd intended to make his first contact with her on the first Monday in March but on the last day of February, he awoke with an overpowering feeling that he *must* see Kitty that very day, if only for a few minutes. Then he could give her an outline of his ideas for their future, so allowing her time to think them over before he met her in March.

It wasn't long after having come to his sudden, new decision that Pat was washed, dressed and eating the breakfast Anne had made for him. He ate in silence, preparing what he was about to say to Kitty. He left their cottage with only a brief wave to his wife.

Anne stared thoughtfully after him as he strode away, spade over his shoulder.

There was still a lot of work to be done on 'Miser's land' in preparation for planting the year's potatoes before St Patrick's Day. Soon he was vigorously digging manure mixed with seaweed and kelp into the ground. He did this for a few hours, after which he took a long swig of his butter milk, but instead of continuing work afterwards, he set off immediately to walk the couple of miles to the 'Coaching House'.

Going round to the back entrance as usual, Pat saw Margaret out in the yard feeding the hens with their morning's 'mash'. She had her back to him so he called out, "Good mornin' to ye Miss Keating, I'm wonderin' if ye would ask Miss Kitty if she could spare a minute for a quick word with me before she goes on her walk with Master Thomas?"

Recognising the voice, Margaret swung round to face Pat, her face red with anger, the empty pan in her hand. "Well now, if it isn't that fine figure of a man, Pat Dowd! So it's Miss Kitty ye want to talk to is it? I doubt it'll be about the present ye left in her belly! I wonder ye have the nerve to come here after what ye've done to her. Ye bastard! Now get out before I get the Master to see ye off!"

Brandishing her pan, she moved towards him, calling out every obscenity she knew. All Pat's attempts to speak were drowned by her voice. So, at last, he decided to leave before others inside the house heard the commotion and came out. He needed time to digest and think over what he'd just heard.

Chapter 19

The Secret is 'Out'

It wasn't long after Pat left the 'Coaching House' that he was back digging on Murray's land. "Holy Mother," he mused, "I've been given plenty to think about now, and that's fer sure!"

In fact, after the first shock, the thought of Kitty carrying his child had filled him with pride. He even went on to regard this new development as a sign that the two of them were meant to be together, and also that Anne would now understand more clearly why he had to leave her. After all, on hearing of some husband having an affair, hadn't Anne often said, "I'm tellin' ye now, Pat, though I know ye have an eye for a pretty woman, if ye ever betray me like that, ye 'll be out of here faster than a fiddler's elbow."

But his next thought was regarding whether Kitty's opinion of him was the same as Margaret's. Did she really consider she'd been seduced by him? Then he began to recall again the events of that night. Hadn't she *agreed* to that kiss? And hadn't she seemed as eager as he'd been to let their bodies join together? It seemed Margaret's view of him was simply her own. Certainly not Kitty's! And with his baby on the way, she would now be needing him and his love.

In a few days she'd be visiting her family again. And he'd be waiting for her near Seamus' cottage.

As Kitty and Thomas returned from their walk that same morning, a smiling Margaret greeted them in the kitchen. "I'm to tell ye that the Mistress would like a word with ye in the parlour. I spoke to her early this morning and I'm thinking the news will be good."

Kitty had been dreading her first meeting with the Laverties now that her pregnancy was certain, but Margaret's expression had reduced her anxiety. So with less apprehension, she made her way to the parlour door. Here, she knocked twice and then entered the room where Mrs Laverty was putting young Master Joseph in his cradle for a midday sleep. She turned as Kitty came in, saying, "I've heard about your news Miss Kitty. I am both sorry and surprised to hear it. But please take a seat and we'll have a talk about the matter."

She indicated the wooden, high-backed chair and, having checked that Joseph was settled, she sat down in her armchair facing Kitty. Her expression serious, but not unfriendly.

"Miss Keating told me about the baby due in late August." Kitty nodded. "I was also told that the father is in no position to marry you, being a married man. And I believe he seduced you." Kitty was about to interrupt, but Mrs Laverty raised one hand saying, "No, please let me finish before you speak."

"As you know, Margaret has worked here for a long time and proved herself to be trustworthy and hard-working. More than that, she a very good judge of character and has a very high opinion of you as a person and as a teacher. And so do Mr Laverty and I. Additionally, Master Thomas' affection and respect for you is obvious."

"So Miss Kitty, there'll be no recriminations - what's done is done. But I'd like to know about your situation at home. Miss Keating implied that your family has concerns about finance, and that you help by handing over most of your wages to your mother. Is that correct?"

After affirming that Miss Keating had been correct, Kitty described how her father's health seemed to be steadily declining along with the family income.

"Well, Miss Kitty, after speaking about this sad event with Mr Laverty, a decision has been made. Despite my husband's great disappointment in you, he agreed that you may remain in employment here until the sixth month of your pregnancy. It's your first child and so it should be fairly easy to hide the baby's growth beneath your apron and shawl. However, both of us need your assurance that you will have nothing more to do with the man responsible for your condition. Do we have that assurance?"

"Ye certainly do Mrs Laverty. And thank ye for such kindness." Kitty's response was immediate.

Her employer continued, "Of course, this arrangement is also dependent upon you remaining healthy and being able to carry out your present responsibilities. I take it you understand that?"

Another quick response from Kitty, "I do Mrs Laverty. This is all more than I deserve, and I'll see I'm fit to work until my sixth month."

"That's settled then. We'll speak no more on this subject, so you may go now and supervise Master Thomas' studies."

As Kitty was about to leave, Mrs Laverty called out, "You have a lot to thank Miss Keating for."

That evening up in their room, Kitty talked with her friend until well past midnight. Indeed Margaret seemed as happy as she was about the good news.

The first Monday in March arrived all too quickly for Kitty. On reaching home, Mam and William were, as usual, at the door to greet her. But she imagined her mother's words sounded decidedly pointed as she asked, "And how's my teacher- daughter feeling today?"

After a non-committal reply, Kitty went inside the house where she saw Dad. He face looked grey and haggard as he slept in his chair by the fire. She looked at Mam questioningly.

The latter shook her head wearily, "He's nae good lassie, nae good. He's been up all night with that blasted cough of his."

Bending over him, Kitty planted a light kiss on her Dad's forehead, guiltily thinking she was no longer his 'ray of sunshine' but an unmarried daughter bringing shame upon the family. Then, tip-toeing away, she unpacked her basket of food.

As always, she had brought with her a selection of foodstuff for the family from Mrs Laverty. Some of the cheese was eaten with the lunch-time meal, a rare treat for everyone. However, the whole family had been affected by Dad's steadily worsening health, and there wasn't the same banter as usual. The only good news was that Edward would soon be back on one of the Sligo cargo ships. Meanwhile, he was doing road mending in the town. Back-breaking work which paid only a pittance.

In the afternoon, Kitty began ironing a huge pile of the family's clothes whilst Mam sat near her knitting long woollen socks for Edward. Casually, she asked, "Did I tell ye that our Mary Anne's expectin' another bairn sometime in September?" Trying to sound equally casual, Kitty replied,"No, ye didn't tell me, but that's grand news. George is a making good progress in the tailoring trade, so in a year or two they may be able to afford a bigger cottage."

"Aye, she has a good, reliable man in George Peattie. Sure it makes all the difference to have a husband when a bairn's on the way." A piercing look from Mam accompanied the remark.

Kitty could bear no more of this 'loaded' conversation, so, replacing the iron back by the fire, she faced her mother, saying, "Aye Mam, as ye probably know full well, I'm expecting a bairn - but *I* have no husband. Mrs Laverty has promised I can stay on until I'm six months gone, so I'll be working until the end of May. I can give ye money till then, and if it's better for ye all, I can get the money *sent* to ye." Defiantly, she added, "So ye won't be feeling shame at having your disgraced daughter in your home!"

Shocked at the last words, Mrs Tooey put down her knitting. "Aye Kitty, 'tis true I wish this hadn't happened to ye! And if Dad was well, he'd be round to the bastard that fathered your child, knocking the living daylights out of him! But *you* Kitty have been Dad's favourite since ye were a wee lassie. And always will be." Tears began to well in her mother's blue eyes. Then she continued, "So whatever ye've done, you're our flesh and blood. Our daughter. And always welcome in this house, so I'll be givin' ye all the help I can ma lassie."

Kitty's defiance immediately left her. She knelt down in front of her mother, and spoke quietly, "Ach Mam, I'm sorry, so very sorry. This was never meant to happen. All I've ever wanted is for you and Dad to be proud of me."

Her mother patted her head and sighed. Then in a business-like tone said, "Anyway lassie, there's much to be discussed, so we'll talk as we get on with our work. Ironing and knitting doesn't do itself. As well ye know!"

Of course, her mother wanted information about the child's father. Kitty refused to name him but admitted he had a wife and children. A reply which received a look of displeasure and some head-shaking. There followed questions regarding where Kitty would live after she left the Laverty household. To this her daughter had no answer.

But Margaret Tooey had an idea. Firstly, she explained that it wouldn't be practical for Kitty to return to her still crowded home where her very sick father needed constant attention. However, she carried on to say she was sure Kitty would be welcome to stay with her elder sister, Mary Anne. Her cottage in Drumfin was only a couple of miles from Riverstown, and the sisters could give each other companionship and support since their babes were due only a month apart. Finally she added, "Of course, once ye've given birth, things will have to change. But that can be discussed later."

Mam's idea sounded a possible and practical solution to Kitty's first big problem. It could work well provided her sister and husband were agreeable. Though never having been close to Mary Anne when young due to the seven years' difference in ages, the two had become quite friendly as they grew older. Kitty also smiled to herself at the fact that Mam hadn't asked her when her babe was due. Clearly, she'd had it worked out weeks ago.

The journey back to Riverstown was another period of varied reflection by Kitty. Firstly, she felt relieved that she had been able to talk to Mam about her pregnancy and make some preliminary plans. But secondly, even if Mary Anne agreed to the plan, where would she go after the birth?

She wouldn't be able to afford even the cheapest of dwellings, and she certainly didn't want to move into a Sligo workhouse. Although children and nursing mothers received better food there than other inmates, once babies were weaned they were separated from their mothers. Their mothers were then expected to work long hours doing domestic jobs such as cleaning and cooking. And those in charge at workhouses generally regarded inmates as the 'parasites' of society.

Kitty's ponderings then turned to Pat. Now that he'd been told of her pregnancy, what would his thoughts have been? Perhaps, now realising the consequence of their union, he would think he'd had a lucky escape. And that would be the last she would hear or see of him.

Meanwhile, as dusk fell, Pat was anxiously standing some distance from Seamus' cottage. He didn't want to miss Kitty's arrival so he'd already been waiting there for some time. At last, a pony's trot and tuneless whistling was heard in the distance. He delayed making his presence known until Seamus and his pony were out of sight. Then stepped forward to greet Kitty.

An amazed Kitty stood rooted to the spot.

Resisting the urge to take her in his arms, Pat's first words were reproachful, "Ach, my darling, why didn't you let me know about our child? I am so happy and proud to know that, though unplanned, you are carrying *my* baby. This changes everything Kitty, and I need to talk to ye about the plans I've been making for us."

Unprepared for these totally unexpected words, and also very much aware of her promise to Mrs Laverty, Kitty replied quickly, "Pat, this is all wrong! Ye belong with your family- not making plans for *us*." Then, aware of time, she said decisively,

"I'm going now, Pat. Ye can be sure that Margaret will be waiting for me!"

Relenting a little when she saw Pat's crushed expression, she added, "But ye can walk back just half of the way with me. Then we *must* separate."

Relieved, Pat replied, "Aye, I hear what ye say. So half-way it is. But please listen to what I have to say as we walk. As I told ye just now, things are different now that my child is in yer belly!"

Kitty looked as though she were about to say something, but Pat put a gentle finger to her lips, and carried on to outline all the thoughts he'd had since their last wonderful meeting. These included the various reasons which appeared to him to make it easier for the three of them to be together.

He assured her he would always see that his wife and sons were well provided for by giving them the main part of his wages, explaining,

"And ye see Kitty, if we went to Scotland for a time, there'd always plenty of work for me, with better wages too. Also, I could make extra money by playing the old tin whistle in pubs. A lot of Irish men find work there, such a sentimental bunch when away from home. So when they hear Irish tunes, they're generous with their money."

Having reached the half-way point of their walk, Pat halted. Then said, "Ye see, I've kept to my word." A slight pause. "Now ye must go, Kitty, if ye want to be back in time for Margaret's 'watch'."

Kitty could hardly believe all she'd just heard. She looked both astonished and angry. Noting her mood change, Pat again placed a finger on her lips, and whispered, "Hush now my love. I know we made promises when we last met. But ye must see that a baby makes the situation quite different. Say nothin' yet. But please think over what I've said, and planned for us. I'll be waitin' in the usual place on the first Monday in April, so ye can tell me then what ye think of my ideas."

Though scarcely able to hold her tongue, Kitty did as bidden, and said nothing. She just stood motionless as Pat turned, then walked in the direction of his home. As she recommenced her walk to the 'Coaching House' she heard Pat call out, "And if ye *do* come away with me, I promise ye'll never regret it."

He continued on his way - but not back home. He first wanted to find some quiet spot where he could think over how he would tell Anne the whole story that night. Including his plan to leave her.

Chapter 20

Cards On the Table

The three boys had been asleep for some time. But Anne couldn't sleep that night, she was both angry and apprehensive as she awaited Pat's return. Things hadn't been normal for some months now. She never knew what mood Pat would be in. One day he would be finding fault with nearly everything she did. Similarly, Frankie and Michael would be told they were making too much noise or not doing their fair share of work in the *gairdeen*. And if young John cried, Pat would sigh in exasperation.

Yet, a day or so later, he could be praising her, saying things such as, "Ach, it's a fine mother ye are, Anne. I'm lucky to have someone like yerself as a wife." Then he would spend time talking to or playing with his sons.

She'd no idea where he'd gone, and no longer believed his 'tales' of checking if everything was alright on Murray's land. But tonight she must tell Pat what she should have told him in January. And whatever his mood, she was going to tell him her news as soon as he got back. She wouldn't even ask where he'd been.

Anne was just beginning to think Pat wasn't going to come home at all when she heard his foot-steps outside. Rising to meet him, her expression a mixture of anger and apprehension, she enquired, "So ye decided to return home before the cock awoke, did ye? Well, I'm not after asking where ye've been, but I *am* asking ye to sit down and listen to what I have to tell ye."

Taken aback by this greeting, Pat went over to his chair, but before he sat down he said firmly, "Right. But first ye must listen to what I need to get off my chest - *then* ye can have your say."

Without mentioning Kitty's name, Pat told her the whole story. He began from when he'd first seen her, and moved on to his growing attraction for her through their 'chance' meetings. He emphasised the fact that she had not 'led him on' but admitted he'd quickly fallen in love with her - despite knowing it was wrong. Finally, he told of their unplanned act of love, her pregnancy, and the rationale for his decision to leave Anne, and make a new life with his new love and their child. His astounding news was followed by him taking Anne's hands in his, and saying, "So ye see Anne, ye don't deserve to have to put up with me staying here. All the time, knowing I love someone else. Someone who's carrying my child."

Anne's look was stony. Pat tried to sound reassuring as he continued, "I have great respect fer ye, Anne, and I love my sons. So ye can be sure I'll always see my family is well-clothed and fed."

Anne continued to look at him. Still she said nothing.

Pat tried again. "I'm so sorry, dear Anne. But don't ye see that leavin' will be the best for all of us?" Pat looked up at her expectantly.

A response finally came. "Ach, Pat Dowd, ye tell a fine tale alright - a fairy-tale! So what you're about to do is simply because it's best for everyone, is it? And ye have great respect for me, do ye?" Anne fixed him with a bitter look. "Well here's my tale. So listen well."

Her tone was now one of sarcasm.

"So it seems ye've been very generous with your seed-sowing, Pat! Not only have ye put some poor hoor in the family way, but ye've kindly given me the present of a fourth child as well! Due sometime in August this year." Before turning to go, Anne added, "Anyway that's my news. Have a think about *that!* I'm off to bed now before the cock does crow.!"

A dumb-struck Pat gazed after her as she got up and left him.

That night he remained by the fire, just staring into the flames until they turned to dying embers as a new day began to dawn. That brought him reluctantly back to the present. Not being able to sleep, think clearly, or face Anne again, he got up and rekindled the fire. At least the house would be warm for her.

Then before she should also decide to get up, he set off with his spade to continue working on Murray's land - he needed time alone. He had to sort out his thoughts in view of this latest unexpected and unwelcome news.

❧ ❧ ❧

Since her last encounter with Pat, Kitty's thoughts had started to take a different route. This had begun when she'd felt the first flutter of the baby in her womb. From that moment, she became truly aware of her responsibility for this new little being. She had never, like many young girls, simply wanted to find a man, get married then have children. However, given the present situation, she determined that this child must have the best life she could give it.

Yet how was that possible in the present circumstances? After the birth, where would she go? She couldn't continue to live in Mary Anne's small cottage. And Mam's already overcrowded house was out of the question. What she needed was somewhere comfortable where she could look after her love-child. But that required money. She still had no intention of allowing Pat to leave his wife. But he ought to take some responsibility for his baby. Then she recalled him having talked about being able to make money by playing his tin-whistle. This thought gave her an idea; perhaps he could afford to give her some money by doing just that. Yes! She could save it up until her babe arrived. These thoughts cheered her considerably.

She realised that not everyone welcomed unmarried mothers, but with some money, she could at least give it a try. After all, once she'd weaned her child and regained her strength, she ought to be able to find work again and become self-sufficient. So she wouldn't be asking Pat for money for long.

The more such thoughts threaded their way through Kitty's mind, the more feasible they sounded. Of course, the 'stumbling block' might be his wife. What if she became aware her husband was giving her money?

Anyway, that would be Pat's problem, not hers.

With these ideas continually at the back of her mind, the rest of March passed fairly reasonably for Kitty. Not only had her morning vomiting ceased, but she also felt more positive about her future as a mother on her own. Also, work with young Thomas was still enjoyable, and despite some cold days of rain with keen winds, there were enough fine ones for them to go for walks. They watched the development of frog spawn in the pond near the main street in Ardkeeran, and also took pleasure in spotting the first primroses and violets opening in 'Caw' Wood.

Moreover, Kitty was able to look forward to her visit home in April since Mam knew about the baby - though she was still very concerned about Dad's health. She was also anxious, and yet hopeful, that her meeting with Pat would result in a mutually amicable plan.

March brought nothing but tension between Pat and Anne. There was constant torment in his mind regarding the future he'd had planned for himself and Kitty. He knew where his duty lay, and how much Anne quite rightly expected his understanding and care now she was with child again. But what about his duty to Kitty and her child? How could he possibly go back on all he'd said to her only a week or so ago?

Anne clearly expected him to promise he'd immediately end the 'sordid affair' with 'whoever she is'. She took the view that the 'hoor' had known full well he was a married man, and that pregnancy might result from their adultery. Consequently, she ordered Pat to put the woman out of his mind saying, "Let her lie on the bed she's made, and pay for her mistake!"

It was in vain Pat tried to convince Anne that the woman involved was no hoor but an intelligent and moral lady. That they'd fallen in love without intending to. And moreover, she'd been the one to remind him of his duty to his wife and children, saying they must never meet again.

In fact, at the end of this defence of Kitty's character, Anne had given a sarcastic laugh, remarking, "Would ye listen to yourself, Pat Dowd! It's obvious that if this model of modesty really did remind ye where your duty lay - then, for sure, neither of ye were listening!" Her tone turned to bitterness. "And never ever use the word 'love', when what ye feel is just pure '*lust*'!"

So days passed with neither making any attempt to see the other's viewpoint. It was a stalemate of silence. Repressed anger on Anne's part, and tortured, fluctuating thoughts on Pat's.

Eventually, just before the first Monday in April, it was broken by Pat admitting to Anne that he would be meeting the person concerned in a day or two, but only for a brief time. During that time, he'd inform her of the child his wife was expecting. The two would then discuss what would be best for everyone concerned.

Anne was fearful when she heard this from Pat. She dreaded the possible outcome of a further meeting of the two. She felt he'd become so obsessed that he'd lost all logical reasoning and objectivity. Also, she feared this other woman. She'd always known Pat would sometimes flirt with attractive women, but he was also an intelligent man. Not one to be 'taken in' by some pretty, stupid little tart. It was possible that Pat had met someone who was educated as well as attractive. One who could be a *permanent* threat to their marriage - no matter what the outcome of the proposed meeting.

Soon it was April, time for Kitty's visit to her home. On this occasion, though still looking very ill, Dad had been awake to greet his 'Ray of sunshine'. She had gently kissed his forehead, glad that Mam had previously agreed to hide the fact of her pregnancy from him. This deceit being aided by the pinafore which hid her small 'bump'. Her siblings, apart from the three younger brothers, had been told about the baby but had sworn not to mention it in front of Dad.

As she and Mam got on with jobs of washing and ironing, Kitty learned that though Dad had kept awake to see her that day, and was not worsening significantly health-wise, he was still coughing for a large part of the night.

However, there was good news about Edward who had been able to return again to his work on a cargo ship in Sligo. Best of all, Kitty was told that Mary Anne and husband George had agreed to her staying with them in Drumfin for the last three months of her pregnancy.

Kitty left home to catch the earlier train from Sligo in order to see Pat. Mam waved her off saying, "Make sure ye take good care of yourself, my lassie."

Chapter 21

More Decisions

On nearing Seamus' cottage, Kitty had the coins ready for him so she could jump down quickly from his cart. She'd caught the earlier train in order to arrive before dark as she didn't want to be seen with Pat in daylight. So having paid Seamus, and waved 'goodbye', she waited until he was out of sight, then turned to walk a little way in the direction of the 'Station' pub. It was then that Pat appeared at her side. He'd been watching her from beneath the overhanging branches of the large ash tree close to the pub.

"Kitty, my darlin'!" He spoke quietly and with some apprehension.

A little startled, but also relieved that he was already at the station, she began to speak urgently. "Pat, I've given everything a deal of thought this past month and I've a lot to discuss with ye - though it may not be what you're wanting to hear."

Not fully aware of the implications of her words, Pat simply replied, "Aye my love, we'll make for the path at the back at the pub, it's usually muddy but we should be alone there."

Soon the two were standing under the cover of another ash tree. Pat, anxious to get his news over and done with, said quickly, "Before ye speak Kitty, I'm dreading what I have to tell ye. But anyway, here it is." Pat swallowed, then continued. "Just after I'd made all those plans for us, Anne told me she was expectin' our fourth child this August."

He paused, letting it sink in. Never had he felt so guilty, so helpless and so anxious.

Kitty stood there speechless. Her first thoughts were of anger mixed with jealousy as she pictured her lover lying with his wife. But quickly she saw how unfair and pointless those thoughts were. Then she realised the news also meant it would now be impossible to expect money from Pat. Of course it would also make her decision not to go away with him easier. But that was small consolation.

She remained silent a while longer, needing time to adjust her thoughts to this new situation.

Taking the silence as a sign of Kitty's contempt for him, Pat hastily assured her, "But I still want us to be together Kitty - only it'll be later than I'd hoped. I owe it to my wife to stay with her for a while, and I owe it to you to provide for our child.

"I've already told Anne about your pregnancy, and I've told her I'll be startin' a new life with you in the future because I love you."

Scarcely able to believe Pat was still intent on pursuing his initial plans, and had told his wife everything, Kitty responded exasperatedly, "Ach Pat, that was a cruel thing to do - sure isn't she needing your support and affection more than ever right now? And if ye'd just waited until this meeting, all that would have been unnecessary. Ye see, I'd already made up my mind that I would never be responsible for breaking up your family."

It was Pat's turn to be amazed. He'd been so sure she'd want them be together. Yet here she was, not only dismissing his plans for their future, but also criticising him for telling Anne the truth.

At last he spoke. "Kitty, my darlin', I thought ye loved me and would *want* us to be together. Do ye realise how hard it will be for ye in the future? An unmarried woman with a child to care for, little money, and having to share a home with your large family. Have ye thought what that would be like?"

A blend of sarcasm as well as anger were in Kitty's reply, "Yes, Pat, I've thought about it day and night ever since I found I was expecting your baby!" Then more calmly she continued, "As regards loving ye and wanting a life with ye -well I admit I'm in love with ye. But I've always known that I could never live with myself if ye left your family for me." A momentary pause, then she looked directly into Pat's eyes, saying, "But I'm going to honest with ye Pat. What I *had* hoped for today was that somehow ye'd be able to start allowing me a small sum of money. I could save it up, and try to get lodgings after the birth."

Kitty went on to describe the position she was in. The impossibility of living at home, her father's illness, and the family's lack of money. Then she told Pat that, though she would be able to stay in Drumfin with her sister and husband in June, she would need to move out once the babe was born.

She ended all this with a simple statement of fact, "But of course, now your wife is expecting a fourth child, *all* your money will be needed for them."

After listening with growing horror to Kitty's account of her desperate financial situation, Pat was quick to try to give her some reassurance. "Sure, money will be needed for my growing family, but remember that won't be immediate. There's over four months before Anne gives birth, and even then her milk will provide most of the baby's needs for quite some while. And during that time I'll be able to give ye some money each week. Also, I'll be honest with Anne and tell her what I'm doing and why. And, in view of your decision not to *allow* me to leave my family, I'll tell her I'll be staying with her and trying to repair our marriage."

In fact, Pat had decided that, though he *would* say all that to Anne, he felt sure that once a year had gone by, he and Kitty could find a way to share a life together. Unsure that Pat's promise of some allowance would materialise once his wife got to hear of her husband's plan, Kitty just nodded doubtfully saying, "Well, we'll see, we'll see. Now I think we've both said all that there is to be said for the time-being. So I'll bid ye farewell, Pat."

She turned to go, resisting his attempt to take her arm. "No, Pat. Leave it at that." Then she moved from the shelter of the tree and walked away. Pat looked helplessly after her until she disappeared from view.

❧ ❧ ❧

It took Pat a few days before he felt able to talk with his wife about the conversation he'd had with Kitty. And when he did, he'd found her reaction far from expected. Instead of expressing any relief at him staying, she'd remained silent and thoughtful, gazing into the fire.

Anne's sharp brain was warning her to be quite sure she understood the full implications of what Pat had just told her. "On the face of it" she thought, "he's just told me he'll stay with me as long as I agree to him giving money to his mistress. But I'm wondering just how much he hasn't told me. I don't know her name, where she lives, how long these payments will go on for, and how he's going to get the money to her."

"Ach! That's the real question! Will he be intending to give her the money himself? After all, he never said he'd parted with her for good. That woman has a hold on my man, that's for sure, and I need to know a lot more before I agree to anything."

After what seemed an age, Anne finally looked up and spoke firmly, "Now Pat, I want full and honest answers to all these questions. Or not a penny goes to your mistress!"

Pat hesitated a few moments before he decided he'd answer her questions. But in *his* way, and only after a solemn promise from Anne that she'd never pass on the information to anyone else.

He told her Kitty's Christian name and her place of work in Riverstown. He also told Anne that payments would only start in June when Kitty left work and moved in with her sister in Drumfin. Finally, Pat said money would cease once their baby was weaned, but that he hadn't yet given thought to *how* it would be given to Kitty.

Anne took in this information, still feeling some facts had been omitted. Then she spoke wearily, "Right, Pat. That's a lot for me to be thinking about. Ye must wait until the morning before I give ye any decision about this idea of yours." Slowly she rose from her chair saying. "Good night, Pat. I've had more than enough for one day."

Chapter 22

Anne Calls the Shots

It was the following evening when Anne told Pat her decision. "Well now, Pat, we can give your mistress some money to help her find lodgings. But *I'll* be handing it over to her myself when she moves to her sister's."

Alarmed at the thought of the two women meeting and of what might be said, Pat was also concerned about losing the opportunity to see Kitty again. He responded with, "But Anne, ye'll be six months pregnant by then, and Drumfin is nearly three miles away. It isn't a good idea fer ye to travellin'. Also it isn't a good idea fer the two of ye to be meetin' in the circumstances."

Anne smiled knowingly, retorting, "Aye, I thought ye might be afraid of what we both might learn about ye! Have no fear about that! We've better things to be discussing than the man who betrayed us both! I want to meet this woman - much younger than me, I'll warrant. As for getting there, I'm sure ye can arrange one of your deliveries so that you drive to the 'Station' pub in Ballymote by way of Drumfin. Here, ye drop me off, go and get on with your business, then pick me up later." Anne concluded with, "So it's easy. I get to meet Kitty, and she gets money." She paused, then added, "For a *little* while."

Pat thought his wife's tone had a hint of threat and finality in it. So he sighed and nodded.

When the time came for Kitty to leave the 'Coaching House', there were tearful scenes and hugs from Mrs Laverty and Margaret who wished her 'Slanagas' (God bless). Young Master Thomas bravely held back tears, though his face betrayed sadness as he handed her a drawing done by him whilst in 'Caw Wood'. Mr Laverty avoided the scene by busying himself in the public room. He considered that Miss Kitty, though an excellent teacher, had brought disgrace upon herself and the family.

Old Seamus was already waiting with his faithful pony at the front of the pub, whistling as usual. As Kitty climbed up on to the cart (less nimbly than usual), he caught sight of the small swelling under her white apron. His whistling stopped momentarily. Then giving a sigh and shake of the head as he met Kitty's eyes, he recommenced his tune and the cart moved off.

It was early morning in Drumfin, the second week of June. Through the half-door of the cottage (which let out the smoke from the fire), Kitty stood stirring a pan of potato peelings she was boiling for the pigs. The four-year old twin girls, Mary and Jane were just tall enough to peer over the door and watch their mother, Mary Anne, who was outside feeding the hens whilst toddler, George, held on to her apron.

It was then a pony and cart stopped near to the cottage. A woman was helped down by the driver who immediately got back on the cart, flicked the reins, and went on his way. It was clear that the woman was heavily pregnant. She looked around, noticed Mary Anne, and walked slowly towards her. The latter, noting the unexpected visitor was with child, thought to herself, "Holy Mary, I'm hoping it isn't another pregnant woman coming to stay."

The woman, explained she was looking for a Mrs George Peattie and her sister, Kitty. She wondered if they lived nearby.

Surprised by this question, Mary Anne introduced herself and told her that Kitty was inside. Looking thankful to have located them, the woman introduced herself as Mrs Anne Dowd, and expressed the wish to speak with Kitty.

A few minutes later, Anne was inside the cottage sitting in a chair facing a bewildered Kitty who was nervously trying to arrange her pinafore so that her 'bump' was less obvious. Mary Anne had diplomatically gone out again with George.

Anne spoke first, "Well now Kitty, you're not how I pictured ye, but I can well understand why Pat has never had you out of his thoughts these past months. You're not actually beautiful, but your eyes give ye a look of child-like innocence."

Kitty began to stammer out, "Oh Mrs. Dowd, I'm- I'm so very..."

Quickly Anne interrupted her, "I know! I know! You're sorry - and well ye might be! But all the 'sorries' and tears are pointless, and change nothing. Young as ye are, ye should have known by now that men will always heed the voice in their breeches more than the one in their brains! Anyway, let's get to the point. I've got a question to ask ye, and I want an honest answer to it."

Kitty was surprised by Mrs Dowd's 'matter-of-factness'. On being told the name of the visitor, she'd expected to see a furious, ranting wife.. Anyway, she promised to answer the question truthfully, though couldn't imagine what it might be.

The question, and what followed it, was certainly unexpected.

"Are ye sure ye'll be able to provide for this child once you've left here and have to find a home for the two of ye? I've agreed to let ye have some money each month until my baby's weaned. But it won't be very much."

Pleased that Mrs Dowd had agreed to providing some money, Kitty replied, "For sure, things are going to be far from easy, even with your kind promise of money. To start with, there's no guarantee that any lodging place will take in an unmarried mother - well, not without increasing the price. However, to answer your original question, what I *can* provide for my child is continual love.

Anne shook her head in disagreement at the latter statement. "Ach Kitty, sure no one can live on love - though the words sound fine enough. Ye'll need to find work, and then ye'll have to leave the child with someone, as well as paying them. And Pat tells me it can't be your mother." Anne looked at Kitty very seriously, asking, "Now what kind of person will *you* be able to afford? Probably some poor, unmarried woman like yourself! And what kind of home and care will she be able to provide? Especially for a child that's not hers!" There was a slight pause as Anne let her words sink in. Then she summed up with, "And after working all hours to pay for this so-called 'care', how will love compensate for your continual absence from a child brought up by stranger? Face it Kitty. That's the real cruel. truth of your situation."

Kitty was near tears as Mrs Dowd finished speaking. Desperately she replied, "But I wouldn't let that happen - I'm sure I'd be able to cope - somehow."

"But ye cannot be *sure* about that, can ye, Kitty. It's likely that you and your unfortunate child will be in for a hard life. Isn't that right now?"

Kitty, stroking the swelling beneath her pinafore, and looking totally miserable, gave no reply.

"Cheer up! I've a suggestion to put to ye," went on Anne.

"What if I told ye that I know a married couple who *could* and *would* provide your baby with all the love and security a child needs? But ye'd have to agree to certain conditions. Would ye be interested in such an agreement?"

A kaleidoscope of questions spun round Kitty's mind. Had she heard Mrs. Dowd correctly? Did she really know a couple willing to care for her baby? Why was she so willing to help her husband's mistress?

Aloud, she replied, "Well, firstly, I'd need to have more details about this arrangement before I say if I'm interested or not. I need to know the names of this couple and their circumstances. Also, I'd want to meet them both."

Anne smiled, saying, "The woman's name is Anne Dowd, her husband's called Pat." Then, with a touch of sarcasm, she added, "I think ye know him well!"

A startled Kitty felt she was in a kind of dream. After some reflection, she asked, "Why are ye so willing to take care of my child - one fathered by *your* husband?"

"That's easy!" was Anne's prompt response. "Despite his faults and his betrayal, I still care for Pat, and I also need him to help me bring up his children. But he's besotted by you. And as long as you remain in Ireland, he'll never settle with me. Sooner or later, he'll be off in search of you and his child."

"However, if ye give the baby to Pat and me as soon as it's born, we will love and care for the child. After all, he is the child's father and I can surely love what is part of my husband. All this should be made easier by the fact that both our babies are due only a few weeks apart, so it will be simple to bring up the two as twins."

Seeing that Kitty was about to speak, Anne warned, "No! I don't want ye to say anything until ye've heard this second part of the bargain" Anne took a deep breath. "I want ye to leave this part of Ireland for good once ye've had the child. Go anywhere, as long as it's nowhere near County Sligo."

Anne saw that Kitty had been stunned by her words. She continued quickly, "I know both parts of this agreement must seem very harsh at first, and will need some thought before you decide anything. But they may turn out to be the best decisions you'll ever make. Pat's told me a little about ye. How ye've a good brain and had a good teaching job which ye've had to leave because of your pregnancy."

At this, there was a slight nod from Kitty who still looked stunned.

"Just think about it, Kitty, ye won't have money to worry about, and ye'll know your child will always be loved and cared for. Pat and I will pay for your travel plus a few pounds besides. It'll start ye off. Sure, a young, intelligent girl like yourself will be able to begin a new life anywhere, and end up doing well."

During this 'rationale' of the proposed agreement, Kitty's face had taken on a look of fury. She now rose to her feet, and stood in front of the seated Anne. "Well now Mrs Dowd, here was I thinking ye'd come here with an offer of money for me and my babe. But it was simply to make sure *you* could hold on to your husband. You're going to take my baby from me, and also have me move from my family and friends to a place far away. Somewhere that Pat can't follow me! So how in God's name is this arrangement going to end in me 'doing well' for myself?"

It was Anne's turn to stand now. Slightly the taller of the two, she glared down at Kitty, her forefinger wagging in her rival's face. "Now look here, *Miss* Kitty, just listen to me - and ye'd better be listening well!" The finger-wagging stopped and she continued. "So ye think you're the loser, do ye? Well think about what happens if ye keep the child. Ye'll be shunned by most folk wherever ye live. Ye've committed a great sin, and to many you'll be seen as nothing but a slut and a hoor! And without money, ye'll soon be asking for charity. And here am I, giving you and your baby a chance in life!"

She continued, "And what about me? Over the past months, I've had to watch my husband gradually 'disappearing' from my life and the boys' lives. All the time knowing there's someone else he cares for, but keeping silent in the hope he sees sense before long. Then I'm told about you, your pregnancy, and the fact that he's leaving me - even though I'm expecting his child. How's that for a 'winner'?"

Anne paused letting her words sink in. She then went on, "So what do I do in order to try to hold on to the man I now need more than ever? I think of a plan which could benefit everyone. But it's also one at a great cost to me. For a start, it means that instead of having four children, I'll soon find myself with five! Five to feed and clothe. And one of those children, despite the fact I'll love it as my own, will remind me that my husband once betrayed me." And with that, Anne sat down saying. "So *don't* try to tell me you're the loser"

Kitty, who was sitting down again, was looking at Anne sorrowfully. She still needed a little thinking time, but now she spoke calmly and decisively."You're right Mrs Dowd, of course you're right! In all of this sorry mess you are the innocent one. At least your idea provides me with the opportunity for a new start. Though giving up my baby and leaving this part of Ireland and my family will tear at my heart, that's for sure. So I'd like a little time to discuss it all with my sister. Are you agreeable to me giving you my final answer in a week or so? I could write it in a note, then ask my brother-in-law, George Peattie to deliver it to your home - though he'll need to know where ye live."

Relieved, but trying not to show it, Anne replied, "I'll agree to a week's delay, but no longer! Mr Peattie seems a good choice of messenger. Then, opening a brown bag, she handed Kitty a piece of paper, "I've already written out the directions to my home. Just make sure Mr Peattie gives the note to me and *not* to Pat!"

Kitty asked, "I take it that Pat's in agreement with these plans?"

"Ye take it correctly, Miss Kitty. He wasn't at all happy at first, but he slept on it for a night or two. And now he's decided it'll be the best thing for all of us."

This lie was one which Anne would be repeating 'in reverse' to Pat, later on.

She then stood up once more, ready to depart now that it seemed her mission had been accomplished. As Anne moved towards the door, she turned, saying, "If ye do accept these arrangements, I'm thinking it for the best if Mr Peattie lets me know as soon as your labour starts. Then I can make arrangements for the baby to be brought to me as soon as possible. My child is due about the end of July." Then, having reached the door, her final words to Kitty were, "Good day, and may the Holy Mother protect us at our birthing-times."

Kitty rose to accompany her to the door, but Anne stopped her with the warning, "No, stay inside! 'Tis better that we are not seen together."

As requested, Kitty remained inside the cottage. For some time she sat in a daze as she reflected on all the implications of the morning's meeting.

Chapter 23

The Sting

After conversations with both Mary Anne and her brother-in-law, Kitty was convinced that the arrangements suggested by Pat's wife were the best that could be made - given all the circumstances. Also, George seemed quite willing to deliver Kitty's note to Anne Dowd. Indeed, he was secretly quite relieved that Kitty would be departing once her baby was born, leaving more space for his growing family.

During the last week of June, Margaret Tooey made the journey to Drumfin to see how her heavily pregnant daughters were. She also had some sad news for them. Looking pale and strained, she told them the doctor in the area had visited her husband recently and confirmed what she'd suspected for some time. Namely, that he was not long for this life. Three or four months at the most.

"Aye ma lassies, the only good thing is that Dad's suffering will soon be ended. Indeed, he's sleeping most of the time now. He doesn't always recognise his children - so luckily he's not aware that the two of ye haven't been round for a while."

Mary Anne hoped he might live to see her and her fourth baby, due in September. Kitty's initial shock was tinged with some relief at the news of Dad's failing memory. At least she was able to keep the news of her pregnancy from him. But hoped she would be able to see him before leaving Sligo.

Also, though apprehensive of her mother's reaction, Kitty knew she must today tell her about the plan Mrs Dowd had suggested. An opportunity came when Mary Anne left them alone whilst she worked in another part of the kitchen.

Mam listened carefully, only interrupting when informed that Pat Dowd was the father. She nodded, saying, "Aye, he'd be the one who helped ye with Master Thomas during your 'blackberry meeting'. I suspected as much!"

When Kitty had finished speaking, Mam's reaction was surprising. "I canna say I could ever have given up one of *my* bairns, but then I've had a husband with a good job to support me. I'm just sorry I'm not in a position to have you and the bairn back home to live. So it's lucky for you that Mrs Dowd has come up with this option - *and* hold on to her man as well. A canny woman all right!"

She thought for a few moments, then concluded, "Given the alternatives, in your place, Kitty, I *might* have done the same. But, I'll certainly miss ye when ye leave Ireland. However, Mrs Dowd is correct in saying that, with your brains, ye could do well for yourself anywhere. But I'm not sure how well she's thought about the part where your bairn is smuggled to her without anyone knowing."

Looked slightly worried, Kitty said, "Well I was hoping Mrs Dowd would come up with a plan. Have *you* any ideas on the 'smuggling' part?"

"Well here are my thoughts. Nobody round here knows me, so I can be 'midwife' for ye when the time comes. Then, as soon as it's safe, I'll carry the bairn to the Dowd's home. Of course, the wee mite will have to be 'disguised' somehow. I'll have to give some thought to that." Another pause, then she went on, "Here's a further idea. Mrs Dowd can tell neighbours I'm the midwife, come to check on her before her bairn is ready to be born." Kitty's mother gave a wry smile, "What a surprise for everyone when they hear she's had twins!"

Diverse thoughts were spinning through Kitty's mind. She was still surprised at Mam's reaction to the plan, and even more at her willingness to help carry it out.

"Aye" she thought, "Mam's just as canny as Mrs Dowd. And after ten children, very well-qualified to deliver a baby!" Then her mother spoke again, "Of course, I'll be needing to have a word with Mrs Dowd in person for these plans to be plausible. She'd better be pretending her bairn is due in late September. Twins tend to come early, so nobody will be surprised if 'twins' arrive in August. Also, when she does gives birth to her own child, she mustn't tell anyone outside her home about it. To everyone else, she only gives birth when its 'twin' arrives."

There was another brief period of reflection as Mrs Tooey pondered over the logistics of these amendments to the quite complex plan.

Then decisively she said, "And the sooner I talk with her the better. So would ye mind, Kitty, if I have a meal with you and Mary Anne earlier than usual? Then I can take a walk to Riverstown today."

Kitty was not at all sure that Mrs Dowd would want to listen to advice from her mother. Still, Mam's ideas seemed to 'tie up' all the loose ends. However, she felt it necessary to ask her mother if she were really well enough to take on all these commitments, with Dad so ill. Mam was quick to reassure her, "Despite all my present worries about your Dad, I must admit the challenge of helping you safely through these difficult days will take my mind off them for a while. As I told ye both, he sleeps most of the day, and Madge is there for him."

Indeed, Kitty need not have concerned herself regarding the outcome of the meeting between the two women. After Anne's initial reluctance to speak to the rather severe looking Margaret Tooey, she very much welcomed the advice given. It certainly made a lot of sense to inform any neighbours who enquired about the forthcoming child that its birth was not expected until September.

Mam's visit had made Kitty aware that she needed to think about where she would go to make her 'new life'. There followed many discussions with Mary Anne and George regarding possible destinations. They had both considered moving away from Drumfin sometime in the future to better themselves, so were able to provide Kitty with more optimism regarding leaving County Sligo.

George was apprenticed to a high-class tailor in Sligo Town. Wages were low at present but there were good prospects for the future. He proposed to move to Belfast eventually where he and his family hoped to find a 'better life'. Here, with his skill in tailoring, he hoped to become a Master Tailor in due time.

"But that doesn't necessarily mean Belfast's the place for you Kitty," was George's advice. "Ye've to think of where there'll be good opportunities for work. I believe sister Sarah is thinking about New Zealand. People say there's a good life to be had if ye don't mind work. But I'm thinking the opportunities in that country are mainly for men. However, I do know that, with the coming of industrial revolution in England, many Irish folk are thinking of emigrating there. Work of all kinds is said to be plentiful. And besides, if things don't work out, ye could always come back to Ireland." With a smile, he concluded, "Mam Tooey's right; beggaring off to New Zealand like Sarah intends to do, is like an eejit booking a one-way ticket to the moon or another planet!"

George paused, inhaling deeply from his clay pipe. This was followed by a hearty chuckle, as he again pictured Mrs Tooey giving her opinion of that country.

But the inhalation hadn't mixed well with the chuckle, and soon he fell into a fit of coughing. Mary Anne leaned forward and thumped her husband's back enthusiastically, saying, "Wise words, Georgie, wise words."

And though laughing at George, Kitty was now wondering if emigration to England wasn't such a bad idea.

August arrived and so did Kitty's mother. She was carrying a large brown leather bag as she walked determinedly into the Peattie's cottage. Two days later, Kitty's back started aching in the evening, but it wasn't until the next day that her waters broke. It was then that Mary Anne, now in her eighth month of pregnancy, was called upon by her mother to be her 'ancillary' nurse.

There followed a long day of Kitty walking round the kitchen, then pausing with each pain. Mrs Tooey regularly checked on the extent of her daughter's dilation. Meanwhile, Mary Anne gave words of comfort to her sister, made drinks of oatmeal and water, and saw there was a good supply of boiled water to hand. Her hardest job was trying to keep her three youngsters occupied in the garden with their toys. They were forever trying to get back in the house to see what all the fuss was about.

It was seven o'clock that night before 'pushing' time came. Then, whilst still pressing hard on her sister's hand, Kitty gave a final grunt, and out slithered a blood-covered little child.

Next moment, Mam stood triumphantly holding Kitty's baby. A fine boy.

She cradled her Grandson, saying tenderly, "Welcome! Welcome ma laddie! I wish ye a life filled with happiness. And may the Lord bless ye."

With tears in her eyes she gently kissed the child's forehead, and turning to an exhausted, tearful Kitty, asked, "Do ye want to hold your son?"

"No Mam - or I'd never let him go! But I'd like ye to hold my boy so I can have one good look at him - then ye must take him away - and do what has to be done."

As her mother held the tiny boy closer, Kitty spoke softly to him. "I love ye my son and always will. And though I have to let ye go now, it's only so ye will have a better life than I could ever give ye. I promise that one day I'll be back to see ye, my son." Then she closed her eyes and prayed, "God forgive me, and watch over this child." Finally, with tears running freely down her cheeks, she kissed her baby's forehead.

Of course, by then, George was home from work and ready to help where needed. A weary Kitty was left resting after her labours of the day. Mrs Tooey, having helped her to express some milk, had given it to the hungry baby. Then she'd wrapped him in a blanket and placed him in the small wooden cradle which had been made for Mary Anne's children.

Whilst Kitty, her baby and the Peattie children were sleeping soundly, the three adults thankfully sat down to have a late meal. Mrs Tooey announced that it would be best if the baby were to be taken to the Dowd's cottage that night. Already, it was gone eight o'clock and she knew that darkness would set in about nine. An arrival at dusk would be ideal for her purpose. Everyone helped in putting warm covers in her large bag, and gently transferring the sleeping baby to it.

Carrying the slightly open bag with great care, the 'midwife' set out to walk the three miles to the babe's new family.

Chapter 24

Crossing the Irish Sea

Kitty now seemed to be recovering quite well, and Mary Anne was there to look after her until she felt ready to begin her journey to Liverpool. So her mother left Drumfin, anxious to see how Edward was faring in Sligo Town. On arrival home, Madge assured her that Dad had remained about the same whilst she'd been away. He'd slept most of the day, still eating very little, with the coughing and vomiting still occurring mainly at night. Next she wanted to hear about Kitty and her baby. Though she knew her sister would be giving the baby into the care of 'good parents', none of the family knew who they were.

In fact, Kitty was soon was up and about again, and had asked brother-in-law, George, to book her a third class rail ticket from Sligo Town to Dublin on August 20th, and also a night steerage ticket from Dublin to Liverpool. She planned to spend the morning of that day with all her family. It was her dearest wish that Dad would be awake and recognise her before she left for England.

Mary Anne, though heavily pregnant, felt well enough to travel with her, and so on the morning of August 20th the two sisters, along with Mary, Jane and young George, caught the train from Ballymote to Sligo Town. Both were apprehensive regarding their Dad's condition. However, as they entered their family home, a lovely and totally unexpected surprise greeted them. Dad, though thin and haggard, was propped up in bed awaiting their arrival. He greeted Mary Anne first, "Ach, ye look well, and ye'll be giving me another grandchild soon. For sure, it's grand to see ye and the children again." Then he turned to Kitty, "And it's grand to see you my 'Ray of Sunshine'- I've been missing that smile so much." Then in a whisper, he repeated, "So very much."

An emotional Kitty managed a smile as she placed her hand on Dad's.

The two sisters were happy to be able to speak with their father for a while, having feared that, even if awake, he might not have known who they were.

All ten Tooey children were gathered at meal-time that day, conversing with each other both inside and outside the house. They recalled and laughed about past family incidents, though Kitty became pensive as noon approached.

When the time came for her and Mary Anne to leave, she bade farewell to each member of her family, apart from Dad. He was sleeping again, his breathing punctuated by low throaty moans. The two sisters kissed his forehead and walked to the door with Mam.

Mary Anne was told by her mother to take great care of herself during this final month of pregnancy, and a kiss was blown to each of her three grandchildren. After looking at Kitty with an expression of love and sadness, she took her daughter's face in her hands, saying, "Be sure to write to me with all your news. Have a good and safe journey to England. And if ever ye feel homesick, as we Scots say, 'Haste ye back'!"

Once at the station, Mary Anne and her children boarded their train back to Ballymote. There was a brief period of 'farewells,' then Kitty was left, a lone figure waiting for the Dublin train.

From nowhere, a figure appeared at her side, and a familiar voice spoke, "Kitty, luveen, I couldn't let ye leave Ireland without seeing ye."

Startled, she turned to see the man she'd fallen in love with. Her first expression was of joy, but it quickly changed to one of consternation. "Pat ye shouldn't ..."

Before Kitty could say more, Pat assured her, "Don't worry. Anne knows I'm here! And she also knows I'll be returning to her when I leave here. I'll be forever sorry that I caused ye all this distress. But I want ye to know ye go with my love and wishes for happiness in England. May the Lord take care of ye on the journey and in your new life." Then he looked deeply into her eyes, saying softly, "And I've the strongest feelin' my darlin' that somehow, some day, we'll be together with our son."

Before Kitty could make any response, he'd turned and was out of sight.

Alone again on the platform, Kitty stood thinking over Pat's words and the babe she'd left behind. Then she crossed herself, quietly praying to the Holy Mother.

By the time the train eventually came, other travellers had joined Kitty on the platform. However, being now the afternoon, it wasn't as packed as the morning trains, and she was able to obtain a seat. It was going to be a journey of about eight hours, so, having had an emotional day, she closed her eyes and drifted off to sleep.

But it was a disturbed sleep, one in which she saw a baby looking at her pleadingly. *Her* son, born out of wedlock, so not 'worthy' of a church baptism! Next a young child appeared asking why she'd abandoned him.

She awoke with a start, murmuring, "Sorry, so sorry" to herself. Then she noticed a young woman next to her, eating a large slice of potato apple cake.

The woman, having seen Kitty's agitation as she awoke, said kindly, "I'm sorry for your trouble, but I'm thinkin' ye'll be feeling hungry after that restless sleep. Would ye like one of my oatcakes?"

She then reached down into her large travelling bag, took one out and offered it to Kitty who gratefully accepted it, having refused Mam's offer of a packed meal. She was also glad to take her mind off the dreams she'd had.

Soon the two were in conversation. The woman introduced herself as Margaret Rougham from Westport in County Mayo. She said she was travelling to Dublin, and from there would board the night boat to Liverpool to find work and start a new life. Kitty was pleased at this coincidence since it meant she would have a companion on the journey. Also, having taken a liking to this erstwhile stranger, she suggested that they could together look for suitable but cheap accommodation in Liverpool. From there they could try to find work. At this, Margaret gave a derisive laugh, "Sure I've no intention of seeking work there, Kitty. I've heard that most labouring jobs have already been taken by earlier Irish immigrants. And most of the decent jobs advertised usually state, 'No Blacks - No Irish.'"

Taken aback by this, Kitty enquired where Margaret intended to look for work.

"Luckily, I've already been given the name of a Mrs Rourke who runs a small boarding house in the Lancashire town of Wigan. She's willing to take me in for a reasonable rent. I'm told it's a growing town with plenty of work available."

She paused whilst Kitty took this news on board, then continued, "And now I'm thinking that if you're still of a mind to keep with me, 't would be grand if ye came to Wigan with me. Maybe if we share a room, Mrs Rourke will take ye in too. So what do ye think?"

Whilst Kitty was reflecting on this unexpected, but possible change of plan, her companion rubbed together the thumb and forefinger of one hand, observing, "Sharing a room should mean a cheaper rent for us, and a bit more money for Mrs Rourke."

There was a fairly quick reply, "Well, I must admit I like the idea of saving money on the rent. But how far is Wigan from Liverpool? And what will this extra journey cost us?

"No problem there." Margaret's reply was also quick. "The Liverpool train runs to Wigan for only a few pence. It's roughly only twenty-odd miles north."

Kitty was still not quite sure if she wanted to change her plans so suddenly, but she liked Margaret and had found out she was twenty-five years old. It seemed a good idea to travel with someone who'd had more experience of life than herself.

So finally, she said, "Well, Margaret, I think I'll be joining you in Wigan."

It was dark when they reached Dublin, and though fairly warm, a steady drizzle had set in as they walked with their luggage to their ship, 'City of Dublin Steam Packet Company'. It was already waiting in the Dublin dock. Having both booked steerage passages to Liverpool, they made their way downstairs to the area below the deck of the vessel. Crowds of passengers were already there, but by elbowing their way through them, the two found a spot at the side of the ship. The majority of passengers seemed to be Irish; the rest seeming to be mainly from England, though Kitty detected a few Scottish accents here and there.

Once the boat set sail, it wasn't long before a strong wind got up as they reached the Irish sea. And after less than an hour, the ship began to roll. Soon, people were being sick, and the stench of vomit became overwhelming. Women were moaning, children were crying, and Irish men added to the chaos by cursing the weather, their wives - and the 'Bloody English'.

Kitty and Margaret proved to be good sea travellers, but since sleep was quite impossible, they began observing the rest of the passengers and listening to the assortment of accents. Nearby was an English woman travelling with a young boy of about eight. He'd started to make the retching sound which usually precedes vomiting.

Anticipating this, the woman yelled, "Don't tha dare be sick o'er tha new clothes Jack, or I'll give thee such a good pastin'!" She held up her hand, ready to carry out her threat, whereupon Jack, turning to avoid the hand, proceeded to be sick all over her woollen shawl. Immediately, she let out a cry of, "Christ, me bloody best shawl! Can tha do nowt reet?"

The hapless Jack then received the pasting he'd been promised.

Though seeing a funny side to this scene, the two friends felt sorry for the lad.

At last, the long and exhausting sea journey was over and the ship docked in Liverpool. By the time the two companions had disembarked, it was seven o'clock in the morning - still windy and now raining heavily. Glad the sea journey was at an end, they both felt exhausted and hungry, so Kitty put forward a suggestion, "If we carry on walking towards the city centre, we might see somewhere we can get something to eat, and then we can find out where we catch a train to Wigan."

Actually, the truth of the matter was that Kitty was disappointed at what she could see of Liverpool. Though it was August, the rain, wind and tall, grey buildings seemed to loom threateningly around her. All of which heightened her feeling of being a stranger there, though she was glad to have Margaret for company. Also, no matter what Wigan was like, it surely had to be better than this place.

Nodding in agreement, Margaret took her arm and the two went briskly towards signs indicating the city centre. They hungrily ate their first Lancashire meat pies. They'd been bought from a street vendor who called Kitty 'queen' as she paid for them. Eventually, they found the station where trains travelled from Liverpool to Manchester, one of its stops being at Wigan.

On the journey there, Kitty was pleased to note that the train travelled through some pleasant agricultural areas. These included a place called Burscough which was by a canal, and one was called Parbold. However, as the train neared Wigan, dark grey, built-up areas came into sight.

Soon, a Lancashire voice was heard announcing, "Wiggin! Wiggin Station."

They climbed a flight of steep stairs up to ground level. Here Kitty noticed a number of advertisements, mainly about coal and mining. With very mixed feelings, she walked out of the station, and on Margaret's instructions turned right. Then the two headed for somewhere called 'Walker's Yard.'

Chapter 25

Enter Mrs Rourke

Kitty was glad the rain had ceased, but even so, clouds still loomed threateningly overhead. As she looked around, she saw large hostile buildings, blackened by soot and grime. It all filled her with foreboding. Margaret tugged at her arm, "Come on with ye, Kitty! Plenty of time for looking round Wigan when we've made sure Mrs Rourke has saved the room. Then we can start looking round to find work for ourselves."

Wallgate was busy as crowds of people, mainly women, hurried along the streets. Most of them wore long, dark skirts covered by aprons. Shawls covered their shoulders or heads. The clothes looked quite similar to those to be seen back home, the main difference being the footwear. Many wore heavy black clogs with brass studs along the front edges. Some had a kind of iron on the soles which made a clattering noise as they walked over the pavement.

But it was their faces which held Kitty's attention. So many had deeply-etched lines, and wore expressions of hopeless resignation. Faces like the ones described by her Dad and Pat when talking about the dreadful years of the famine.

"Holy Mother," thought Kitty, "is this the Godforsaken place where I'm going to be finding my fine new life?"

Loud, raucous voices were then heard yelling in the distance. People seemed to be selling things, and Kitty was reminded of Market Days back in Sligo Town. But the voices here were low-pitched and alien to her ear. As though confirming her thoughts, Margaret said, "Ach, it seems we've arrived on one of their Market Days. But I'll be damned if I understand a word they're saying! Anyway, never mind them, I was told Walkers Yard's not far from the station, so I'd better start asking if we're going the right way."

The person Margaret stopped was a woman of about thirty. She was walking in the opposite direction and grasping the hand of a three year-old girl who wore a small pair of clogs similar to her mother's. What caught Kitty's eye however, was the large bulge clearly visible under the woman's apron and shawl. Immediately, her thoughts returned to the son she'd left behind. Then Margaret's voice interrupted her sad recollections. "Would ye kindly tell me if we're heading the right way for Walkers Yard? I believe Lyon Street's there."

An amused look crossed the woman's face as she heard Margaret's accent. Smiling, she said, "Aye, tha's nearly theer. Only five minutes or so away." In an ironic tone, she added, "A reet bonny place it is too! The likes of thee should fit in reet well." Then tugging the child's arm she said, "Come on, an' stop tha gawpin'. Nowt to look at theer!"

The encounter served only to confirm Kitty's first impressions of Wigan - and its people. Even Margaret was taken aback by the derision implied in the woman's words. However, she simply took Kitty's arm and they continued walking.

Not much later, they found themselves on unpaved, uneven, muddy roads which were criss-crossed by clog prints. Here and there, cinders had been put down. Eventually, they saw Lyon Street, it was amongst rows of back-to-back, terraced houses, the bricks blackened by smoke. Seeing a young girl of about fifteen in a long black dress emerge from one of them, Margaret again took the lead in speaking.

"Could ye tell me if Mrs Rourke lives near here?" The two friends were surprised and certainly cheered to hear her reply in a familiar brogue, "Sure, 'tis the one at the very end of this row."

Then, pointing to the large bags they both carried, she said, "I expect ye'll be the new lodgers from Ireland. Mam told me Mrs Rourke was expectin' new people today. Welcome to ye both. Not a pretty place - but ye'll find ye have many friends here."

A heartened Kitty replied. "Ach, 'tis grand to hear an Irish voice again, and thank ye for the welcome."

Then the two made their way to the end of the grimy houses. Soon they were introducing themselves to a dark-haired, sharp-featured woman wearing a long, brown dress with a white pinafore over it. She wiped her hands, white with flour, on her apron before she greeted her guests. On her head was an old velvet hat, and fixed to its side was a faded red rose on a longish stalk. Though the rose seemed entirely incongruous, Kitty found something endearing in it. And despite her former pessimistic thoughts about the people in Wigan, she felt she was going to like this woman. Smiling, Mrs Rourke welcomed them into the house, "Failte! Come in, come in with the two of ye. I trust the crossing wasn't too bad?"

Without waiting for a reply, she went on, "Now I'm thinkin' ye'd like to see your room. Then we can discuss the rent." Giving a wink, she added, "Business first is what I always say."

And with that she led them into the kitchen which boasted an old settee in one corner and two wooden chairs near the fire. By the fire, a kettle bubbled away on its stand. They came to some stairs, and after turning left, they followed Mrs Rourke up to the top of them arriving at a tiny room at the back of the house.

A double bed filled most of it, though there was just about enough space for a small wooden stand which held a basin and jug for water. Proudly, their landlady announced, "There ye are Margaret and Kitty! A fine and comfortable clean bed, water that'll be changed every day, a chamber pot that'll be emptied every day - and besides that," at this point, Mrs Rourke went over to the window, "this window opens! For sure there's many a lodging house without even *one* window that can be opened properly. All due to subsidence caused by the mining, of course!"

Whilst uttering the last sentence, she shook her head vigorously from side to side in strong disapproval. However, the movement caused the rose to mimic the side to side action of her head, and the new friends found it difficult to refrain from laughing. So it was with some restraint that Margaret managed to say, "That sounds just fine, Mrs Rourke. So what will ye be expecting as rent - considering there's now two lodgers, but we'll be sharing this bedroom?"

"Well now, I charged my last male occupants two shillings each. They were from Wigan, but were of the Catholic faith, so I didn't mind them too much. They worked for a couple of butchers in the town for a year and left a week ago to set up their own business in Standish. Since ye were recommended by a friend, Margaret, *and* from Ireland, I'm willing to reduce the price to one shilling and ten pence each. But that's provided ye'll be staying here at least six months, and can pay three months in advance. What do ye say?"

Kitty replied first, having quickly calculated three months' rent as being five shillings and six pence each. She had four pounds over from her travel money, and so could help out Margaret if necessary.

"Mrs Rourke, would ye give me and my friend a few minutes to discuss it? We'll be downstairs in a minute or two to give ye our answer. Are any meals included in the price?"

"Aye. Meals are provided in the morning and early evening. It's seven o'clock sharp at week-ends. I can arrange week-day meals according to your working hours. And since ye won't have had a proper meal for a while, I'll have an extra one ready for ye this dinner time. That's if ye decide to stay!"

She gave a meaningful nod, and the rose bobbed again. Then she left the room, closing the door behind her, and made her way downstairs.

Once they were sure she was in the kitchen again, Margaret and Kitty discussed the price. Both agreed that, though in a very grim area, the price was very reasonable. Margaret knew that many boarding houses had four or more people sharing a room. Also, the bed and sheets (after a close inspection for fleas) were found to be clean, so was the room itself. As for Mrs Rourke, both considered she seemed not bad for a landlady. They found her old hat and 'rambling rose' most amusing and, in a strange way, it suited her character. It seemed to declare, 'I might look a bit battered now - but once I was something to take note of!'

They also took into consideration the fact that with two meals a day included, they could save a reasonable amount of money, provided they found work quickly.

So the decision to stay being made, they made their way down to make their advance payment. Mrs Rourke smiled as she took the money and shook hands formally to acknowledge the agreement. Next she told them to sit at the table in a small room adjoining the kitchen, adding that their meal would be ready soon.

Whilst preparing it, Mrs Rourke called from the kitchen, "I forgot to tell ye about the privy. It's outside. There's one to every four houses, and they're emptied every night."

When a meal of tripe, boiled onions and slices of buttered bread arrived, the young women regarded it suspiciously. Then they looked questioningly at each other. Mrs Rourke, noting these exchanges, was quick to reassure them, "Ach, I see ye've not had tripe before. Well, let me tell ye, it's a fine, nourishing and tasty meal. Highly popular in these parts. So get it into your bellies."

And to their surprise it didn't taste too bad. So after unpacking, and a brief rest on their bed, the two got up and had a quick wash. They were now ready to find out what work was available.

Chapter 26

Looking for Work

It was mid-afternoon by the time they were in the town centre again. Mrs Rourke had told them a shop called 'Starr' often displayed information regarding available work. However, they decided to 'get the feel' of the town first and then find 'Starr'. From the distance the sound of hooves could be heard, and about five or six horse-drawn carts came into sight. All the carts carried several large wicker baskets. Most of the drivers wore caps, though one, boasting a straw boater, looked at them admiringly, doffed his hat and called out. "'Ow do ladies?" Like the other men, he had on a rather soiled waist-coat over rolled-up shirt sleeves, and of course, the ubiquitous clogs. Both women acknowledged his greeting with a smile, and Kitty remarked, "Well, that's an improvement on the 'welcome' we got from that woman this morning! I wonder what's in all those baskets?"

Smiling, Margaret replied, "Yes, it was nice to be greeted in a friendly way. As to the baskets, I'm guessing they hold all the goods not sold at the market this morning."

They continued exploring the town, and both were impressed by the variety of shops and occupations to be seen. For some while they watched one of the town's many farriers as he expertly nailed a new iron shoe to a horse's foot whilst it stood there patiently. They were also impressed by the number of men wearing battered top-hats, their faces covered in soot, and carrying an assortment of brushes over their shoulders. Many called out, "Swee-eep, swee-eep."

"I'm thinking *they're* never out of work with all the chimneys they have here," commented Kitty as she surveyed the buildings, all topped by tall chimneys. "I suppose that accounts for all the coal advertisements we saw at the station."

As they walked on, Kitty saw the usual variety of shops which she might have seen in Sligo Town in Ireland. These included fishmongers, drapers and the like. One of the many butchers' shops particularly caught Margaret's eye. There were the usual large carcasses of farm animals hanging outside as well as various sizes of hens and chickens. But what amused her was a large notice which read, IRISH eggs for sale inside.

"So it seems, Kitty, that Wiganers don't despise everything that comes out of Ireland!" was Margaret's comment. Then both began to laugh loudly. This brought tuts of disapproval from a female passer by who was carrying a baby in her shawl. She stopped and glared, declaring, "I'm glad *tha's* getten somat to laugh at. There's bugger all meks *me* laugh these days!" Then she 'clattered', grim-faced, on her way.

So they carried on with their sight-seeing in mock solemnity for a while. Coming to a fairly new, large shop which was three storeys high and had the name, CO-OP printed in large letters at the top, they paused to look in the windows. Here they saw a range of men's, women's and children's clothing on display. Both felt it would be an interesting shop to look round sometime, though it was likely to be expensive. Also, since it was getting late, they decided to ask for directions to 'Starr'.

Luckily, it was in the Wallgate area and was quite a large shop with a double-fronted window. It specialised in books, book-binding, maps and various types of paper. Just inside the door was a board which displayed an assortment of cards giving details of employers seeking workers, and cards written by those needing work. There were plenty of jobs available in the many nearby mills and collieries, but these were ignored by Kitty and Margaret. They'd heard enough about the long hours and dangers these jobs entailed. Yet to their dismay, they found that when they read about the more suitable jobs, these always ended with, 'No Blacks. No Irish'.

Kitty immediately turned to Margaret in disbelief saying, "But didn't ye tell me that Wigan wouldn't be like Liverpool?" Equally devastated, Margaret replied, "I'm sorry, Kitty. That's what my friend was telling me, and for sure she seemed so positive, I believed she must be right."

Disheartened, they continued looking through the cards. Finally, each found one with no stipulations regarding colour or nationality, though the jobs were a far cry from what they'd originally had in mind. Both were in

Public Houses, and both had work for only one applicant, though luckily the hours were almost identical.

"They'll do for the time being until something better comes along. But I think we should be applying for them now to make sure they're not taken," observed Margaret.

Kitty nodded, though she was only too aware that many Irish people looked down on women who worked in Public Houses.

'The Bowling Green', Margaret's choice, was in Wigan's centre, whereas 'The Packet', Kitty's choice, was near their lodgings. So they decided to go to their respective pubs separately, then hopefully meet up in time for the evening meal.

It was about six o'clock when Kitty arrived at 'The Packet'. There was already quite a noisy crowd inside. Going somewhat apprehensively up to the bar, but trying to look casual, she asked a thick-set man with greying hair if she could speak to the proprietor. She was promptly told, "That'll be me. I hope it's a job tha's after!"

He looked relieved to hear that it was indeed the purpose of her visit, and asked if she could commence work immediately. Kitty explained about her long journey that day, but said she was able to start work on Monday morning.

Clearly disappointed, he replied irritably, "Well mek sure tha's on time. We start at six prompt. Tha wipes o'er all t' tables and cleans t' tankards. Tha works from six till ten, then tha comes back at six at neet and works till midnight. Tha'll be on 'alf-pay fer a week while I see how tha's shapin' And think on, I stand no messin'!"

Relieved she'd managed to get the job, though far from happy to be working for half-pay for a week, Kitty made her way back to Walkers Yard. It was about half-an-hour later when Margaret arrived back. She too had been successful in obtaining work. Similarly, the 'Bowling Green' proprietor had tried to insist she began work that evening, but like Kitty, had promised to start the following Monday.

At seven o'clock, they went downstairs ready for something to eat. Here they noticed a little girl of about three years sitting on the old settee and using a wooden spoon to eat something from a bowl. Next to her was a man of indeterminate age. He had a lined face, though his black hair contained only the faintest hint of grey. On seeing the two young women, he nodded, saying, "Aye, go through. The table's set. I'll join ye when the scouse is ready."

They nodded, went into the room adjoining the kitchen, and sat down at the table. It was now covered with a blue and white oilcloth on which four plates and spoons were set out. To their surprise, a young boy of about seven or eight entered the room via the kitchen. Looking at Kitty and Margaret in turn, he said brightly, "Evenin'. I've just finished work. Mam's havin' another babby, so she's sent me round to Granny's for a meal. I don't mind though cos I love her lobscouse."

Smiling, they introduced themselves. The boy replied, "I'm Patrick - like Granddad, but I like to be called Pat."

Kitty's felt her cheeks redden as she heard that name once more.

Luckily, at that moment Mrs Rourke entered the room, carrying a large, fire-blackened pan, and proceeded to drop several dollops of its contents on each plate. The man they'd seen in the kitchen had followed her, carrying a plate of bread.

"Dig in!" he ordered whilst seating himself in front of the fourth plate. As he took a large piece of bread and spread a spoonful of lobscouse on it, he said, "Welcome to ye both. I'm Patrick Rourke, married to this fine figure of a woman, Annie. And, apart from choosing one of the handsomest men in Ireland for a husband, the next best thing she did was learn to make a *perfect* lobscouse."

The 'fine' Mrs Rourke, standing by his side, gave him a friendly clip on his ear, saying, "Would ye listen to the man! Now I'm off to see if young Molly's asleep." Turning to Pat, she continued, "And you, me young gasureen, can scrape the pan, but only after ye've brought the empty plates to me. Then home to Mam!"

Turning, she walked briskly into the kitchen, the red rose bobbing on her hat.

Kitty and Margaret ate hungrily and with relish, clearly they had the same opinion of lobscouse as Patrick and Pat - and they mopped up their last mouthfuls with chunks of bread. Once Pat had finished, he took the empty plates to the kitchen.

Mr Rourke watched him go, then addressed Kitty and Margaret, "I expect ye'll be wondering who the children belong to. The little girl ye saw in the kitchen is Molly. She's our grandchild and lives next door with her Mam, our daughter, Mary. After having our Pat, she lost two children before Molly was born. Now she's pregnant again and not feeling too grand, so me and Annie help out by having the little one here overnight. Young Pat often comes for a meal."

"Pat said he worked, Mr Rourke? What work would that be?" asked Kitty.

"Ach, call me Patrick, please. Our Pat goes round with the travelling butcher and his horse and cart. He knocks on doors and shouts, "Meat! Fresh meat!"

He's a popular little beggar and a hard grafter, but the pay's poor. Still, every bit helps. And he's a damn sight better off than those poor lads who used to work for the chimney sweeps and were sent up the chimneys to loosen the soot."

Here, Margaret chipped in, "We saw a few sweeps in the town centre - surely young boys don't do that now."

"No, they don't! But it was only about three years ago that the government passed a law to get it stopped for good!" ([1]) Mrs Rourke then came into the room.

"Anyway, you two young ladies," said Mrs Rourke, cheerily "enough about chimney sweeps! How did you get on with finding a job?"

And so Kitty and Margaret told her the whole story of their big disappointment when looking for job vacancies in 'Starr'. They ended by admitting they'd reluctantly decided to apply for jobs in local pubs despite the poor pay. Mrs Rourke seemed relieved to find that at least they'd both obtained jobs.

"Well as ye say, you've both *got* a job!" she observed. Then continued, "The pay may not be much, but two young, capable and intelligent women like yourselves should soon be moving on to something better."

Patrick then chipped in with, "Aye, Annie's right - as usual! It isn't too bad a place to start ye off. And thank God ye didn't settle for hellish work in a factory!"

Before either of them could comment, Mrs Rourke broke in with, "Talking of women doing hellish work, the pits were even worse! I know an old lady who worked down the pit as a young woman. Her job was dragging tubs of coal to the surface. She had to wear a harness round her waist with the chain going between her legs. Just like an animal!"

The two were duly horrified at the very thought of such a job.

However, much as they'd found the evening and the meal informative and enjoyable, exhaustion from their long journey had finally crept up on them. So after bidding Mrs Rourke and Patrick, 'Good night', they made their way upstairs to their bedroom.

Whilst undressing, Margaret remarked to Kitty, "I'm thinking Patrick has had an education and keeps up with the news. They're both quite chatty and I like them."

Sleepily, Kitty replied, "So do I. Goodnight"

Footnote[1]

In 1875, George Brewster was still working as a chimney sweep's boy when aged twelve years - much too big and old for the job. He became stuck half-way up a chimney. One side of the chimney had to be pulled down to get him out but he died soon afterwards. The government declared such work by children illegal. Regular inspections helped to enforce the law.

Chapter 27

Sunday in Wigan

It was still early when Kitty awoke to the sound of movement downstairs and the voice of Mr Rourke quietly persuading young Molly it was time to go back to her mother's house. A few minutes later, she called up the stairs, "We'll be off to St. Joseph's in about twenty minutes. Would the two of ye care to join us?"

"Of course!" thought Kitty, "It's Sunday - I'd forgotten what day it was after all our travelling." Hastily, she sat up in bed, rousing Margaret as she did so, then called down the stairs,"Thank ye Mrs Rourke, we'll be down in a few minutes to join ye for Mass."

Once out of bed, Kitty washed her face with water from the jug then asked Margaret,"Wonder if Mrs R will be wearing the same hat? Or will she have a Sunday one for 'best'"?

Sleepily, Margaret replied," Sure she'll keep a special one for Sundays."

Once dressed, they went downstairs to meet the Rourkes who were patiently waiting for them. Both were surreptitiously looking at Mrs Rourke's hat, but both were wrong! She wore her old hat - but now the faded red rose was replaced by a slightly less faded trailing white one. Suppressing their amusement, they set off for the church. Once inside, Kitty's mind became occupied with recollections of the church in Riverstown, also named St Joseph's. Indeed, it was a relief when the congregation filed out and they were all walking back for breakfast.

After the meal of porridge, bread and butter and mugs of tea, Margaret suggested they should take the opportunity to explore more of Wigan. She'd been told by her friend, Maria, that the lodging house was near a canal. So asked, "What do ye think about us starting there first, Kitty?"

The idea appealed to Kitty since she had always lived near water.

Mrs Rourke told them the most direct way to the canal adding, "Sure, ye won't find it the prettiest way, but 'tis the quickest. The towpath shouldn't be too bad since there's been no rain since ye arrived. Ye might also want to go to the Market Place afterwards, the women are holding another Temperance Meeting there today. Sure it could be a bit lively if the men are there as well."

Following the recommended direction, they soon reached the canal. After less than a mile, a sort of lunar landscape surrounded them. It was formed by 'hills' of grey slag-heaps. "'Tis certainly a far cry from the Ox mountains and the clear air of Cloonacool!" observed Kitty as she surveyed the ugly scene.

Margaret nodded, saying, "Well we *were* told it wouldn't be pretty!"

The canal towpath was just earth covered by cinders, and the canal water was dirty and murky. They both assumed the transport of coal along the canal was responsible for its colour. By mutual agreement their walk along the towpath was cut short and seeing a cinder path leading off to the left they made for the town.

Before long they heard the noise of laughter and shouting and came across a group of children playing on a slag-heap. A group of boys were trying to race each other up the heap, becoming helpless with laughter as the loose waste products of coal mining sent them tumbling down. Another group of girls and boys were taking turns in carrying a largish piece of wood up the 'hill', then sitting on it to slide down again amid more laughter. Their clothes and faces 'decorated' by greyish-black streaks.

Kitty remarked, "Well it's good to see the children are still able to enjoy themselves amongst all this poverty and grime."

Following the path still further, they came to a row of terraced two-storey cottages. The road here was cobbled. A few women and children stood near doorways, but one woman in particular caught their attention. Looking to be of middle-age and wearing an apron made of sacking, she stood by a pile of coal heaped against the wall of her house. Next to the coal was a large pair of scales and also a large dog.

"I wonder if she's selling the coal?" queried Margaret.

"Not sure about that." replied Kitty. I thought men delivered it to houses in bags. Anyway, Patrick should have an answer for us at supper tonight."

Margaret nodded, and they walked on hoping to arrive at the Market Place.

It was about twenty minutes before they reached their destination and already they could hear laughter and shouting. This time it came from a crowd of adults, mainly women. Several of them held large banners and were chanting slogans. What surprised Kitty and Margaret were the number who wore tailored linen skirts and high quality blouses of brocade or cotton, 'set off' by stylish hats. However, the majority wore familiar long dark skirts covered by white aprons. Dotted round the Market Place were some men, usually in groups of six or seven, all wearing caps and working clothes. A few men in tailored suits were spotted amongst the women.

The first banner they saw bore the words:

LIQUOR

NEGATIVE EFFECTS ON HEALTH, PERSONALITY

AND FAMILY LIVES

Whilst four women held the banner, they and those standing behind, chanted loudly and forcefully,

"DOWN WITH DRINK! DOWN WITH DRINK!"

One of the groups of men standing nearby, began chanting,

"UP WITH SKIRTS! UP WITH SKIRTS!"

This, of course, caused much raucous laughter amongst them. The response was glares from the women. One of them called out, "They all needs a good punce in th' 'ead." Another amended the suggestion with "Nay! Punce 'em where they've getten feelin'. In their bloody trousers!"

Both friends found the exchanges amusing - though Margaret had had first hand experience of the evils of drink from within her family. And Kitty was recalling how her Presbyterian mother had often declaimed against the evils of drink. The two then walked on to a second banner some distance away. This one bore the words:

LIPS THAT TOUCH

LIQUOR SHALL NOT

TOUCH OURS!

The large group of women there, including the banner holders, began to chant the whole message in unison, coming to a 'grand finale' as they slowed down and emphasized "NOT TOUCH OURS!"

Again, another group of men were laughing loudly and some blew kisses to the women. One of them, who looked as though he'd already had a 'bellyful', pointed to a very plain, severe looking woman who was helping to hold the banner. He called out, "Eeh Missus, I wouldn't touch *thee* - even if I were sober!"

More laughter from the crowd.

The two stayed on for a while listening to the banter from both 'sides' then had a further exploration of Wigan. Of course, all shops were closed but it was interesting to look in shop windows. So it was after five when they were again walking back down Walkers Yard. Both were looking forward to their evening meal - and to asking questions about their eventful day out in Wigan.

When it was nearly seven, they went downstairs. As they glanced to their right, they saw young Molly on the old settee by the side of Patrick and both gave a quick wave to her and her Granddad. On entering the dining-room they saw that Pat was already seated at the table. He greeted them cheerily, "Evenin' Miss Margaret, evenin' Miss Kitty. I've been doin' jobs for Mam most of the day, so as a treat she's let me eat here again. Did ye enjoy your day out?"

Margaret told him of their walk by the canal and seeing all the children playing on the slag-heaps. Pat grinned saying, "Ach, it's a grand place, ye can have plenty of fun there slidin' down the cinders. But it can be a bit rough on yer backside!" Pat then looked wistful for a moment, concluding with, "But Mam says I'm too old to play there now."

At that point, Patrick came in carrying a dish of boiled potatoes and a dish of carrots mixed with turnips. He was closely followed by Mrs Rourke who carried a plate of boiled beef. Pat's sad face was replaced by one big smile. Mrs Rourke commanded "Now be sure to eat up! I've made a special Sunday meal for ye and there's rice pudding afterwards." Then off she went, her red rose bobbing wildly.

During the meal Patrick asked the two friends how their day had been. They asked him about the woman who appeared to be selling coal. His answer tallied with their guess. "I'm thinking you're correct, especially as there were scales beside the house. It would be sold to poor people not able to afford to buy coal by the hundredweight." He paused, asking, "But did ye not get to the Market Place then?"

"For sure we *did*!" replied Kitty with a laugh. "We wouldn't have wanted to miss that." Then the two of them described what they could remember of the slogans and chants, and also the responses of the men.

Also amused, Patrick replied, "Of course these meeting have been going on, a good while. Until about a hundred years ago, Wigan was a small rural town, I believe its population was around four thousand. However, the Industrial Revolution quickly changed things. Ye see, as mining and mills appeared in Wigan, more and more people came here to find work. I think the population is now about forty thousand."

Another voice was heard from the kitchen. "Aye and people - especially the *men* - were wanting some relaxation from work." Mrs Rourke then came in the room, wiping down her hands on her apron. "And relaxation usually means pubs and the drunken behaviour that goes with it." ([1])

"And how is yourself feeling about the Temperance Movement, Patrick?" Kitty ventured to ask.

"To be brief, Kitty, back in Ireland, I was one of those eejits who filled his belly with porter and was then not responsible for what my fists did!"

"Well now, that's one way of putting it!" Mrs Rourke remarked. Touching her hand, Patrick continued, "The truth of the matter is that I was after wanting to marry Annie, here. Times had been hard for many people but I'd been lucky enough to have a family who could give me a good education and so I became a white-collar worker in the Post Office. But I was like a mad beast when I had the drink inside me, and I lost my job. Annie was having none of it. She told me to choose - either the drink or her. Twelve months it took me to give it up entirely - and only then did she agree to marry me. We decided to find a new life and emigrate here. And I haven't touched a drop since!"

Kitty nodded. "I admire ye for it." Then a further thought struck her and she continued, "I'm wondering if, with your education, ye managed to obtain a decent job when you arrived here?"

Patrick gave a wry smile," I might have the education, but I'm still Irish! The answer is that I could only get a job as a road mender- and that's still my job."

Once everyone had finished their meal, Kitty, suddenly feeling sleepy after the busy day said, "That was a grand meal Mrs Rourke, thank ye so much. And thank ye Patrick for all your information and patience with our questions. However, I'm thinking Margaret and I need an early night as we start work at six tomorrow morning. So 'Goodnight' to everyone."

Accordingly, Margaret rose from the table, bade the other three 'Goodnight' and headed for the bedroom with her friend.

Footnote[1]

With the advent of the Industrial Revolution, mining and work in the newly-built mills became the main occupations in Wigan. Soon, people began to move there to find work and the population rose to 40,000. Public Houses emerged where the increasing population could meet to relax and drink together. However drunkenness and lawlessness also increased. At first, gin was thought to be the main cause, with beer being regarded as relatively harmless. Around the 1840s, women's organisations got together to form the Temperance Movement. Women opened up gin barrels and drained out the contents. Later, all kinds of liquor including beer and whisky were 'attacked'. Wealthy women led the movement and were soon prepared to go to any lengths for their cause. Poorer women soon joined them.

Chapter 28

'The Packet'

By five o'clock next morning, everyone in the Rourke household was up - except of course for little Molly who was still asleep upstairs in her Grandparents' room. There was just enough time for Kitty, Margaret and Patrick to have a quick breakfast of porridge and a mug of tea before setting off to their various jobs.

It didn't take Kitty long to reach 'The Packet' well before six. As she entered by the main door she found Mr Wood already busy changing one of the barrels of ale, so she coughed and introduced herself. He looked up, greeting her with, "Tha's in good time, lass. Just mek sure tha keeps it like that! Yon floors want a good clean, so will all t' tables and chairs. Then there's all t' mirrors and brasses -and don't forget t' pumps. Oh aye, and there's some tankards that got left on Sat'dy neet. Brushes and all t' cleanin' stuff's in a cupboard in t' back room. I suggest tha gets agate (get busy). Plenty to be done!"

So Kitty got 'agate'. She found the mirrors hardest to clean, streaks kept appearing which Mr Wood immediately pointed out. His hawk-eyes watched her closely as he went about his work. It wasn't long before customers started arriving. The first two were elderly men who sat together in a corner of the pub with their tankards of ale and pipes. A few men, possibly mill workers, were standing at the bar having their liquid 'breakfast'. The latter watched Kitty with interest and whispered to each other, but said nothing to her.

At ten o'clock Kitty was relieved to be told that she could finish for the morning but she must be sure to return promptly for six o'clock that evening. Mr Wood added, "Mondays are usually quiet, but tha never knows."

On arrival back at Mrs Rourkes, she went upstairs and lay on her bed until dinner at eleven o'clock. Her work at 'The Packet' had emphasized again the fact that she was amongst strangers in a town which bore scant resemblance to places she'd known back in Ireland. Then images of her baby began to dominate her thoughts and she wished she had at least held him in her arms before she'd left to come to this place. Tears began to stream down her face until blessed sleep overcame her. In a dream she heard her Mother speaking, "Away with those tears. Your laddie is in safe and loving hands!"

When Kitty awoke from her brief sleep, she soon had a positive plan for her free time that afternoon. She would write letters to Mam and Mary Ann. Yes! And also she'd write to Master Thomas.

Just as she was getting out of bed, Margaret, who had also taken the opportunity to have a rest, stirred and declared, "What a morning I had! The boss's wife was there to supervise my work - and she followed me round the whole time. It seemed that everything I did was wrong! And I wouldn't like to repeat the language she used. Anyway, I'd already decided to leave the job. But then Mr Wright comes in. He looks all around the room, smiles and says...." here, Margaret tried to imitate his Lancashire accent - "By the 'eck, lass, tha's done a grand job!"

Then laughing, she sat up on the bed, "Ye should have seen Mrs Wright's face, Kitty! If looks could have killed, I wouldn't be sitting here now!"

Smiling, Kitty replied, "Well, it seems we've both had miserable mornings. But I tell ye what Margaret. Ye do a grand Wigan accent!"

Soon they were cheerfully and hungrily eating the meal Mrs Rourke had prepared. It was quite a substantial one and included some of the braised beef from Sunday's meal and plentiful helpings of boiled potatoes and carrots.

Whilst taking away their empty plates, Mrs Rourke explained, "Patrick's working some distance away, so I'll save his meal for later. It'll just be something light for the two of ye at tea-time."

Once in their room again, Margaret suggested they take a walk into town to have a look inside the Coop shop. But Kitty had her own plans for the afternoon and began writing as soon as Margaret had left. She used the small wooden table as a desk after removing the water jug and bowl.

The letters to Mam and Mary Anne were easy to write. She told them all about the journey to England, the meeting with Margaret, and her decision to move on from Liverpool to Wigan. Mr and Mrs Rourke were described in some detail. She knew Mam would be especially amused by her landlady's hat with its trailing, bobbing rose. Of her work experience, she wrote little except to say it was very different from her work at 'The Coaching House'.

The letter to Master Thomas needed a bit more thought. After all, she wasn't sure that his father would want him to receive a communication from the 'disgraced maid'. However, Mrs Laverty had been very sympathetic towards her, so she wrote a brief one addressed to Thomas in which she asked if he were still walking and drawing. She also told him about the children playing on the slag heap, describing the clogs they all seemed to wear.

Having finished the three letters, Kitty was soon making her way into the town with her precious envelopes. As she placed them carefully into the letter box she felt that part of her would soon be travelling home across the Irish Sea.

The two friends plus Patrick and young Pat were seated at the table just before five o'clock. Margaret began talking about going in Coop's to see what kind of garments were for sale and what the prices were like. She paused when she saw Patrick looking puzzled, and then amused. "What's funny?" she wanted to know.

Laughing, he replied, "Ach, ye 'll be meaning the big 'Co-operative' shop in town. It's often shortened to 'Co-op', though most folk pronounce it as 'Cwop'".

"Right then," obliged Margaret, "I found the *'Cwop's* prices quite reasonable."

"Aye, 'tis a good store, I've heard." Then as on previous nights, Patrick had more information to impart. "The co-operative movement started in the mid- forties in Rochdale, about twenty miles from here. It soon spread, and now Wigan has its own 'Cwop'. Folks round here are happy to become members. Ye see from time to time, they get some money back depending on the money they've spent."

Mrs Rourke must have been listening because as she entered with two warmed-up meals, she included her own contribution to the conversation, "Patrick's quite right, members save up their 'divvies' and then they can use the money in any *'Co-op'.*" She emphasized her use of the correct abbreviation whilst placing meals in front of her husband and grandson. Then continued, "I'm not a member myself, for though it's a good idea, I find I can get things cheaper by shopping at the market." With a wink, nod and bob of her rose, she explained, "Ye see, we Irish know just *how* real bartering works!"

The meal for Kitty and Margaret was black peas with buttered bread and mugs of tea. Though new to them, they found the black peas quite tasty when sprinkled with vinegar.

They didn't chat long after they'd finished their meal because of their early start that night. Soon they took their leave of everyone and went upstairs to get ready for their shifts. Both wondering what the evening held in store for them.

Chapter 29

The Night Shift

Mr Wood was again busy as Kitty arrived at 'The Packet' a few minutes before six. This time he was pulling pints for a couple of men, one of whom was wearing a straw hat. Kitty could only see the side view of his face but she felt sure he was the one who'd greeted her and Margaret so cheerily on their first day in Wigan. However, at that point, the landlord spotted her, "Tha's just in time, Kitty. There's a load of tankards need washin' o'er yonder, and t' tables need wipin' too. Bin busier than usual today." Both men turned to look at the object of the Landlord's instructions.

"Well, if it isn't the lass with the lovely green eyes! Didn't think I'd see thee agen! As the man spoke, he doffed his straw-hat to her, adding, "Good evenin' to thee. Miss Kitty, I think? My name's Billy, Billy Trodden."

Kitty acknowledged his greeting and question with a smile and brief nod then made her way to where tankards were stacked beside the stone sink. She was thankful that running water was readily available in Wigan, it certainly made her work much easier. Once the pile of tankards were clean and draining on the slop-stone beside the sink, Kitty set about wiping down tables and collecting empty tankards. A group of four men sitting at a table near to the bar, and presumably having heard the earlier remarks of 'Straw-hat', called her over.

"Eh, Kitty! This table needs a good wipe o'er," called one of them. He was young and short, but well-made with a blue scar on his nose. Glancing towards the group, Kitty finished what she was doing before moving over to their table, trying to avoid eye-contact with any of them. As she leaned over to mop up some spilt ale the speaker gazed at her saying, "By the 'eck, Kitty, tha *as* got bonny green eyes." At the same time he was running his hand over her buttocks whilst she leaned over the table. He further remarked, now looking at her breasts, "And that's not all tha's got that's bonny."

Without thinking, Kitty ceased her wiping, slapped the man's face sharply, and said angrily, "I'll thank ye to keep your hands to yourself in future." She then grabbed two empty tankards from the table and was about to set off towards the bar but was prevented by the man grabbing her arm tightly. He held his other hand to his smarting cheek as he enquired derisively, "Oh, so tha's Irish? I should've known! Who the hell does tha think tha are? Over from Ireland and tekin' our jobs! And don't try to tell me tha doesn't enjoy a bit of teasing. We all know wot you Irish girls are like!"

Before Kitty could reply to this tirade, 'Straw-hat' had moved quickly away from the bar and stood facing the man who'd addressed Kitty. He spoke quietly but with threat in his voice. "That's enough, Jim Butterworth. Now tha'll let go of this young lady and apologise to her!"

"I'll let go of 'er, and gladly - but I'll be damned if I'll apologise to the likes of 'er. Any road, it's got nowt to do with thee, Billy Trodden!"

And though shorter by a head than 'Straw-hat', Jim glared at him, looking ready to pull a punch if necessary. Before 'Straw-hat' could speak, Kitty, now freed, said to him, "I'm grateful to ye for your help. Thank ye. But I don't want an apology from *him*. Sure, I'm Irish and proud of the fact! And an apology from that ignorant man would be meaningless. So I'll be getting on with the job I'm paid for." A pause, then she added pointedly, glaring at her 'assailant', "A job which I took from no one!"

Then with a nod to 'Straw-hat' and head held high, she walked towards the sink with her tankards.

Looking angry and aggrieved, the man identified as Jim Butterworth turned to the other three at his table, two of whom had been watching the drama with interest. The third, an older man, had merely continued drawing on his pipe whilst reading a paper. Jim addressed him, "Did tha not see all that rumpus with th' Irish trollope? Then yon Billy Trodden comes o'er and interferes?" Jim had a further thought and announced decisively, "I've a good mind to go o'er and give 'im a good puncin'!"

"Eeh lad," said the man, taking his pipe from his mouth and shaking his head in exasperation, "Sit thasel down an' drink up tha ale! Bloody women!" He reflected on women for a moment and concluded, "I'd rather have a good pratie pie any day!" Then replacing his pipe, he continued his reading.

Clearly, not the response Jim wanted. But in the end he settled for glowering over at Billy whenever he glanced his way, and making obscene gestures at Kitty when she worked anywhere near him.

By now, Kitty was aware of a hostile atmosphere in other parts of the pub too. Fortunately, this didn't seem to apply to everyone, and the man in the straw-hat gave her an encouraging grin whenever she passed by him.

And so Kitty managed to get to the end of her shift without feeling too angry at the earlier incident. Instead, she concentrated on thinking about her letters, now starting their journey back to her homeland.

When at last Mr Wood informed her, "It's twelve, time for thee to get off," Kitty was ready to leave the pub quickly, but paused when he looked at her sternly and continued, "but before tha goes, I need to warn thee about sommat. I saw what tha did to Jim Butterworth. Now I know him well. He's allus lookin' out fer good lookin' lassies. And he only did what he allus does when he sees one."

Here, he gave Kitty what he thought was a conspiratorial smile, asking, "After all, a little pat on t' backside doesn't do any harm, does it?" Receiving no response from Kitty, he explained, "Tha sees - Jim and them other miners are some o' me best customers. And besides that them miners are a tough lot, they may look small, but I can tell thee, it's all muscle! And we don't want any fights startin' in 'ere, do we? So think on. Keep tha 'ands to thasel! It's nowt but a bit o' fun!"

Though inwardly fuming at the fact that *she* was the one being reprimanded for Jim's actions and words, *plus* the implied threat of dismissal, Kitty had somehow managed to keep her thoughts to herself. After all she needed the money. So with some difficulty she replied, "I'll do my best, Mr Wood. Goodnight."

It was some fifteen minutes later that Margaret joined her in the bedroom that night. She seemed to have fared better since Mr Wright had been 'in command' during the evening shift. Unlike Kitty she was very sleepy and, aware that it wouldn't be long before she was up again at five, she was soon dead to the world.

Not unnaturally, Kitty was awake for some time as she went over the events of the evening, wishing she could have told Mr Wood exactly what she thought of his idea of fun. Now, all that cheered her a little was the hope that she could try to find alternative work once a little time had passed. In the meantime, she would carry on as she was. Also, she decided to say nothing about her experience to Margaret next day.

Chapter 30

Sad News and New Friends

The following weeks passed fairly quickly for the two friends. In fact Margaret felt reasonably settled in her job since Mr Wright had made it quite clear to his wife that he was more than satisfied with their new Irish employee and didn't want to lose her. It was probable that his opinion of Margaret as an asset to the pub was partially due to the fact that a fair proportion of his customers were Irishmen who had been impressed by the friendly and attractive new Irish employee.

And for Kitty too, work in 'The Packet' seemed more tolerable. She was now receiving her full pay. Mr Wood had ceased watching her every move and even gave her an occasional smile of approval. In addition, Billy Trodden came in regularly after Wigan's Market Days and always exchanged some friendly greeting with her. Friday and Saturday nights were, as Mr Wood had warned her, the busiest days for the pub and so work was non-stop then. However, that was greatly alleviated by the fact that they were also the days when a group of Irishmen usually gathered at 'The Packet'. The four miners still came in regularly but the Irish 'gang' was more than a match for any of the derogatory comments made to Kitty.

One of them had a tin-whistle, and as the night wore on one or other of the men would say, "Come on Seamus, give us one of yer tunes". And Seamus invariably obliged. These were bittersweet moments for Kitty as she recalled how Pat had talked about playing the tin whistle to make money for her and their unborn child. But at the same time, the music helped her to feel closer to Ireland.

In addition, both friends were now used to their long hours and routines so their work didn't seem as hard. After all, both of them had already known what hard work was like back in Ireland.

However, on the first day of September a letter arrived from Kitty's mother containing the sad news of her father's death. Again she longed to be home with Mam. Although she'd known for some time that Edward Tooey wouldn't last much longer, his death still came as a shock to her. And now Kitty bitterly regretted the fact that she hadn't been there at his bed side, able to hold his hand when his last moments had come. At dinner-time that day she shared her sad news with Margaret and Mrs Rourke. Both were extremely sympathetic and accompanied her to St Joseph's to offer prayers and to light candles for her Dad that same afternoon.

Of course she wrote back immediately to her mother trying to give some consolation through her written words - though they seemed totally inadequate. The following day, she received a letter from Mary Anne who had been equally devastated by their father's death. She wrote that Dad had died peacefully in his sleep, adding that it was a blessing after his months of suffering She further wrote that the burial would take place the following Thursday at ten o'clock in the morning. And of course, their father's wake would be held the previous evening. This would be shared with neighbours and RIC colleagues. The latter group had promised to send a wreath of lilies for the coffin, whilst the younger members of the Tooey family would simply pick wayside flowers to place in their father's grave.

Mary Anne then followed on with the usual enquiries about how Kitty was faring in Wigan. However, a post-script to the letter served to increase her feelings of both helplessness and guilt. It read: "I don't know if I should be telling you this, but we are concerned about Mam being able to manage financially now that Dad has gone. We know she will get his pension of sixty-six pounds each year, but money has been short for some time and now there is the funeral to pay for. Besides that, Edward is talking about getting married soon and is trying to save up his money. To make things worse, Anne still hasn't been able to obtain work, and the four younger ones are still at school!"

"George and I will be giving Mam a little money each month but, as you know, we expect our fourth child soon. Forgive me, Kitty, but I thought you'd prefer to know rather than have the facts hidden from you."

Immediately, Kitty began to plan how much she'd be able to save from her wages to send to Mam. She wished it hadn't been necessary for her sister to remind her of her mother's financial problems and accused herself of having spent too much time thinking about her own welfare.

Amidst all her grieving and guilt, Kitty was pleased to receive good news later that month. It came in a letter from George Peattie telling her that Mary Anne had safely given birth to a fine boy on 28th September. He was to be baptised George. The letter also contained thanks from her mother for the money she'd received.

By November, both friends had become interested in the Temperance Meetings held regularly in Wigan. Some of them took place in the home of one of the reasonably wealthy supporters, Mrs Nelson, who lived about two miles away in Mesnes, a district of Wigan. So when Margaret suggested they should join the movement, Kitty was happy to go along with her since she welcomed the chance of making new friends. Besides that she found the area around Mesnes much less depressing than the area near her lodgings. And, best of all, she loved going into Mrs Nelson's home and seeing the spacious parlour with its upholstered chairs, grand piano and long beautifully carved oak table - not to mention the indoor lavatory and bathroom which she discovered later.

Both Kitty and Margaret generally rested a little while after their early lunches, so they had plenty of time to look around the town centre or take interesting 'mystery' walks around different areas of Wigan. Often they would see groups of miners who, according to Patrick Rourke, would have worked on the morning shift which lasted from six until one-thirty in the afternoon. They would be walking home from the pits, their clothes and faces blackened by coal dust so that only their eyes and reddish lips would be visible. As they clattered along in their clogs, they seemed like beings from another planet. "Wonder how many kettles of boiled water it takes to clean off that dirt and grime?" Margaret queried.

There was no response from Kitty. She continued to look in admiration at these men who walked so uprightly with their shoulders back- despite having been bent double for most of the day. The friends had learned from their 'Fount of Knowledge', Patrick, that the miner's upright stance was a normal reaction to the hours spent bent, underground.

And so Kitty's social life was becoming far more interesting and tolerable, though her work at the 'Packet' gave her no feelings of satisfaction. Yet she had to admit that work did have a couple of redeeming features. One being week-ends when the Irish 'gang' drank at the pub, the other being her friendship with Billy Trodden.

In fact the two were soon having regular though brief chats prior to Kitty commencing her evening shifts. As time passed, she gradually learned he had a wife and a three year old son. The latter apparently being a fine boy with his mother's handsome looks. Along with this information, Billy had added, "Aye, the little beggar can be glad of that! Folk used to tell me I had a face only a mother could love!"

In turn Kitty would tell Billy humorous tales relating to her Presbyterian, Scottish mother and nine siblings. In this way they both got to know a little about each other's lives. Kitty enjoyed these periods of interaction with Billy, especially because she knew it was a genuinely platonic friendship. 'No strings attached'.

Soon it was Christmas - a difficult time for both Kitty and Margaret, but the Rourkes helped to make it more bearable. Snow had been threatened so fires needed to be well-stoked. Here, young Pat had made his contribution to the family Christmas. Along with some of his friends, he'd gone with a sack to the nearest slag-heap where crowds of women and children were already kneeling and scrabbling to find coal amongst newly-tipped 'dirt' dropped from one of the pit's trucks. Many pieces were only as big as an egg or smaller, but that didn't matter. Pat was agile and quick and soon had his sack filled. He was eager to return with it to Granny.

Meanwhile, Mrs Rourke had managed to make a delicious Christmas dinner which included a large chicken with chestnut stuffing, roast potatoes and vegetables. It was followed by suet pudding made with raisins and figs.

So Kitty, Margaret and the Rourkes together with their daughter, son-in-law, Pat, Molly and their new 'babby', Michael, all sat down to quite a feast. And with a big blazing fire too.

Chapter 31

Letters and a Tram Ride

The new year seemed to arrive quickly and moved on in more or less the same pattern as the previous five months. Kitty wasn't exactly happy but neither was she unhappy. The longing for home wasn't as urgent, though thoughts of her baby never left her. Of course letters to and from Sligo usually gave her much pleasure. Yet one which arrived in late February gave Kitty great cause for concern. It was from her mother and contained shocking news about her thirteen years old sister, Anne. Though she was aware that her sister had been unable to obtain work since leaving school, Kitty had not realised how depressed Anne had become by seeing her mother struggling to put food on the table. She blamed herself for not being able to contribute to the family's income. So one bitterly cold day in mid-February, she'd simply left the house saying nothing to anyone of her intentions or destination. With only her shawl to keep her warm over her long woollen dress and pinafore, she'd begun to beg for money in Sligo Town. For three days, she'd continued to do this, wandering about the outskirts and sleeping in shop doorways at night.

Of course Mam, Sarah, and Margery had taken turns in searching for her but it was all in vain. Then on her third day away from home, a member of the RIC had brought home a pale, pathetic shivering Anne. Naturally, Mam was overjoyed to know her daughter was safe, but then came the news that Anne would have to appear before Sligo Court for the 'offence' of begging. Subsequently, she was sent to work in St Laurence's Industrial School in Sligo for two years. It was a place where young people deemed to have been abandoned or neglected, were sent to learn skills or trades. Mam and Anne were devastated. Moreover Mam blamed herself for it all.

Kitty immediately wrote to her mother. She tried to comfort her by saying how much she was loved and respected. On finishing the letter, it did occur to Kitty that now Mam had one less child needing food. Also, on the positive side, Anne was learning a new skill which might improve her job opportunities. At the same time, Kitty was well aware that Industrial Schools were known to have very strict regimes and very severe members of staff.

However, after a few months her mother's letters became more cheerful since finances had improved slightly and Anne had been allowed some home visits. Her daughter seemed pleased with her new learning - though she hated most of the staff.

The next letter Kitty received contained some very good news from Mary Anne. Apparently her husband, George, had been seen by Pat Dowd on a Market Day in Sligo Town. (The two having met briefly during the period of the 'baby smuggle'). Pat had asked him if his wife could tell Kitty that Denis was doing well and had her green eyes.

Of course, Kitty was overjoyed to have news of her son and felt she had to share it with someone. So that night she confided part of her 'story' to Margaret. "Well me girl," Margaret remarked, "isn't that just grand news! Ye must be so relieved to know the child with *your* green eyes is being well looked after."

Several years passed in the same vein for Kitty. She was still working at the 'Packet' but was now settled into a routine which balanced working life with quite a good social life. Not unnaturally, Irish politics now concerned her less than when she had lived there, but in the early 1880s she received promising news about Ireland from brother Edward. He wrote that Gladstone seemed quite sympathetic to the aims of Charles Parnell, leader of the Home Rule party. His letter concluded, "So ye see, Kitty, 'Home rule for Ireland 'may well be in sight if that bloody lot in Westminster keep to their words." Kitty said a quiet, "Amen to that." as she finished reading.

Also during these years, Kitty and Margaret were able to enjoy rides out on the recently introduced steam locomotive trams for their Sunday afternoon outings. These had replaced the previous horse drawn trams with metal wheels which ran on iron rails. On fine days, the two would choose one of the nearby districts of Wigan to visit such as Pemberton or Orrell. Here, they would have one of their 'mystery' walks round the area before catching the tram back. They discovered that a bowling green had been introduced to one of the places they visited. And it was during a trip to Pemberton on a warm Sunday in June that Margaret suggested they should watch a game of bowls taking place near the 'Bowling Green' pub in Spring Bank. It seemed she'd occasionally seen men playing bowls on Saturday afternoons at the 'Bowling Green' where she worked.

And so the two friends joined the small group of onlookers who were watching the players closely. They were both impressed by the green itself, expertly cut and as green as the grass to be found in Ireland. There were only eight spectators besides the two of them, three of them being women. Two were young and one was considerably older. At the other end of the green stood a group of about twelve men who, according to Margaret, were players waiting their turn. They hadn't been there long when there was a short interval during which mugs of tea were brought out to the players. When it seemed the game was about to recommence, the older woman loudly addressed one of the young bowlers ready to go on the green."Mek sure tha shapes lad. Wi' a bit o' luck, we can give these Pemberton beggars a run for their money!"

The lad walked on to the green accompanied by a mixture of cheering and jeering from the onlookers. He stood waiting, ready to roll a small black ball along the green. Then a rather stout man came running out from behind some nearby bushes. A notebook in one hand, and the other fastening his flies. He shouted, frantically, "'Owd on, 'owd on! I'm not in place yet! Tha can't start without a Ref." One of the home team turned, and seeing who it was, exclaimed,"Get a bloody move on, Tom. We nearly started without thee!"

One of the spectators called out, "It wouldn't mek much difference if they 'ad started! Yon dozey bugger's as much use as - as …" He searched to find the right words. Then he said triumphantly, "as much use as a bog-eyed bloater!"

A roar of laughter came from the crowd.

The friends had been watching the second part of the game for about twenty minutes when Kitty became aware of one of the spectators watching her. He was quite a good-looking man, tallish and with a moustache. On turning to glance at him again she received a broad smile and the young man began to walk over towards her. Touching his cap to both of the young women, he addressed them politely,"Good afternoon ladies. I think tha must be new to the area and I'd like to welcome thee to this match." Then he grinned, adding "Even if tha supports the Wiganers!" More formally he said, "I'm Robert Gibbs and I support Pemberton."

After introducing herself and Margaret, Kitty explained, "This is the first time we've seen a game of bowls. We travelled from Wigan on one of the trams and came across this place by accident."

Margaret chipped in with, "But now we know Wigan's playing, I'm thinking we may well be supporting them."

The three continued to chat together. Robert commented on their accents, asking what part of Ireland they were from. On hearing they were from the north-west, he nodded, observing, "Ay, I should've known! With that lovely lilt in tha voices, tha couldn't be from anywhere else!"

From time to time, Robert kept them informed of some of the bowling terms. The latter included the small black ball which was called a 'jack', whilst the two larger balls which each player had were called 'woods'.

It was soon clear that it was Kitty who held most of his attention. And when the game was over with a win for the home team, Robert spoke to Kitty quietly, "Listen Kitty, as a 'Horseshoe' supporter, I've been asked to go for a drink to one of the lad's houses after the match. But I'm very keen to see thee agen. Would tha mind if I came to Wigan to meet thee somewhere next Sunday?"

Kitty hesitated. She liked this young man but didn't want to rush into anything quickly. Also she knew little about him, and didn't want him to know where she lived.

Cautiously she replied, "Well now, Robert, I'd prefer to come to Standish on the horse-tram if I'm to see ye next week. Margaret will probably come too, but we'll still be able to talk to each other." Then she paused wondering where they could meet. Finally she said, "How about waiting for me where the tram stops at Spring Bank."

Robert agreed to Kitty's suggestion. Inwardly, he was praying she would come on her own.

Back on the tram, the two chatted at some length about Robert Gibbs. Margaret's opinion was that he seemed a friendly enough chap and very personable. She also pointed out that he'd seemed to have a touch of the blarney about him. By the time they'd arrived back in Wigan, Kitty had decided to give Robert a chance, and Margaret had promised to accompany her the following Sunday.

Yet as she lay in bed that night, Kitty lay wondering whether or not she really wanted another man in her life. After all, she and Margaret were reasonably settled into their jobs, and they were enjoying their leisure time in each other's company. Yet she did miss the company of a man. And she did quite like Robert and his sense of humour. Yet what did she really know about him? He could be married! Yet before falling asleep, she'd told herself, "Well, Kitty, there's only one way to find out!"

Chapter 32

Robert

Kitty was glad that the week seemed to pass quite quickly. Soon it was Sunday afternoon again - time for her trip to meet Robert. On this occasion, as well as her best green blouse and cream skirt, she wore a cream-coloured hat trimmed with tiny green leaves. It was actually a 'cast-off', originally given to Margaret by one of the ladies who organised the temperance meetings.

It was a sunny day in July when the two friends boarded the tram which would take them to Pemberton. On the journey there, Margaret informed Kitty, "Now I've been thinking hard about your meeting today with Robert. For sure ye'll never get to know anything about him with me tagging along. So when we reach Pemberton, I'll stay long enough to bid him 'Good day', and then I'll take myself off to explore on my own. We can meet again at the tram stop in time for our return journey. Would two hours give ye enough time to 'inspect' him?"

At first Kitty wasn't having any of this. But Margaret was adamant. So the end Kitty agreed, replying, "Well, I can see ye've made up your mind." Then she added, "Though of course he may not turn up, having decided there are better fish in the sea!"

However, as they drew near to the 'stop' in Pemberton, they caught sight of a smartly dressed Robert wearing what seemed to be a brand new cap. He was anxiously watching out for the tram's arrival.

Margaret nudged her friend, remarking, "Seems there's no better fish. So he's had to settle for you, Kitty!"

"Away with ye! I'll see ye in two hours." And Kitty stood ready to alight from the tram. As arranged, Margaret greeted Robert briefly and told him she was off on a 'mystery' walk round Pemberton. She then waved 'Bye' to him and walked away.

Surprised at the speed of it all, Robert gazed after her for a moment. Then he remarked, "Well, me Irish Colleen, that was the fastest 'Hello' and 'Goodbye' I've ever had! But I can't say I'm sorry to be left alone with a pretty lass like thee."

"That'll be enough of the blarney, Robert Gibbs. Or I'll be joining my friend!"

His response was immediate, "I'm sorry. I just wanted to let thee know how much I've been lookin' forward to this moment." He paused, then asked "Shall we start walking down this road? There's some open country further on that should please a lass from Ireland." Then he proffered his arm to Kitty, who hesitated for a moment, then placed hers through his.

After they'd walked together for a while making 'small talk', Kitty asked him about his accent. She told him the way he spoke was similar to people in Wigan but there was also a nasal sound to it. One like the voices she'd heard in Liverpool.

"Aye, I reckon that's about right, Kitty" was Robert's reply. And he explained that he'd been born in Liverpool and hated going to school. Though he never 'got the hang' of reading, he could write his name well, and had been happy enough with his mother. But after her death when he was eleven, his life there had been miserable. His Dad had soon remarried, and from the start he'd never got on with his step-mother. So living in a large seaport, he'd left home at the age of fourteen and become a deck hand. He described life at sea as being an escape from home and a source of independence. But for these, he'd paid a high price. Poor food and pay, cramped conditions, months at sea with frequent storms. A wry smile accompanied his next words, "And that's only the half of it. Anyway, now tha knows somat about my life, maybe tha'll tell me about thine in Ireland?"

In turn, Kitty told him about her nine siblings, her schooling, and the lovely rural Cloonacool and Riverstown. She also mentioned her unusual parentage of a Catholic father and a Presbyterian mother. Instinctively, she omitted mentioning her father's occupation, recalling how members of her family had often been viewed with suspicion and distrust by many. So her final words were, "Though it disappointed Mam, only her two elder daughters were christened in the Presbyterian Chapel. The rest of us were baptised in the Catholic Church."

On hearing about Kitty's baptism, Robert said proudly,"Well Kitty, talkin' of baptisms, I'd like thee to know tha's now with a man who were baptised in 'Saint Nicholas Catholic pro *Cathedral*' in Liverpool!"

At this boast, Kitty adopted a look of exaggerated admiration, replying,

"Bejaysus and begorrah! A cathedral is it? Sure I'd no idea that I was in the presence of a member of England's gentry!" And she made a low curtsey to Robert.

There was a guffaw of laughter from him as he took her arm and raised her to her feet. Once she was facing him, Robert admonished her with mock severity.

"Nathen, Kitty Tooey, I'll have less of tha cheek! Or I'll have to give thee a good spankin'. So think on!"

He now found he was very close to her, looking down into emerald eyes with a twinkle in them. Meeting his gaze, she responded, "And I'd like to see ye try. So *you* think on too!"

He made no spoken reply but bent to press his lips firmly on hers. For what was only moments Kitty was lost in the urgency of his kiss and the flash of electricity which surged through her body. Then, as though waking from some wonderful dream, she abruptly pushed him away, saying, "No Pat! No!"

Startled by the suddenness of her action, and puzzled by her words, he regarded Kitty enquiringly, saying "Pat? Tha called me Pat."

It was only then she realised what she'd said. She was silent for a while before replying, "Ach, I'm sorry. Pat was just someone I knew years ago - he's been long forgotten. Would ye mind if we just carried on with our walk?"

Robert nodded and the two recommenced walking. But now there was an awkward silence and he made no attempt to offer Kitty his arm. Both were busy with their own thoughts and they walked on without speaking for a couple of miles. It was then Kitty noticed a row of terraced houses standing where the fields and hedgerows of hawthorn ended. On nearing, she saw that one had a sign over its front door.

'Temperance Bar - Come inside'

Turning to Robert, she said, "I realise I've hurt your feelings. But let's not be spoiling the day. May I buy a drink for a man who was baptised in a Cathedral?" Robert couldn't resist the smile she gave, so he nodded and they made for the door. Soon they were entering a room which had once served as a kitchen and living-space. Chairs and four small tables were spaced around it. Three women were seated at one of them. Each had a tall thin pot from which they were drinking. All of them paused to glance up at the new customers.

At the back of the room was a long counter on which stood several large jugs, each one with its own label. These included: Sarsaparilla, Dandelion and Burdock, and Ginger Beer. Next to them were three smaller jugs which bore the labels: Raspberry, Chervil, and Thyme. An elderly woman in a long black dress and white apron sat at a counter to their right, her white hair was scraped back in a bun. On seeing the two entrants, she 'inspected' them over rimless glasses, then spoke, "Afternoon! Tek a look at what's on offer, mek yer choice, then sit yerselves down and I'll bring it o'er to thee." She gave Robert an appreciative smile, remarking, "Men are allus welcome. Shame we don't get so many."

They both passed the time of day with her and did as requested. Kitty assumed the smaller jugs contained herbal tonics and thought the drinks in the larger jugs would be more refreshing. Within a few minutes they were sitting at one of the small tables with drinks, Kitty had sarsaparilla, Robert had chosen ginger beer.

He pointed out, "At least its name meks me *think* I'm drinkin' ale" He took a long swig, grimaced and gave his verdict, "Christ, it tastes more like tom-cat's piss! I'll be honest with thee Kitty, if I wasn't with a lovely lass like thasel, tha'd never get *me* in these sort o' places."

Kitty made no comment. However, she gave him a warning look, and a nod towards the three women who were now looking over at Robert with some animosity.

Realising he'd voiced his opinion rather loudly, Robert, took a sip of his ginger beer, and smiled disarmingly at the ladies. Turning back towards Kitty, he now looked more serious, "Listen Kitty, I know tha said that this man, Pat, was in the past and forgotten. But I'd like to know if tha ever intended to marry him?"

Kitty replied firmly, "No, at no point did I ever consider marrying him." Wanting to move on from any further discussion about Pat, she asked, "And what about yourself, Robert. I'm sure you must have had some serious relationships?"

At this, Robert paused and looked down at his hands. Then he faced Kitty.

"I'll be honest. I got wed three year ago. Elizabeth was her name, but t' poor lass died a year after. So what tha sees now is a widower. A single chap wi' no ties."

During Robert's long hesitation, Kitty had thought to herself, "'Ach, here we go, he's married with children." Now a feeling of relief filled her. She had to admit she liked him. However, to make sure everything was clear between them, she said, "Losing Elizabeth so quickly must have been a great blow for ye. But I'm thinking there must have been other 'special' people in your life afterwards?"

Robert shook his head, looking quite amused, "Kitty luv, since Lizzie I've not met anyone I'd want to wed. That is until a week ago."

Meeting the steady and meaningful gaze he gave her, Kitty smiled back and put her hand on his. Though pleased and surprised at this implied suggestion, she didn't feel ready to commit herself to anything yet, so merely replied, "Thank ye for being honest with me, Robert. I look forward to more meetings when we can *really* get to know more of each other. But just now, I think we should start walking back to the tram stop to meet Margaret."

Not the answer he'd hoped for, but at least she'd spoken of further meetings.

"Reet lass, we'll get on our way then." He stood up and touched his cap to the three ladies, smiling as he did so. All three treated him to a stony stare. Then with his hand in his pocket, he made as if to pay the elderly lady at the counter who'd dozed off.

Quickly, Kitty intervened with, "Have ye forgotten? Sure this is my treat."

She then crossed to the counter where the bespectacled woman had awakened, and paid for the drinks. The woman thanked Kitty, but it was Robert she smiled at as she said warmly, "Good day, sir. Think on, tha's welcome any time."

Outside, Robert let out a loud laugh and remarked. "By the 'eck Kitty, so now I'm a 'Sir' am I? Well I'll thank thee to remember that! But tha can forget givin' me any more treats of ginger beer!"

Also laughing, Kitty put her arm through his and they walked back leisurely to meet Margaret.

Chapter 33

Kitty is Confused

During the coming few weeks the Sunday meetings between Kitty and Robert continued, and by a lucky coincidence, Margaret had also attracted the attention of a widower who lived in Mesnes. After his wife's death the previous year, he'd started accompanying her to temperance meetings in the home of Mrs Nelson. So now, on Sundays, the two friends went their separate ways.

Kitty now felt ready to meet Robert in Wigan. She thought the 'Starr' in Wallgate would be a suitable meeting place as she hadn't yet told him where she lived or worked. Usually they would walk the two miles from the centre to the recently-opened Mesnes Park. Here, they would stroll round the beautifully laid-out gardens and lawns, then later Robert would suggest they find one of the more secluded areas where there were benches.

So far, neither one had told the other what their employment was, so it was during one of their 'bench' chats that Kitty had asked Robert what kind of job he had in Standish. He sighed, saying he'd only been able to find work as a labourer for a building firm. He explained,"Tha see, I'd worked a long time on a transatlantic paddle steamer, 'Scotia,' owned by Cunard. One of t' fastest steam ships of its time. It carried passengers as well as mail. But my job workin' as a deck hand, didn't really give me many useful skills fer workin' on shore. But there's one thing I *can* do - and that's climb! That's because paddle steamers have sails, and often when there's a strong wind the sails are unfurled to mek it go quicker. By the 'eck, Kitty, tha should've seen me go up. Faster than a rat down a sewer I were! Now, since I've met thee, I keep thinkin' I should get a better job with more pay. I reckon I could get a job as a roof slater."

Quite impressed by Robert's description of climbing up high sails in strong winds, Kitty told him that with his personality and climbing ability he should be able to get work as a slater fairly quickly. Looking pleased with her opinion, he replied, "Well lass, if tha's got faith in me becomin' a slater, maybe I should see if any jobs are available." Then taking her hand in his, Robert said, "Anyroad, let's be hearin' what *tha* does for a livin'. Tha's never talked about it."

She smiled nervously, "To tell ye the truth, I've been feeling ye might not approve of my job here. Back in Ireland I loved my work because part of it was spent in teaching the young son of my employers to read and write. However, as an Irish immigrant, I had to settle for a cleaning job. I work at the 'Packet' in Wallgate."

Gently, Robert put his arms around her saying, "Eh, lass tha's no need to worry about what I think - I love thee whatever work tha does!" And with these words, he bent forward towards Kitty, and the two were soon lost in an embrace.

It was some time later before they rose to make their way back out of the park. They walked in silence for a while, simply holding hands, each very aware of the other. Kitty's thoughts were dwelling on Robert's words, 'I love thee.' It was the first time he'd actually told her that in the couple of months they'd known each other. Yet how did she feel about him? She had to admit she enjoyed the company of this plain-spoken man who made her feel happy and alive. But hadn't Margaret warned her not to rush things?

Their regular meetings continued, and only a couple of months later near the end of October Robert had some news for Kitty. He looked happy and excited. "Nathen my pretty colleen, didn't tha tell me my skill in climbin' could lead to better things? Well, begorrah and bejaysus, tha's now looking at a slater! And one wi' good prospects ahead!"

Of course, Kitty was also very happy for Robert, "Sure isn't that just grand? Congratulations to ye!" Then she put up a warning finger, saying "But we'll have less of the 'begorrahs'! Or ye'll be feeling the weight of my shillelagh on your back!"

Laughing loudly Robert replied, "Tha's a hard woman, Kitty! A hard woman!" He then went on to explain that whilst in the pub with some workmates, he'd heard about a builder in Wigan who was desperately in need of a first-class slater. So he'd asked one of his mates to tell their boss he'd be a bit late for work next day due to getting his 'sprained wrist' seen to. Early next day he'd duly introduced himself to the builder and briefly told him of his seafaring background. Robert was then asked to demonstrate his skill by going up to the roof of the house his gang were working on whilst carrying a bucket of cement and a trowel. The task was accomplished with ease and speed. Approvingly, the builder spat on his hand and shook Robert's, telling him he could start next day.

Robert concluded by saying. "So I've been workin' in Wigan for three days now, gettin' up early to walk there. But it'll mek more sense if I get meself lodgings in Wigan. That would mean I'd be able to see thee more often, specially if I tek my nightly 'jars' in t' 'Packet'. What does tha think, Kitty, love?"

But Kitty was not at all sure that she wanted him to see her whilst at work. So her reply was cautious, "Sure it makes sense for you to live in the area where ye work. Also we'll be able to see each other on Saturday afternoons. Yet I don't think it a good idea for ye to be coming to the 'Packet.' My boss, Mr Wood, is the very divil if he sees any of his workers chatting to customers."

Robert grinned as he replied, "Eh lass, don't thee worry! I'll be havin' a 'quiet' word with Mr Wood if he ses owt to thee!"

This did nothing to reassure Kitty about Robert's intended visits.

It wasn't long before Robert had found new lodgings in Regent Street. It seemed that though he had to share a room with three others, he got on well with Dick, the man who shared his bed. Also, Dick, worked in Trencherfield Mill which meant he and Robert rose for work at the same time. And as Robert pointed out, "It's a beggar if ye share a bed wi' somebody that starts earlier. They seem to tek pleasure in mekin as much noise as they can."

Now that he was living in Wigan, he was soon asking Kitty to meet him on Saturday afternoons to spend a few hours together before her work at the pub. Often, they would have a walk round the Poolstock area which was a pleasant change. But one cloudy and decidedly chilly Saturday in late October, Robert suggested they take a walk round Wigan's open market. He explained, "I want to buy thee somat, Kitty. I can't afford much yet but that'll soon change now I'm on better money."

As they explored the variety of stalls, he eventually saw one displaying woollen scarves, men's long stockings and also women and men's gloves.

"What does tha think about gloves, Kitty, love? It'll soon be winter and they'll keep yer 'ands warm." Then, with a twinkle in his eye, he added, "O' course, when we get wed, I'll be able to warm more than yer 'ands!"

Taken by surprise at this sudden and unusual implied 'proposal' of marriage, Kitty chose her next words carefully, "Ach! Away with ye Robert Gibbs! For sure gloves will be grand. But there's no way we can afford to get married."

From Robert there was just another grin, then he tapped the side of his nose replying, "We'll see. But I notice tha didn't say 'no' when I mentioned marriage."

So some gloves were purchased and they continued looking round the market stalls. When it was time for Kitty to get back for some tea before her evening shift, Robert had another surprise for her. As she turned to go, he called out, "I'll be seein' thee tonight when I mek my first visit to t' 'Packet'."

It was a worried and apprehensive Kitty who ate the light meal of buttered bread and brawn placed before her by Mrs Rourke. Though usually more than ready for meals, she was scarcely aware of the food she ate. Her mind dwelt on the events of the afternoon. Had she actually agreed to marry Robert today? Surely not! She liked him- but did she want to marry him? She may not have directly rejected the idea of marriage but, Holy Mother of God, she hadn't agreed to it either! Yet he seemed to think she had! And he was coming to the pub that night! Her final thought was, "Kitty, me girl, what in the name of all that's Holy have ye got yourself into?"

Chapter 34

Kitty Decides

It was the usual busy night at the pub and Kitty was working non-stop whilst at the same time keeping one eye on the door. It wasn't long before Robert made his entrance, looking relieved as he caught sight of her. Going straight to the bar he ordered his drink and, on receiving it, raised the tankard to Kitty. She acknowledged it with a smile. Robert blew a kiss to her and remained standing at the bar.

Five minutes later, Billy Trodden arrived with friend, Michael. As they stood at the bar waiting to be served, he noticed the man standing next to him. Feeling sure he'd seen him before, he enquired, "Tha'll excuse me, but didn't I see thee at t' market today? Tha were with our bonny Kitty."

Robert turned in surprise. He'd no recollection of seeing this man before, and he certainly didn't like him referring to 'our' Kitty. "Still", he thought, "better not cause any trouble on my first visit." So his reply was reasonably polite, "Sorry, I don't remember seein' *thee*, but tha's reet about me bein' wi' Kitty. We're engaged tha knows. After a pause he added, "And by the way, She's *my* Kitty."

"Well all I can say is, yer a very lucky bloke! I've known young Kitty more than five year now. She's a good lookin' lass with a lot o' spirit."

"She is that!" Was the curt response. Robert had taken an instant dislike to this man who wore a straw-hat despite the onset of winter. It was obvious he was nothing but a show-off, intent on letting him know of his prior friendship with Kitty.

Another thought occurred to him, "By God, it'd better have been no more than friendship! Or he'll damn well live to regret it!" Aloud and unsmiling, he said, "Now if tha doesn't mind, I'll tek me drink over to yon table."

As Robert passed a table where Kitty was clearing away the tankards, his broad smile returned and he said in a voice loud enough for everyone to hear, "Evenin' me darlin'. I'll be seein' ye tomorrow."

Kitty's response was quiet and brief. "Good evening Robert." Then she moved over to the next table with empty tankards on it.

Once again, Kitty's thoughts were spinning like tops. She'd told Robert the landlord didn't like his staff being spoken to. Yet here he was, addressing her in a voice which could be heard a mile away.

At the bar, Billy was also pondering on the words and actions of this recent friend of Kitty's. Turning to Michael, he remarked, "I'll tell thee what, yon chap's a rum bugger! He reckons she's engaged to him, yet I've never seen him in t' pub afore. And I've never seen him wi' Kitty afore today." He paused and with a puzzled shake of the head repeated, "A rum bugger!" Michael took another swig of his ale.

The remainder of the evening passed with Robert sitting at his table making no further attempt to speak to Kitty - though his eyes remained on her all night. When he rose to leave just before midnight, he waited until she was near before he spoke, "I'll meet thee tomorrow at one o'clock my darlin'."

Regretting her earlier curt attitude, Kitty replied quietly, "Yes, one o'clock will be fine, Robert."

❧ ❧ ❧

The two friends attended church together next morning with the Rourkes. Mrs Rourke, as usual, was wearing her Sunday hat with its trailing yellow rose. As they were all walking back to Walkers Yard after the service, Margaret whispered to Kitty. "Ye tossed around last night as though ye'd a brigade of demented bed-bugs in there with ye! I'm guessing Robert Gibbs was responsible."

Apologetically Kitty replied, "Ach Margaret, I'm sorry if I disturbed ye, but I had a lot to be thinking about, and I'd certainly be glad of a chat."

And so when the two were in their room a little while later, Kitty described some of the conversations and events which had led to her confusion about her feelings regarding Robert. She told Margaret that his behaviour in the pub had made her feel he was declaring ownership of her to everyone. Also, she'd noticed that Robert had had a lot to drink that evening.

As Kitty ended, her friend remarked, "Well now, it seems to me that here's a man you like a lot and would like to keep as a good friend for the time being. Yet he seems to be regarding you as much more than that and has marriage on his mind. I think ye *do* need to consider a couple of things carefully. Firstly, you felt he was trying to show his 'ownership' of you in the pub - which many women find flattering. But if possessiveness continues into married life, it can result in a desperately unhappy woman, totally under the control of her husband."

Kitty looked thoughtful but made no reply.

Margaret continued, "Then there's the point ye made about him drinking quite a lot last night. Tell me now, was your man actually drunk as he left the pub? I mean, was he steady on his feet? What was his speech like?"

Kitty thought for a moment, "Well now, he did speak, but it was very quiet and controlled, and it was only to arrange the time of our meeting. As far as I can recall, he walked normally. I must admit I felt a bit sorry I'd been so off hand with him." "Well, it's probably a good sign that he wasn't staggering as left the pub and that he wasn't slurring his speech. Yet, remember he's a man who likes the ale, and as time goes by, he may start drinking more."

"Anyway, I've said my piece. There's only yourself can make the final decision." She paused. "And now I'm off to the Temperance Meeting at Mrs Nelson's."

Once alone, Kitty began to consider whether or not she was content with her present life. Of course, she'd been very lucky to have met Margaret and found accommodation with the Rourke family. Yet still didn't much care for her job in the pub, though Billy Trodden had made it bearable for her. And of course, she'd enjoyed Margaret's friendship and also the Temperance Meetings. But she realised that she had only really felt *happy* when she'd been in the company of Robert. And, maybe all his showy talk was merely his way of expressing his feelings for her in front of others. Also, he did seem to have his drinking under control.

Next, she began to think of how her life might change if she *did* decide to marry Robert. Well he had a good wage as a slater and, if she added her wage to his, there was a chance she could have quite a comfortable life with this man who made her happy. Yes! Perhaps marrying Robert might not be so bad after all. Moreover, she was sure Mam would be pleased to see her daughter settled and married.

So the weekly meetings continued - and with Kitty now happy to regard herself as Robert's 'intended'. He continued to frequent the 'Packet' most Saturday evenings, but was more discreet in his greetings and attitude towards Kitty. Yet he always made sure to sit where he could keep a watchful eye on Billy Trodden.

On a bright but bitterly cold afternoon, two days before Christmas, Kitty and Robert were again taking a walk round Mesnes Park. She was telling him how much she and Margaret had enjoyed helping Mrs Rourke to decorate the house with holly and ivy. But Robert wasn't listening. Suddenly, he placed a finger on her lips, took her by the hand and led her to their favourite bench. Here he motioned to her to sit down. Kitty did as bidden, and found Robert kneeling on one knee, asking, "Will tha marry me, Kitty?"

Without hesitating, she answered, "Yes, Robert, I will."

Only a few days later, Robert told Kitty that Dick (the collier who shared Robert's bed at his lodging house) was getting married in January the following year. Moreover, he would then be moving into the lodging house of his future wife since it was nearer to his work at Trencherfield Colliery. Robert went on to explain, "So tha sees Kitty, there'll be a nice space left in my bed, ready fer my new missus when he goes. So what does tha say to that, Kitty love?"

Though sharing a room with two other men besides Robert wasn't an ideal start to marriage, Kitty agreed to the suggestion - with the hope they would soon be able to afford something better.

Subsequently, the couple decided they would get married in Wigan Register Office on Monday, 14th January 1884. Kitty had been initially surprised at his choice of a working day, but Robert had explained that Saturdays were sure to be fully booked for the first two months of the year. Doubtful about having the morning off work, Kitty suggested that the wedding could be booked for after lunch.

"I reckon tha's reet, lass" agreed Robert. I'll book it fer about one o'clock."

That evening, Kitty shared her news with Margaret and the Rourkes. They were delighted and felt quite honoured when she asked both Margaret and Patrick to act as witnesses to the marriage. Mrs Rourke also said they'd be pleased if Robert would come to share Christmas dinner with them all. She also declared her intention of obtaining a new rose for her hat to wear at the marriage.

Just before getting into bed that night, Kitty asked her friend,"Are ye thinking it might possibly be another *trailing* rose?"

Chapter 35

Married Life

January 14th arrived with Kitty looking very attractive in a long, light-grey skirt, new cream blouse with a narrow frilled panel down the front, and a small hat trimmed with cream-coloured roses. Being a winter wedding, she also wore Mrs Rourke's best cream shawl, the one she'd worn at her own wedding. Robert was waiting outside the Register Office looking smart in his best Sunday suit and bowler. He greeted his future wife with a smile and the simple words, "Tha looks lovely, lass."

Margaret wore a turquoise dress trimmed with pink over warm underskirts. Her hat was also turquoise and trimmed with pink roses. As forecast, Mrs Rourke had indeed bought a new *trailing* rose for her old hat. This time it was a deep-red colour which predictably and rhythmically bobbed up and down with her sobs as the couple were pronounced 'man and wife'.

Kitty looked happy as she and Robert kissed after the brief ceremony. There was applause from the select group attending the wedding. Then the bride, groom and witnesses were asked to assist in completing the registration form. The registrar, by the name of James Jolley, asked Robert to sign his name which Robert duly did (Robert James Gibbs). Then he asked the three Irish participants to *spell* their names so they could be written down on their behalves by him. Kitty looked in amazement at Margaret. This became indignation when the three were asked to verify his writing with a cross.

However, since neither Margaret nor Patrick had queried anything, Kitty felt her wedding day was perhaps not the time to make a fuss. But she couldn't resist an aside to Margaret, "Dammit! Not only does he think we Irish are all illiterate, but just look how the eejit's spelled 'Tooey'. He's written it as 'Towhy'!"

Luckily, Kitty had been allowed to have the rest of the day off, so after the ceremony everyone returned to Walkers Yard. Here, Mrs Rourke had prepared a meal of potato soup, roast beef and vegetables. As a special surprise, she'd baked a biscuit mixture containing sultanas which she'd named 'Bride's Tart'. Also on the table were letters and cards of good wishes from her mother and siblings. As Kitty had guessed, Mam had been pleased to hear her daughter felt much more settled in England, and was marrying a man who could provide for her. She sent special wishes of happiness, signing off with, "May the Good Lord bless you and keep you safe."

As she read the card, Kitty felt a great longing to have had her mother there to witness her marriage. However, her moments of sadness were curtailed by Mrs Rourke looking at her affectionately and saying, "Ye've been like one of the family for some years now Kitty, and we've grown fond of ye. So we wish ye well in your new life as Mrs. Gibbs."

Then the two embraced warmly. Wet cheeks touching.

It took a little while for Kitty to become accustomed to sharing a bedroom with two other men besides her husband. However, Robert reassured her by saying their current situation wouldn't last long. He was quite confident that, in a few months of 'hard' saving, their combined incomes would enable them to afford the rent on one of the empty two bed-roomed terraced houses in Dobbs Fold. Here they could take in a couple of lodgers who would occupy one of the bedrooms. To speed up his prediction, he'd also promised to restrict his pub visits to once a week.

Robert's plans gave Kitty the feeling that life with him would bring contentment and happiness for them both.

It was six o'clock on a frosty morning in mid-March, Robert had already left the lodgings for his work on a house in Baker Street. Kitty should have left for work too, but earlier that morning a familiar feeling of nausea came over her. Certainly not a welcome one since her wages were an important part of Robert's plans.

"Holy Mother," she pleaded, tightly grasping her rosary beads, "I know the gift of a child is truly a blessing, but please Holy Mother, not yet, not just yet!"

It was seven before she arrived at work. Mr Wood looked annoyed, telling her to "Get agate - an' be sharp about it!"

As the weeks passed, it seemed the Holy Mother had ignored Kitty's plea, and by the end of the month, her suspicions were confirmed. That night she decided she *must* tell Robert the news, yet she was apprehensive of how he'd react in view of his plans. At first, he was silent, then he asked if she was sure, and if so, when did she expect the child to be born. After being told there could be no doubt about it and that she thought the baby would arrive in November, he fell silent again and sat down on the bed. Kitty stood quietly by, now *very* nervous about his response.

Abruptly he looked up, took her hand in his and gave her a broad smile, saying, "Well me lovely colleen, I must say I thowt we'd have a bit more time together before a babby came on t' scene, but if that's the way it is, then it's reet by me! It'll be a fine lad and we'll call 'im Bob." He stood up and kissed Kitty gently.

In fact, the Holy Mother must have decided to relent a little, since only a month later Robert was made foreman at work *and* Mr Wood told Kitty she could stay on as long as she felt well and able to do the work.

Spring gave way to summer, and life was going well for Kitty, especially when her morning sickness came to an end. And for Robert, long periods of good weather had given him plenty of work and he was able to see their combined wages increasing week by week. He was now hopeful they'd be able to afford the move to a home of their own *before* the arrival of his son in November.

By mid September, Kitty, now heavily pregnant, had left her employment at the 'Packet'. Robert had already arranged for them to move to the empty house in Dobb's Fold by mid-October, and even knew two work-mates eager to lodge with them.

Now that Kitty had more free time, she began preparations for her baby. She'd bought a piece of linen from the market and was cutting it out to make into clouts (nappies). Already, she'd received several long dresses and under-skirts from Mrs Rourke's daughter, Mary. Margaret had knitted a soft, white shawl for the baby, and Kitty was delighted to see her pile of baby clothes growing. Mam of course had been happy to hear another Grandchild was on the way and was also knitting for the baby.

As she did her cutting, Kitty recalled her first, and only, glimpse of her son Denis. Then she began wondering how he would look now at six years of age. These reflections were interrupted by a loud knocking at the door. Rising somewhat clumsily from her chair and laying aside her scissors, she made her way slowly to the door. On opening it, she found an elderly man standing there. He was holding the hand of a little girl who was sobbing whilst squirming to release her hand from his. The man spoke with only a trace of the Lancashire accent. "I'd like to see Robert Gibbs, I've been told he lives here now and is married."

A puzzled Kitty replied, "Yes, Robert does live here but he won't be back from work until about six o'clock. Also, he married me earlier this year, so I'm Mrs Gibbs. Can I be of any help to ye?" The man shook his head.

"Thank you, but no. It's Robert I must speak with first, though my visit *will* concern you. Is it possible to come in and wait for his return?

Kitty was aware of the child still sobbing. Between sobs she pleaded, "Home, Granddad, home!"

Politely, but with a strange feeling of foreboding, Kitty answered, "Of course you may come in, though it will soon be busy as two other lodgers besides Robert will be returning to have their evening meal." Then she opened the door wider to allow both visitors to enter the main room which served as a dining room and kitchen. The child's sobs grew louder. She was clearly reluctant to enter the house.

Once inside, Kitty pointed to a chair by the fire, and asked the stranger to sit down. When seated, the man picked up the tearful child and rocked her gently in his arms whispering, "Sh, sh, sh little Lizzie, close your eyes and have a little sleep."

Exhausted from her sobbing, the little child finally fell asleep. The other two lodgers, brothers Richard and Peter, were the first to arrive back from work. They ate their meals with an occasional glance at the visitors. Then went up to their bedroom.

It was just after six o'clock when Kitty heard Robert's whistle before he opened the front door. She'd placed herself on a chair quite near to it, hoping she could warn him of the visitor. As he entered the house he said cheerfully, "And how's me big bonny lass and son today?"

Ignoring the question, Kitty pointed to the man with the little child, saying, "Ye have visitors." Robert looked at the seated man. Immediately his bright manner changed. He asked in a tone of astonishment, "Mr Pinnington? What brings thee 'ere?" His expression was apprehensive.

"Well, Robert, I think that should be obvious since I believe you've been married for a while now - though you never had the courtesy to inform us of the fact!"

Face black as thunder, Robert turned to his wife and gave the order, "Kitty, go up to t' bedroom - this matter has nowt to do wi' thee."

Shocked, and angry at Robert's words, she replied firmly, "No, Robert. I will not go upstairs! As your wife, I have every right to hear all that is said here."

Between gritted teeth Robert repeated, "Get up to t' bedroom!".

Mr Pinnington intervened. He spoke calmly and with authority, "Mrs Gibbs should be allowed to hear what I have to say. As your wife, it is her right."

Kitty moved to place herself between Mr Pinnington and Robert.

The older man then explained, "I'm here because my wife Ellen and I can no longer look after Elizabeth. Ellen has suffered for some time with stiffness and pain in the joints of her hips, knees and hands. The pain has gradually become more acute. Of course I've been doing my best to help her, but things have been difficult for us both." He then looked directly at Robert. "We love your daughter dearly, and offered to bring her up after her mother's death. But only until you married again!"

The look of guilt had returned to Robert's face and he stood looking down at his daughter shaking his head sorrowfully. His father-in-law continued, "You neither told us of your marriage, nor of your first move from Wigan to Standish! Your contacts with Lizzie lasted only six months."

Whilst Mr Pinnington was speaking, Kitty kept looking at Robert in disbelief. She was willing him to say something to explain his lies and rejection of his daughter.

But Robert couldn't meet her gaze. Instead, tears began to well in his eyes.

"Tha's reet! O' course tha's reet! But I never, ever, stopped lovin' this little lass o' mine!" And he put out his hand to stroke the child's fair hair.

He was prevented by her Granddad saying, "Not yet. Let Lizzie sleep now. "You've still a lot of explaining to do. To me *and* to your wife." Kitty nodded.

Swallowing hard, Robert tearfully expressed how thankful he'd been when Mrs Pinnington had come to stay in his home in Wigan when it was clear that giving birth to Lizzie had taken its toll on her daughter. Amid more tears, he stressed how he'd never moved from his wife's bedside during her last week of life.

"Yes, yes" interrupted Mr. Pinnington impatiently, "I know all that. Now get on with explaining to me and your wife why you broke your agreement with us. Namely, that if we looked after *your* child in our home, you'd continue working in Wigan and living in the house for which *I* paid the rent. You also promised that you'd see your little daughter every Sunday, and that if you remarried you and your second wife would welcome Lizzie back into your home in Wigan."

Sorrowfully, Robert admitted, "Aye, I do recall th' agreement - but I tell thee, losin' Elizabeth fair broke me heart. And I did come to see Lizzie ev'ry Sunday fer a while. She allus looked so content wi' ye both that I used to cry like a babby each time I left her. So I started drinkin' agen, then I lost me job and couldn't face tellin' thee."

For a few minutes Robert, his face in his hands, couldn't continue. His father-in-law appeared unmoved. Kitty remained silent.

"Anyroad," he continued at last, "I felt I wasn't fit to be a Dad. So I decided Lizzie'd be better off wi' out me. I moved from Wigan to Standish to try to find work. After all, I knew Ellen and thee were givin' Lizzie a good life and love."

Mr Pinnington remained impassive. Robert continued, "Fer a while I slept rough, but at last I were given a job mendin' roads and I managed to get lodgins wi' five other lads. Bit by bit, I managed to drink less. Then one Sunday I met Kitty and that were that! I fell in love wi' this lovely Irish lass and I married her."

Immediately a furious Kitty demanded, "And why, in God's name, did ye never tell me ye had a child? All ye said was ye were a widower and had lost your wife some years earlier. And like an eejit I believed ye and felt sorry for ye!"

During Kitty's tirade, Robert had moved nearer to Kitty. Looking miserably at her, he kept trying to take her hand. Each time she knocked it forcefully away. Roused by Kitty's voice, Lizzie had slowly opened her eyes and started looking around at her strange surroundings, and the unfamiliar figures of Kitty and Robert. Then she buried her head in Mr Pinnington's chest, shouting, "Home, Granddad, home!" On hearing her cry out, Robert walked over to his daughter saying softy, "Nay, Lizzie, don't cry. I'm tha Dad and I love thee."

The child glanced at Robert, then cried out again, "Home! Home! Granddad!"

Mr Pinnington spoke softly, "Hush my darling. Nothing to cry for. He's your Dad. He's been working hard, so he's not been able to take care of you until now. But he's come back for you because he loves you. And you'll also have a Mummy to look after you too," he added, pointing to Kitty. "Won't that be grand, Lizzie?"

With tears streaming down her cheeks, Lizzie stammered out, "D-don't li-like him, and d-don't like her! Want Granny and want you!"

Several minutes passed and finally Robert sighed, "Tha can see 'ow it is. It's not lookin' as though 'ers goin' to settle wi' us. 'Er just wants thee and tha missus."

His father-in-law's response was immediate, "Well Robert, I'm afraid it's not a question of what Lizzie wants nor what you want. Ellen is the only person who matters now. And I need to get back to Hindley as soon as possible to look after her!" He then lifted Lizzie from his knee and asked her to be a really good girl for her Dad and new mother. He stood up himself and, before she could cling to him again, asked her more firmly, "Now please stop crying. You know Granny and I love you. And you know how ill she is, don't you?" Lizzie nodded, her shoulders shaking with heavy breaths and sniffs. "I will be round to see you whenever I can. Now I have to go to catch the train back to Granny - so give me a smile for her."

Though Kitty had been devastated by this sudden and life-changing news, her mothering instincts came to the fore. Seeing the little girl looking so woebegone and exhausted, yet now trying her best to 'be a big girl' for her Granddad, she went over and knelt down next to her.

She spoke comfortingly to little Lizzie whose eyes were swollen and red, "There, there, little lass. Ye'll be fine with me and your Dad. Granddad will come to see ye again soon. Shall we go to my special tin where I keep nice biscuits?"

Lizzie looked up questioningly at her Granddad who smiled as he said,"Yes, love, you go and see what's in that tin. Sounds like something good."

Reassured, as well as feeling quite hungry, Lizzie accepted Kitty's hand, and both headed for the biscuit tin. Meanwhile, Granddad made his way to the door.

Chapter 36

Aftermath

Lizzie, having chosen a couple of biscuits from the tin, allowed Kitty to sit beside her as she ate. However her eyes were still swollen, and she was still wary of Kitty.

Robert had watched how Kitty had gradually managed to gain the trust of his daughter and was filled with conflicting emotions. There was admiration but also jealousy since his daughter was still rejecting him. There was guilt too at the way he'd lied to Kitty. And there was also resentment that his deception had been revealed when life appeared to be going well for him and Kitty. In self-pity, he muttered to himself, "Bloody Fate's definitely got it in fer me!"

But noting Kitty's perplexed and angry glance at him, he pulled himself together. Now he must apologise to Kitty and also try to salvage something from the present mess. He began, "Kitty, love, I understand what tha must think of me, but I can ..."

That was as far as he got. Turning to him with a look of utter contempt, she snapped, "I refuse to listen to more of your lies. You listen to me now! I've been thinking about where we'll all sleep tonight. *You'll* be downstairs. I'll be sleeping upstairs with the child you disowned. So go up and bring yourself a blanket."

A dumbstruck Robert just gazed at her. He'd expected things would be 'tricky' between him and Kitty for some time - but not this attitude. Finally, he responded, "But Kitty, at least let's *discuss* what's goin' to happen about sleepin'. Then we need to think about tryin' to move house a bit soo..."

Once again, he was cut short. Kitty's tone was resolute, "Sure the move needs discussing! But before that, ye have a whole lot of explaining to do. But ye can do it when this little bairn's asleep. The lass is worn out. So get your blanket now whilst I rock her for a while."

Without a word, a stony-faced Robert carried out the order.

When he returned carrying a blanket and pillow, Lizzie was fast asleep on the settee. Sitting on a chair, an angry Kitty demanded, "Well now, my braw man, why wasn't I told ye had a daughter when ye asked me to marry ye?"

Angry at the sarcasm, but knowing Kitty had to be placated, Robert replied, "Doesn't tha see Kitty love? I were terrified of losin' thee. And I were sure if I told thee I'd a three year-old child that'd be th'end of everythin'. Reet enough, I were bein' dishonest, but I weren't really *lyin.'* As tha knows, I'd lost me job. And seein' Lizzie happy, loved and looked after made me think it best if I were out of her life."

Kitty made no response at first. She could actually follow some of Robert's reasoning. After all, she hadn't told Robert about Denis. And at the present time it was more important that they moved into their new home as soon as possible. So her reply was, "Well ye tell a good tale Robert. Whether I believe it or not's a different matter. Anyway, what about our move? We'll soon be a family of four!"

Robert answered immediately. He hoped his plan would get him into Kitty's 'good books'. "Well love, I'll see our landlord early tomorrow and tell 'im we're movin' out on Friday. Then I'll get round to t' landlord in Dobbs Fold, and ask if it's reet for us to move in on t' same day."

"Well that will be fine with me - *if* it actually happens!" was Kitty's reply.

"Aye, it'll 'appen, Kitty, love. And I'll be a good Dad to our son and my lass."

"Ach, haven't I listened to your grand words before?" Then lifting up the sleeping child carefully, Kitty bade Robert "Goodnight", and made her way upstairs.

It was almost dawn the following day before Kitty finally managed to get off to sleep, and even that was fitful. Luckily, Lizzie had never stirred since the previous night, and so it was eight o'clock before the two finally woke. Finding herself in bed with Kitty, and in a strange room, the little girl murmured tearfully, "Want Granny."

Quietly, and with an arm round her, Kitty explained that Granny was very poorly and so not able to look after her. Then she went on to say, "But your Daddy and I love you and we want ye to live with us." Lizzie was silent. However Kitty's next words brought the glimmer of a smile from the child. "Right! We both need some porridge and lovely toast with jam."

Since leaving work, Kitty had bought and prepared the food for her and Robert instead of paying the 'extra' to have meals provided by the landlady. Once downstairs, it wasn't long before the two were having breakfast. Lizzie ate well - and particularly enjoyed Kitty's homemade blackberry jam. They'd almost finished when the landlady, Mrs Brown, a thin woman with grey hair knotted into a bun, came in from the yard. Carrying two large bundles wrapped in hessian, she placed them beside Kitty saying, "Tha's late this mornin' Kitty. T'other two lodgers were up and off ages ago. Oh, and I'm to tell thee Robert will be a bit late back as he's got to sort things out in Dobbs Fold." Then, glancing at Lizzie, she continued, "We heard tell of your little 'visitor' yesterday."

Whilst the child was busy munching on her toast, Mrs Brown bent forwards and whispered to Kitty, "Child's Granddad came this mornin' and told us 'ow things were wi' his wife." Pointing to the bags, she said, "These are all 'er clothes and some of 'er toys. He said not to let t' child know he'd been." Straightening up she concluded, "Anyroad, good luck in tha move, and good luck wi' tha babby."

It was probably as well that there were plenty of things to do that day. It kept Kitty's mind from dwelling too much on all the recent happenings. There was the washing, the shopping, the preparation of the day's meals, the sorting out of Lizzie's belongings, as well as keeping Lizzie busy so she wouldn't be constantly asking for her Granny.

Luckily, Lizzie seemed reasonably content to be in Kitty's company. And as the day wore on, Kitty found time to play with the child and some of her toys.

By five o'clock the two were eating tea before the return of the other two lodgers.

Once it had turned six o'clock, the lodgers had eaten and gone to the pub. So she took Lizzie upstairs in her nightdress to the bedroom. Realising she was being put in 'that big bed', the child's expression changed completely, and she began to cry. However, being exhausted from a day of non-stop activities, she allowed Kitty to hold her, and gently rock her. Whilst rocking Lizzie, Kitty sang one of her Mam's lullabies. Sleep came fairly quickly. Yet there were sobs in her breathing as she slept. Kitty crept quietly downstairs and sat awaiting Robert's return.

It was almost seven o'clock and nearly dark when Kitty heard Robert's footsteps. Then the door was opened just enough to allow a head to peer round and enquire, "Am I allowed to come in and give good news to me pretty wife? Or is a lass there with a shillelagh in her hand, ready to knock the livin' daylights out o' me?"

Despite herself, Kitty could hardly resist the faintest of smiles as she heard these words. It was a reminder of the Robert she'd first met and been attracted to.

However, she called out in a matter-of-fact tone, "Sure, ye can come in if ye've good news for me. The Good Lord knows I'm needing some. But leave out the blarney!"

So Robert entered the room cautiously, no trace of his usual swagger.

"Aye, Kitty, we'll be leaving these lodgin's and settlin' in our own home on Thursday. And they're leavin' a lot of furniture behind fer us, includin' two beds in each of the bedrooms! We'll soon be able to start afresh and enjoy t' life I promised thee."

Still not having received the appreciative answer he'd expected, he continued, "Can tha not forgive a lad who loves thee? One who thowt he was actin' for t' best?"

Though relieved that the move could go ahead, it was Robert's last words which made Kitty respond sarcastically, "Aye, but ye were only acting for what was best for *Robert*. And though I'm glad we're able to move, I'll be sharing my bed with Lizzie. She not ready to sleep alone yet." Robert looked taken aback.

But Kitty went on, "Anyway Robert, I do agree that the best thing we can do now is look to the future and do the best we can for our baby and your daughter. But it won't be an easy time ahead for us. I can tell ye that!"

Despite the news about sleeping arrangements, Robert felt a great weight had just been lifted from his shoulders, He went over to Kitty and knelt in front of her.

"Thank God for those words me darlin'! I hope tha knows just how much I love thee! And I can promise thee, tha'll never regret stickin' by me!"

"Well, we'll see. But from now on, there's to be no more hiding anything from me! Anyway, I've kept your meal warm so get yourself to the table and enjoy it."

Robert stood up and planted a kiss on Kitty's forehead. "Aye me bonny colleen I'll enjoy it reet enough. And I'll never hide owt from thee agen!"

As Robert ate, Kitty sat with him a little while and they chatted quite amicably about events of the day. Robert was relieved at how things seemed to be going - though not prepared for Kitty's words when he'd finished his meal.

"It's been a long and tiring day for me, so I'll be going to join Lizzie now. I've left your blanket by the settee. Goodnight Robert."

Before he could reply, Kitty had disappeared up the stairs. In fact there was quite a lot that he would have liked to say. Instead, he muttered to himself, "So, Robert lad, it's goin' to be another lonely neet for thee!"

Chapter 37

The Move

The next morning Kitty and Lizzie slept quite late again; both had been catching up on sleep. On waking, the little girl looked round the room, then at Kitty and asked, "Jam Kitty?" Certainly a step forward in terms of the child's acceptance of the situation. So the two got out of bed, used the chamber-pot, washed, dressed and made their way downstairs with Lizzie holding Kitty's hand.

As they were eating their toast and jam, the landlady came over to the table and handed Kitty an envelope,"Robert sent this for thee, he said it were money for gettin' new beddin' today and he said there's a bit extra so tha can buy somat for t' child." Then she continued putting the sheets she'd just washed through the mangle.

After counting the money Kitty smiled at Lizzie saying,"Well now, we've a busy day ahead of us buying things we'll need for our new house. And Daddy has given me some money for ye to choose a little toy for yourself at the market. Won't that be grand?"

The little girl continued munching her toast, her chin stained a dark red colour, she enquired eagerly, "Granny come too?"

The market was busy with shoppers searching for bargains, and there was the usual cacophony of sound from stallholders touting their goods. Kitty thought it best to let Lizzie choose her purchase before they did anything else. *And* she must try to avoid passing near Billy Trodden's stall in case awkward questions were asked about Lizzie. Quite soon they'd reached a stall she'd noticed many times previously. The owner's line of patter had always amused her and Margaret.

"Get yer toys 'ere! Get yer toys 'ere!" All of 'em fit fer Queen Victoria's Grandchilder! And all at 'knockdown' prices!"

Immediately Lizzie's eyes lit on a small toy drum along with a pair of drumsticks. Admittedly the price was a bit higher than anticipated but Kitty was quite an expert in bargaining. So eventually the toys were Lizzie's. Happily she walked round the market, banging away on her new drum.

It was just as Kitty was making her final purchase for Thursday that she heard a familiar voice, declaring, "Well now! If it isn't Kitty Gibbs! And isn't she looking grand! Good to see ye darlin'." It was none other than Mrs Rourke in her 'bobbing' hat. On noticing the little girl playing enthusiastically, if not rhythmically, on her new drum, she enquired "And who does the little drummer belong to?"

Kitty was usually very happy to see Mrs Rourke, but today she felt some embarrassment as she replied "Sure, it's grand to see you again! I'm keeping well and my baby is due early next month. This little girl is Lizzie, Robert's child by his former marriage." A puzzled expression appeared fleetingly across Mrs Rourke's face. Then amid all the noise and bustle, Kitty summed up the salient points of the situation, adding that she'd call on Mrs Rourke soon to 'fill in' more details.

Naturally, Kitty's former landlady was extremely concerned as she listened to the unexpected news, and said she'd be glad to see Kitty at Walkers Yard as soon as she was able. Then the two women parted with warm embraces.

On the morning of the 'flittin', Robert made sure that Kitty and Lizzie were up soon after six o'clock so they could have a quick breakfast and then get all their belongings packed and ready to go. He'd arranged to have a couple of hours off work in order to transport everything to Dobbs Fold in a large wheelbarrow he'd borrowed from his employer. There wasn't a large amount of luggage since it was mainly new bedding, food, crockery clothing and footwear, yet the barrow was soon full. Since Lizzie had been quite tearful that morning, probably confused by all the bustle, Kitty got out the drum and sticks and gave them to her, saying, "Now if you're a good girl Lizzie, you can play your drum all the way to our new home. Remember to thank Daddy for them."

Robert had been standing nearby ready to get under way but hearing Kitty's words to the child, he went over to her, bent down and asked, "Nathen Lizzie, does tha like tha new drum? Show yer Dad how well tha can play it."

Seeing her father's face so close to her own, Lizzie threw down the drum along with the sticks, looked at Robert, and shouted, "Don't like them! Don't like you! Want Granny." Next minute she was clinging to Kitty's skirt and weeping.

With an exasperated sigh Robert stood up, shaking his head at Kitty. She, fearing he might say something inappropriate in front of the child, said quickly to Lizzie, "Do ye remember how Granddad asked ye to be a good girl for me and your Daddy? He told ye how much ye'd be loved by us. If ye pick up your drum and stick and play it on the walk to our new house, Granddad and Granny will be so pleased."

After some hesitation and a few sobs, Lizzie picked up her drum and sticks. Then the three of them set off for Dobbs Fold - Lizzie banging away on her toy drum but keeping close to Kitty. As they drew nearer to their destination, Kitty was thinking, "'Tis probably as well that Robert's not taking the whole day off work!"

There was a busy time ahead as they reached their new home since Robert left for work after unpacking the barrow. Before sorting out the possessions they'd brought with them, Kitty had a considerable amount of cleaning and scrubbing to do. So when there was a knock on the door just after lunch, she was only too pleased to see Mrs Rourke standing there, ready to help with any jobs. She was also carrying a cradle from her daughter, Mary. After she'd handed it to Kitty, she explained, "It only occurred to me after our meeting that ye'd be needing a pair of extra hands today, especially with little Lizzie here." Then she smiled at the child, who had moved closer to Kitty on her arrival, and asked, "Are ye still playing with your drum?" Kitty quickly replied on Lizzie's behalf, "Well, soon after we arrived here, Daddy said it was giving him a headache and told me to ask her to stop playing for a while." Then looking at Lizzie she said, "Perhaps this nice lady won't mind if ye use the lovely cradle she's brought to put your dolly in."

Mrs Rourke, had raised a quizzical eyebrow at Kitty on hearing about the 'ban' on the drum. Now she bent down to Lizzie, saying, "Ach, you're welcome to play with the cradle, darlin'! And I have a little blanket here, ye can use it to keep dolly warm as ye rock her to sleep."

Lizzie looked at the cradle with interest and had soon placed her rag doll in it, covered it with the blanket, and was 'singing' as she rocked her 'baby' to and fro.

"Right now, before we get started on the cleaning, I have a suggestion to make," continued Mrs Rourke, "I'm thinking your Mam won't be able to get here for the birth, so I wondered if ye'd like *me* to be here for ye when your time comes?"

Of course Kitty welcomed the idea and agreed at once. Then the two women started work on all the jobs whilst. Lizzie played happily with the cradle.

By the time Robert returned from work, not only was there a hot meal ready for him but the whole house had been cleaned and was now more or less ready for its new occupants.

Kitty's former landlady returned to Walkers Yard, promising to return as soon as there were signs of an imminent birth. Clearly very pleased with how much had been done in such a short time, Robert was in a good mood after his meal.

"Tha's made a reet good job of sortin' out everythin' ready for us to live 'ere Kitty me love." And he went over to her and planted a kiss on her cheek. She was happy to see Robert looking relaxed again, so when she was about to take Lizzie up to bed, she walked over to him with his daughter. He smiled at her saying, "Night, night, Lizzie. Sleep well." Anxiously, Kitty prayed that Lizzie would, for once, react positively to her Dad.

The child regarded her father dubiously, but after a moment's hesitation she whispered, "Night, night." Then she turned away, holding Kitty's hand tightly.

"The Lord be praised!" thought Kitty. "May only be a small step forward, but it's a step for all that!"

Chapter 38

Lizzie

By November, Kitty was eager to have her 'waiting time' over and to be able to hold her baby in her arms. She told Lizzie there would soon be a new baby in the family and Lizzie asked excitedly "A baby girl?"

"We'll wait and see shall we?" then Kitty added, "I'm sure ye'll love it"

Though Kitty's relationship with Lizzie had become easier, that between the child and her Dad was still rather strained. Also, she still enquired if Granddad or Granny were coming. But on the whole, things weren't too bad - though she did wonder what the reaction would be if the baby turned out to be a boy.

It wasn't long before Kitty felt the back pains which heralded the onset of labour. She told Lizzie the baby would be arriving very soon and asked if the little girl would help by putting the blankets in the cradle, ready for it. Lizzie was only too pleased to be able to see the cradle and blankets again, and asked if she could rock her doll in it. "Yes ye can," replied Kitty, "but only until our baby arrives."

Once Robert had returned from work and had his meal, Kitty informed him it would be a good idea if he now went to ask Mrs Rourke to come round as soon as she could. A broad grin appeared on Robert's face, "Aye my lovely Kitty, I'll be round there in no time. Just rest here and build up tha strength ready fer our son!" And off he dashed into the dark November night.

Being Kitty's second child, the pains had become much stronger by the time Mrs Rourke arrived in her 'bobbing rose' hat. Her daughter,

Mary, came too as she'd volunteered to give help where needed. Kitty was guided upstairs by her whilst Robert was instructed to stay downstairs and provide boiling water. All was progressing well at first. Robert was pacing the kitchen area and anxiously awaiting his son's first cry. Lizzie was still up, happily playing with the blankets and her rag doll. Suddenly, loud groaning was heard as baby Gibbs began to make its way into the world. Immediately, Robert's pacing stopped and he went over to the foot of the stairs, listening for the baby's cry. It was only when he turned that he noticed what Lizzie was playing with. Impatiently he snapped, "Lizzie, tha's not supposed to be playin' wi' them things, they're for t' new babby." Then he picked up the cradle and blanket and placed them by the fire, adding, "Tha should be in bed by now. But if tha waits theer, I'll tek thee up to see t' babby."

At once, Lizzie burst into tears, wailing, "Want Granny and Kitty!"

Robert strode over to her, picked her up, and put her in a chair. He spoke impatiently "Well Kitty won't want *thee* wi' all that bloody noise!"

Lizzie looked afraid and shut her eyes, trying to stifle her tears. Soon weariness overcame her and she managed to escape to the refuge of sleep.

It was another five minutes or so before a baby's cry was heard. At once Robert made a dash for the stairs, but his entrance to the bedroom was blocked by Mary saying, "Ye have a fine son and Kitty's well. Ye can see them both in a few minutes." Though disappointed at the delay, Robert exclaimed delightedly, "A son! I knew it'd be a lad!" Through the partially open bedroom door, he shouted, "Tha's a clever lass, Kitty and I love thee. We'll call our son Bobby."

On a freezing day in December the baby was baptised in St Joseph's Church, Robert Joseph (Bobby).

By March the following year, Kitty and her young son, now aged four months, were bonding well. He was quite a good baby, though could become very vociferous and demanding when hungry. Robert was also bonding with his son, and it was his delight to hold Bobby when not working. On some occasions, the baby would turn its face inwards and begin to suck Robert's shirt, searching for an extra meal. "Eeh lad, tha'll find nowt of interest theer!" Robert would say, passing his son back to Kitty.

Unfortunately, Bobby's birth did nothing to improve Lizzie's relationship with her father - nor even with Kitty. In fact, the tenuous bond established with Kitty was slowly eroding. Lizzie's resentment of Bobby had started when told she had a baby brother. The resentment increased when she realised he now had sole use of the cradle. Worse still, she found Kitty seemed to have little time to spend with her, and would watch jealously as Kitty nursed the newcomer.

One Sunday afternoon Lizzie was sitting with her rag doll watching Bobby being fed. When the baby finished feeding, Kitty placed him over her shoulder and began gently patting his back, saying, "There, there darling. Get that nasty wind up" Soon, loud noises emerged from both ends, Kitty responded with, "What a clever boy ye are." Robert, who'd been reclining on the sofa, went over to Kitty and baby, echoing her sentiment, "Aye, th'art a clever lad, Bobby. Me owd Dad allus said, 'Where e'er tha be, let thy wind blow free!'"

Resentfully, Lizzie continued observing the two adults busy praising the baby. Next, she crept with her rag doll to the cradle and quietly placed it inside. Then she covered it with the blanket and began to rock the cradle, whispering in time with her rocking, "Sh, sh, darling dolly, sh, sh, darling dolly."

It was a few minutes before Robert returned to his sofa, but as he did so he caught sight of the doll in his son's cradle. Annoyed and exasperated, he ordered, "Lizzie, tek yon dirty doll out o' Bobby's cradle! It's not a plaything!"

Lizzie's face crumpled. However she removed the doll from its cradle, went over to the fire and sat down. Then she began rocking it in her arms. Her face a picture of misery.

On seeing Lizzie's face, Kitty spoke angrily to Robert. "Why on earth do ye have to speak like that to the child? No wonder she shows ye no affection. She's afraid of ye! Bobby still hasn't finished all his feed, so won't need his cradle yet!" She paused then continued, "Besides, Mrs Rourke brought us the cradle and *she* allowed Lizzie to play with it. So Lizzie feels she has a share in it."

The little girl had heard Kitty's voice and gathered she was speaking on her behalf. So she ran to Kitty with her doll.

For Robert, that was the final straw. Furiously, he strode over to his wife. "Now *thee* just listen to me! Tha's already said too bloody much!" Pointing to Lizzie, he went on, "If that child's afraid o' me, it's *thy* fault. Reet from t' beginnin' tha' s made Lizzie a reet little mardy. As soon as she starts cryin' tha' s comfortin' 'er instead o' leavin' 'er. Glaring at Kitty and Lizzie, he announced,"I'm off out now and don't know when I'll be back. But when I do get back, I'd best find a wife who knows 'er place and does as I say!" Then. snatching his coat from its peg in the kitchen, Robert went out slamming the door behind him.

A startled Kitty stared at the door for a few moments. Robert's final words sounded very ominous, especially his reference to the pub. Then she became aware that Bobby, still over her shoulder, had fallen asleep. She turned to a frightened Lizzie, saying "Everything's fine. Daddy's just gone out for a while. If I come over by the fire, you can sit by me and play with dolly whilst I give Bobby the rest of his feed." So Lizzie and her doll sat beside Kitty. But her eyes avoided the feeding baby.

As day turned to night, Lizzie was given her tea and later taken to her bed upstairs. Bobby was sleeping downstairs in his cradle. Kitty began to ponder on the events of the day. Robert seemed to think Lizzie's attitude towards him were caused by her. Yet something else troubled Kitty. Going right back to Lizzie's sudden arrival with her Granddad, she recalled that the child had never 'taken' to her father. This dislike had continued even when, on some occasions, Robert had made an attempt to be friendly or kind to her. There was definitely something amiss there.

It was eight o'clock that evening when Robert returned home. He walked over to where Kitty was knitting by the fire and demanded, "Well, has tha thowt about what I said earlier?"

Kitty replied, "Yes, I've been thinking things over. I can understand why ye blamed me for the way Lizzie clings to me, and rejects you. And I'm sorry for that. But my question is, why has she *always* behaved like that ever since her arrival?"

Bitterly, Robert answered, "If tha knew how those damned Pinningtons treated me, tha'd understand why!"

Kitty said quietly, "So tell me, Robert."

Bitterly, Robert then described how the Pinningtons had looked down upon him right from the start. Matters were made much worse when he was laid off from work and then Elizabeth found she was pregnant. Soon they had to leave their lodgings, and the Pinningtons lost no time in demanding that Elizabeth moved back to Tyldesley with them until she gave birth. Meanwhile Robert found himself work and lodgings in Standish for his wife and baby. Unfortunately, the birth was a very difficult one and though the child survived, Elizabeth died two weeks later.

The Pinningtons blamed her death on Robert. He was only allowed to see his daughter, also named Elizabeth, for a few hours on Sundays. This lasted for six months, then Robert decided he'd had enough. During a vicious row, he insisted he should have Elizabeth with him in Standish on Sundays. The Pinningtons refused point blank, pointing out that, when Robert was settled with a good wife, Elizabeth could live with him permanently. Broken-hearted, Robert turned to drink. The Pinnigtons got to hear of it and forbade him to see his daughter at all. In fact Mr Pinnington announced they would make sure that little Elizabeth would hear all about the bad Daddy who had deserted her.

"So now tha knows!" said Robert. As his 'story' ended Kitty rose from her chair and went over to Robert, saying sympathetically, "Well now, all that explains a lot! It seems the Pinningtons did a good job of brain-washing the child against ye. But even so, I think there needs to be changes made by both of us if we are to 'mend' the present situation. I've already told you I'm sorry about seeming to be taking Lizzie's side against ye -so I'll take care not to do that in future. Also, I think it would help if *you* tried not to 'pick' on Lizzie such a lot. Remember it's not her fault that she's been brought up to think you're a bad person. *You* have to prove her wrong."

Having listened to Kitty's views, Robert gave his opinion on the situation. "Well, I'll give it a try, but there's a lot more I want from thee. Tha mun put a stop to all that mardy pettin' tha does. And Lizzie mun learn that Bobby comes first."

"A tight-lipped Kitty asked, "Will ye be wanting your meal now?"

Chapter 39

News from Ireland

Despite Kitty's best efforts, the happy married life she'd been promised had not materialised. In fact, relationships between her and Robert, as well as between him and Lizzie, had worsened. Luckily, seeing young Bobby thriving was one of her few pleasures. A pleasure which Robert shared - on the occasions when he wasn't in a foul temper due to the drink.

Yes, that was the 'enemy' she feared. The demon drink. Already, she was finding the money handed over by Robert scarcely enough to cover the rent and food. The only way forward now was to take in a couple of lodgers as she and Robert had once planned. Yet though there'd be extra income, she'd have to wash clean and cook for two extra adults.

Letters from and to home were still a great source of comfort, especially those from Mam and Mary Anne. The latter was now living in Wigtown with her husband and four children. There, George was doing well in the tailoring trade. Though Kitty was happy for Mary Anne, she couldn't help comparing her sister's life with her own.

Mam's letters were always interesting, and often amusing containing typical comments regarding the family. Recently she'd written that Sarah, who'd been in New Zealand since 1883, had met a man she really liked. He was from Surrey and called Charles Edward Jelley. Mam's only observation was, "Would ye nae think a canny lass who'd travelled nearly to the end of the earth could have chosen a man with a better surname than Jelley?"

Increasingly, Kitty's brief moments of respite came via these letters from Sligo. So when a new Post Office was opened in Wallgate that year, it seemed to be a sign it was time to confide in Mam regarding the true situation in her marriage - including the earlier and unexpected addition of Robert's first child to the family. Naturally, her mother was shocked by the news, but very supportive of her daughter. Kitty felt greatly relieved to have shared her problems with her mother.

However, Mam's next letter held most unexpected news. It seemed that she'd had a visitor. That being none other than Patrick Dowd. He'd informed Mam of the death of his wife, Anne, the previous year after a short illness. Just before dying, she'd told Pat it was her wish for Denis to know the identity of his birth-mother when he was older. Pat said he'd heard Kitty had married and had a child that same year. Now he wanted her to be the one to choose when Denis should know about his 'real' mother. He stressed he'd no wish to cause problems in Kitty's marriage. Mam's letter ended by saying Pat had told her that, despite his past actions, he'd truly loved her and always would.

On reading these final words, Kitty wept bitter tears.

By the end of the year, things were slightly better financially. Two Irish colliers who worked in Pemberton, Arthur and Frank, had become their lodgers. Unfortunately, Robert also saw this increased income as an opportunity to increase the amount of money he gave publicans.

However her spirits were lifted when a further letter from Mam brought news that Pat had again called to see her. He'd asked if she would tell Kitty that Denis, now seven, was a fine lad and, according to teachers was proving to be quite a clever scholar. Also he was learning to play the tin whistle.

Kitty was happy to picture her son as a seven year old playing the tin whistle, just like his Dad. It made part of her want Denis to know of her existence *now,* but she also knew that such knowledge could cause complications in both their lives at the present time.

From time to time Mrs Rourke and Mary called round to see Kitty. They usually brought some soup for her and a few sweets for Lizzie. However, Kitty sensed the real purpose of their visits was to check on Robert's behaviour towards her. But their visits were another bright spot in her life.

Also, her relationship with Lizzie was becoming a little easier. She had started to stand near Kitty as piles of vegetables were prepared for the day's meals. The child nodded eagerly when asked if she would like to help. So a little box was placed by Kitty's side for her to stand on, and she soon proved to be quite an asset in the kitchen.

Moreover, when Kitty told Robert how helpful Lizzie was being he actually gave his daughter a smile, saying, "Seems tha's bein' a good lass, Lizzie." But she would merely give her father a blank look and then continue her work alongside Kitty.

Despite Lizzie's continued indifference towards Robert, he became slightly less ready to find fault with the little girl. And for almost a year there was a sort of uneasy 'truce' between the two. But Robert was continuing to drink heavily and, as Bobby and Lizzie grew older, more money was needed to keep them fed and clothed. In vain, Kitty tried to explain this to her husband, but he remained adamant that she was getting more money from him than most other wives and should be "Bloody grateful."

Soon, Kitty felt forced to join the groups of Wiganers who went round the open market late in the afternoon. They would pick up vegetables and fruit which had dropped off stalls accidentally, or been dumped by stallholders. On these 'outings', Kitty was accompanied by the two children. Bobby was now able to walk, but it was much easier if he were in his pram, another 'hand-me-down' from one of Margaret's friends in the Temperance Movement. Lizzie liked to help by carrying some of the items, the rest were placed at the bottom of Bobby's pram.

By these means, the Gibbs' family managed to keep their heads above water. Also, Lizzie was now almost five, and soon she'd be old enough to attend the local Catholic School. Kitty began planning. She reckoned that she could find part-time work then, which would provide extra money for the family. Money which she would have control over. Of course, as Robert pointed out, there was still Bobby to care for, but Kitty was ahead of him. She'd already checked that, for a small payment, Mary was willing to look after him. So it seemed there might be better days ahead.

But it was not to be. Only a few weeks after her planning, Kitty awoke with severe heartburn which lasted most of the day. This was soon followed by regular morning vomiting. Once again, Kitty turned to her faith for consolation and comfort. She went to St Joseph's church, placed her coin in the box and lit a candle. As she prayed, she looked pleadingly up at the figure of crucified Christ, high above the altar.

❦ ❦ ❦

Eventually, Kitty realised she couldn't delay any longer in telling Robert the news. So that night when Lizzie was in bed and the lodgers had gone out, she broached the subject before Robert too left for the pub. She hoped he *might* realise that, if they were to survive as a family, he must drink much less, or better still, stop. Robert had been standing when Kitty informed him she was pregnant. On hearing the news, he gave a groan and flopped down on the settee. He remained there for several minutes with closed eyes, then opened them, exclaiming despondently, "Well that's it then! No bloody chance of *thee* earnin' a bit of extra brass for us now!"

Kitty was about to reply when Robert abruptly jumped up from the settee, moved quickly over to the door to get his coat, and slammed out of the house.

Hearing his footsteps disappear into the distance, Kitty shook her head asking herself, and not for the first time, "Why in the name of God did I ever agree to marry that man?"

Chapter 40

Mary Catherine

Robert remained 'true to form' during Kitty's pregnancy with their second child. He was out drinking nearly every night. Time and again, she would tell him how much she was struggling to put food on the table for everyone. She even tried to shame him by describing how, for some time, she'd had to resort to picking up 'leftovers' from the market to supplement meals. On occasions when sober, Robert seemed to show some remorse, promising he'd try to cut back on the drink. Yet all his fine words proved to be meaningless. There would follow justifications for his drinking in which he'd maintain his work was demanding and dangerous, besides which there was soon to be another child to worry about. Often, he would 'top up' the extent of his hardships with, "I've all that responsibility, yet Lizzie and thee mek me feel I'm nowt but a piece o' shite!"

For the sake of Bobby, Lizzie and her unborn child, Kitty held her tongue.

Mid-July arrived, and so did the time for the arrival of the baby. Once again, Mrs Rourke and Mary had offered to help with the birth so, at three o'clock one morning, Robert was sent to tell them Kitty's labour pains had started.

As with Bobby's birth, he was asked to wait downstairs. This time, Robert waited whilst looking after his two-year old son as well as Lizzie. He amused Bobby by lifting him on to one outstretched leg which he moved quickly up and down. The lad's happy chuckles as he rode the 'horse' caught Lizzie's attention, and she tried to play the same game with her doll.

Another hour went by before the awaited cry was heard. With Bobby on his shoulders, Robert went to the foot of the stairs and called, "Is it a boy or a girl? Can me and Bobby come up yet?" Mary appeared saying, "Ye have another daughter, she's a lovely lass. Give us a few minutes then you can let Bobby and Lizzie see their new sister."

Robert called back, "Thank God it's o'er! Give Kitty mi love." Then he went back into the kitchen and asked Lizzie, "Would tha like to see tha sister in a minute?"

Keeping her eyes fixed on her doll, she shook her head vigorously.

Under his breath, Robert muttered, "Impudent young bugger!"

Kitty chose the name Mary Catherine for her daughter. The name Mary was chosen in honour of Mrs Rourke's daughter who'd been a great help at the birth. Like Bobby, Mary was baptised in St Joseph's church, Mrs Rourke and husband Patrick being her Godparents. Like Kitty, the little girl had auburn hair, whereas Bobby's hair was dark like his father's.

Although Robert seemed pleased to welcome Mary into his family, he showed none of the delight and pride so evident when his son was born. Bobby occasionally took some interest in his new sister, but when Kitty was not giving him her attention, he seemed quite resentful of her. Young Lizzie's reaction to Mary was unexpected. After the initial indifference shown on the birth of her new sister, her attitude changed. When Mary was being fed she would watch with interest, then often put her rag doll to her 'breast'. Moreover, she was happy when allowed to rock her sister in the cradle, and of course Kitty was only too pleased to have her help.

As in Ireland, English schools began their new year at the beginning of September. So when August was nearing an end, Kitty broached the subject of Lizzie starting school. Robert had been keen on the idea when he'd thought it meant Kitty being able to get part-time work. But of course, Mary's birth prevented that. Now his response to Kitty's query about school was unequivocal. "Nay, tha needs 'er to help thee in t' kitchen and wi' all t' washin'. Tha's bin lookin' tired Kitty, and many a time tha's not cooked a proper meal for me and t' lodgers. They've started grumblin' and we can't cope wi' out their brass!"

Normally, Kitty would have challenged Robert about these statements. However, she just felt too tired to argue with him at the time. "After all," she reasoned, "I can begin teaching Lizzie when I feel a little stronger. And a little later when Mary's a bit older, I'll insist on Lizzie attending school."

After several months or so Kitty had to admit that Lizzie's assistance was a great benefit to her. In fact, the little girl was now helping to bring in coal from outside in addition to helping prepare the meals. And she was always ready to rock baby Mary to sleep.

One day, as Kitty was getting up Mary's wind and Lizzie was busy preparing the vegetables, young Bobby went over to the empty cradle with some of his bricks. Carefully, he placed some inside it, covered them with the blanket, and began rocking the cradle violently.

The noise attracted both Kitty's and Lizzie's attention. Jumping down from her stool, the latter ran swiftly to her brother shouting, "Naughty boy! That's not your cradle!" At the same time she pushed him away from it, causing him to fall and hit his head on the cradle. His loud howls of pain brought Kitty swiftly to the scene. One hand held Mary firmly on her hip, with her other hand, she slapped Lizzie's legs.

Immediately, Bobby's cries were joined by those of his half-sister and, as though in sympathy with their pain, Mary joined her siblings in their 'symphony'. Kitty shook her head, and looking upwards asked, "Dear God! Is this the grand future Mam said was in store for me?"

As it was November, Robert was home before dusk that night. The first thing he did was to pick up his son and spin him round. After laughing with enjoyment, Bobby suddenly touched his forehead, adopted a sad face and said, "Izzie, Izzie." Robert's expression changed as he then saw the red swelling on his son's head. Angrily, he turned to Kitty. "What's this about? Did Lizzie do this?"

Hesitantly, Kitty replied,"It was an accident. Bobby was …"

The sentence was never finished. Bobby was quickly put down and Robert strode over to the fire where Lizzie was standing. Her expression one of fear.

"So, it seems tha's a little bully? Shovin' yer little brother so he gets a big bruise. Well, *this* is what 'appens to bullies!" Then, holding her by the shoulder, he began slapping Lizzie's legs and body. Kitty ran forward and, seizing his raised hand, shouted, "Enough! That's enough!"

Red faced and breathing hard, Robert glared balefully at his wife. Then he stepped away from his daughter. Lizzie looked firstly at Robert, then at Kitty and shouted, "I hate both of you and you both hate me! I wish I was dead!"

The next sound was of small feet running up the stairs.

The extent of Robert's anger vented on Lizzie that night caused Kitty great worry for some time after the event. She was afraid to think what might have happened had she not managed to intervene. Also it seemed that the gradual progress in gaining Lizzie's trust had been totally eroded.

Weeks passed until it was nearly Christmas, and Lizzie, without being disobedient, was still regarding her father with hatred and her step-mother with hostility. So once again, Kitty's life was far from easy though, as always, letters from Mam were a welcome source of respite. Her Christmas letter sent good wishes to: "Kitty, Bobby, Mary, Lizzie and that 'Tatty Bogle', Robert" Kitty smiled at the name which was a Scottish word for 'scarecrow'. She thought to herself, "Don't know about that name, Mam. At least Tatty Bogles are useful, never angry, and never touch the drink!" Also she was glad Robert never tried to read any of her mail.

The next part of the letter brought her special happiness. Apparently, Pat had called round to the house again, this time, accompanied by Denis. Mam described him as, "A braw laddie, the image of his Dad. But there's no mistaking where those green eyes come from."

And for a little while, Kitty was lost in a reverie in which she could picture her son vividly. Then wistfully, she wondered if somehow fate would bring about a meeting with him some time in the future.

Chapter 41

Mrs Rourke Takes Charge

In the years after the incident involving Lizzie and Bobby, family relationships became almost intolerable. In addition to the mutual aversion between Lizzie and her father, the former had become a morose, sullen, and sometimes spiteful girl, particularly with regards to Bobby. And, of course, if Robert ever witnessed or heard of any action taken by Lizzie against his son, there was severe punishment for the girl - usually in the form of beatings. Time after time, Kitty would try to intervene on Lizzie's behalf but she was always pushed away, and threatened with similar treatment.

So when a third child was born two years after Mary, feelings were certainly no better between Robert and Kitty. The baby girl was named Anne, and had her mother's auburn hair. From the day Kitty had told him of her pregnancy, Robert had made it quite clear that he hadn't wanted another child - especially not another girl with a mop of auburn hair just like Kitty's.

Bobby, now aged five years, was attending school, yet Robert was still adamant that Lizzie had no need for schooling since she was being taught to read and write by Kitty. In any case she was more useful helping in the home.

When baby Anne was six months old, she was again in pain due to teething troubles. So of course, Kitty had been up most of the night trying to pacify her - whilst Robert had slept. However, the following morning, he amazed her by acknowledging that, after her sleepless night, Kitty deserved a treat. He informed her, "I won't be goin' to t' boozer after work, I'll be back nice and early. Then 'appen we can 'ave a bit o' time together - like we used to."

Of course Kitty's morning was busy as always, but between jobs she wondered what had caused Robert to forgo his 'boozer time'. Though afraid to expect too much, she was still hoping that if they could talk together quietly, they might be able to improve the present situation, if only slightly.

But that night, Robert had a last-minute invitation to join a group of men in the 'Packet' pub. Here they intended to give a previous workmate, Dave, a good 'send off' before he emigrated to America. Robert had taken little persuading to accept the invitation. And it certainly proved to be a night of rowdy, non-stop drinking, since many of the Packet's regulars also knew Dave. One of the regulars however, did *not* join the boisterous crowd of well-wishers, and that was Billy Trodden. He preferred to observe Robert Gibbs from a distance, having heard several tales of him tottering home late on many nights. Billy wondered how he was treating the lovely Kitty. So when he was ready to leave, he made a detour over to where Robert was standing.

"Evenin' Robert. I hope tha's treatin' Kitty well. Mek sure tha can walk straight when tha's ready to get back to her!"

Robert was just about to take another swig from his tankard when he heard this voice from the past. He spun round at once, "So tha'rt still around, are tha Billy? Still after my wife?" Robert's words were uttered with a sarcastic smile. "Anyroad, 'ow I treat my missus is nowt to do with thee! And so is 'ow much booze I drink. So bugger off tha little busy-body, afore I gives thee a reet good thumpin'!"

At these words, Billy's fists were ready to get in the first blow. But the landlord, Mr Wood, had been watching them and stepped between them saying, "Come on lads, I'm 'avin no fightin'!" He knew that Billy Trodden had once been a much respected bare-knuckle fighter.

Reluctantly Billy relaxed his fist, saying, "It's all reet, Mr Wood. I was goin' anyway." But before leaving, he turned to Robert, saying, "I'll be watchin' thee!"

At nine o'clock that evening, Kitty had abandoned any hope of an amicable talk with her husband. Instead, she'd decided to do a pile of ironing, and by midnight was in a fitful sleep on the settee. She woke to hear raucous singing, "Oh, there was a lusty sailor lad ..." Then the door was flung open and Robert entered, trying unsuccessfully to walk in a straight line to Kitty. She was now fully awake but still on the settee. Her expression registered only contempt.

Robert spoke first, "Well me lov-lovely Irish lass - I'm b-back for thee." A stumble against a chair interrupted him. Then he continued, "So wot about that early neet tha promised?" The next minute, he was on top of Kitty, fumbling under her skirt.

With all the force she could muster, Kitty managed to push Robert off her. Then she watched as he rolled from the settee, crashing his head on to the floor. The pain of the fall seemed to render him sober, and he sat up yelling, "Tha bloody bitch! Tha bloody, bloody bitch! Tha wants teachin' a lesson! If a wife denies a man what's due to 'im, then he teks it!"

Now standing, he made a grab for Kitty's pinafore. But immediately she too stood up and began slapping him as hard as she could across the face, shouting, "Ye useless, selfish bastard! Sure you're nothing but a shitload of fine promises!".

The next thing she felt was Robert's fist on her face. Then she was pushed to the ground.

Panting heavily, a red-faced Robert staggered towards the stairs.

❧ ❧ ❧

Over in Walkers Yard, Margaret, just back from her morning shift at the 'Bowling Green', shared some news with Mrs Rourke. It seemed that the previous night the widower, who attended Temperance Meetings with her, had proposed marriage. And she'd been happy to accept. The landlady's reply was immediate,

"Well now, isn't that grand! And who better than a man with the same views on drinking as yourself?"

Margaret went on to explain it would mean her living in Mesnes, and so hoped Mrs Rourke would be agreeable to accepting her three months' notice. With the rose on her hat bobbing away, her landlady nodded in agreement, saying, "Yes, yes, of course. But ye 'll be greatly missed!"

There was a further question from Margaret who was anxious to share her news with Kitty. Knowing Mrs Rourke visited her friend quite frequently she asked, "Would it be possible to come with ye when ye next see Kitty?"

Mrs Rourke agreed readily, suggesting they visited Kitty that afternoon.

A weary Kitty made breakfast that morning. The side of her face where she'd fallen was badly swollen, as was the eye where he'd hit her. As the two miners ate breakfast, they looked at her face questioningly. But said nothing. Robert came downstairs later, ignored Kitty, and left without a word - and without breakfast.

Despite feeling a dull ache in her cheek-bones, she was able to get on with the day's work. Bobby was at school and Anne had settled well after her feed. Lizzie, after staring at Kitty's swollen cheeks, had volunteered to play with Mary for a while. Kitty wondered if she had heard her and Robert rowing the previous night.

A knock at the door caused Kitty to put her hand to her eye. However, wiping her hands on her pinafore, and self-conscious of her bruises, she went to open it. A smiling Margaret with Mrs Rourke greeted her. But their smiles froze as they caught sight of Kitty's face.

The two friends were invited inside and, despite her initial embarrassment, Kitty felt relieved to be with people she knew and trusted.

Soon she was relating the events of the previous night including the push which had caused Robert to fall and 'crack' his head on the floor. Margaret naturally talked at some length about drink being the very devil incarnate. Mrs Rourke's rose bobbed frantically as she raged about Robert's monstrous actions. Both women knew that wife-beating was all too common, and worse still, it had become regarded as normal by many people. But any further such actions by Robert must be prevented, and both agreed the only course open to Kitty was to give him a shock by reporting the matter to the police. Mrs Rourke was practical with her advice, "Better do it today while the marks are still fresh."

And with no more delay, it was settled that Margaret would see to the midday meal for the children and look after Mary and baby Anne. Meanwhile Mrs Rourke and Kitty would go to the police station and make a report about the beating.

Reluctantly, Kitty agreed to the plan. Margaret stood at the door with young Mary and waved them both off, wishing Kitty 'Good Luck' as she did so. Before returning indoors, a thought occurred to her, "I never even got to tell Kitty the good news about my marriage!"

Chapter 42

Bad Days for Robert

Robert's work that day was on a house in the Poolstock area. He'd left home filled with anger at himself for the way he'd used his fist on Kitty the previous night. But he also felt anger at the way Kitty had spoken to him and then so forcefully rejected him.

"What else did 'er expect after knockin' me to t' floor?" he asked himself, hopeful that this reasoning somehow mitigated his actions. Yet despite himself, as he finally reached Poolstock, he found he was beginning to recall days when he and Kitty had done some of their courting in that area, and his anger began to disperse. That night he went straight home thinking he might even apologise to Kitty.

However, he was both surprised and annoyed to find Mrs Rourke in the kitchen with Kitty. "What the 'ell does she want?" he wondered.

He was soon to find out as Kitty said coldly, "I need to speak to ye about last night. And I want Mrs Rourke to be present. I suggest we go through to the front room ,the children will be fine here." Then Kitty led the way to the other room. Something about the demeanour of the two women caused Robert to refrain from asking questions.

Once there, Kitty looked directly at Robert and gave voice to her feelings. "For over five years now, I've put up with your drinking and the miserable amount of money ye've given me to feed the family and also our lodgers. Ye've made promise after promise to reduce your drinking - but all your grand words have meant nothing!" She caught her breath and went on, "Anyway, last night, your actions were the last straw! Especially when ye left the house this morning without a word of regret. So I've been to the police and made a formal complaint about your actions last night. Mrs Rourke here came with me to give witness to how she found me this morning. So ye'll be getting visitors from the men in uniform soon."

A stunned Robert replied angrily, "Been to the bloody rozzers 'as tha? And do they know what *tha* did to me? I suppose …"

Here Mrs Rouke joined in. "Aye Robert, they know what Kitty did to her drunken bastard of a husband. And if it had been me in her place, ye'd not be fathering any more children - that's for sure!"

Before Robert could reply, Kitty brought things to an end, declaring, "So now Robert, ye know how things stand. Think yourself lucky I'm not walking out on ye. But that's what I'll be doing if ye don't plead guilty. Now, I suggest ye warm up your meal and go in the kitchen. I've no more to say to ye."

Robert appeared before Wigan Borough Police Court some time later. Kitty had gone along with Mrs Rourke who was wearing a white rose in her hat since it was an official occasion. On hearing Robert plead 'not guilty', both women looked at each other in disbelief. The final outcome was a fine of twenty shillings plus costs.

It was only to be expected that both before and after the court appearance, Robert and Kitty scarcely spoke a civil word to each other. Indeed, the only discourse between the two concerned the children. And of course, Kitty was angry that Robert had 'got off' so lightly for his violent behaviour. Admittedly he was making fewer visits to the pub - thus enabling him to hand over slightly money than hitherto. Yet even so, Kitty still struggled to cater for all the family's needs, especially as the children were growing older.

Despite her earlier talk of walking out on him, Kitty had realised she'd never be able to cope on her own with four children to care for. And she'd certainly never leave them with *him* - especially Lizzie who increasingly seemed to invoke her father's wrath - and beatings. But Kitty was now determined not to put up with all her husband's sexual demands - or, as he said, 'his rights'. But she also knew that she could only go so far in denying them.

However, shortly after the court case, Kitty was able to take some 'comfort' on hearing news that Robert hadn't quite escaped scot-free for his act of violence towards her.

It seemed the account of Robert Gibbs' appearance in the Police Court had appeared in the Wigan paper. It was only a brief paragraph, but it caught the attention of Billy Trodden. Immediately incensed by the thought of what Kitty had had to endure from 'That Bastard Bob Gibbs', he muttered to himself, "Tha'll pay for what tha's done. I'll see to that!"

Being June, he knew that Robert would probably work till late most evenings, so he calculated that the latter would probably arrive at 'The Bears Paw Inn' around eight o'clock. Of course, the bastard might even be reducing his pub visits after the court case. But he'd take a chance on him making next Friday such an occasion. By seven o'clock, Billy was already keeping his 'vigil' in the shadows of the pub's side entrance. "Better be on 't safe side," he thought "don't want to miss him."

It was just after eight when Robert appeared in the distance, walking with his usual swagger. Billy waited until his victim was near before swiftly going up to him. Robert hadn't even time to see who was blocking his way before a left jab caught him on the jaw. Shocked by the unexpected blow, he put his hand to his chin. Then a powerful right hook caught him on the left side of his cheek, below the ear. That did it. Robert, now semi-unconscious, fell to the ground.

A self-satisfied grin spread over Billy's face as he looked down at his victim trying, none too successfully, to open his left eye. Then he addressed Robert, "Reet then Gibbs! I daresay tha'll not forget me. Folks didn't use to call me 'Tiger Trodden' for nothin'! Any road, that's a little present for thee."

As Robert managed to half-open his eyes, Billy's expression turned to one of loathing. And he quickly administered a hearty kick to the other's side.

"And that's another! From Kitty. 'Ave a good neet." Then raising his straw hat in mock salute, Billy made his way home, whistling as he walked.

Only a couple of miners had witnessed the scene. They'd watched the drama with interest - both being admirers of Billy. So when 'Tiger' was out of sight, they went over to Robert who was still on the ground. Looking down at him, they began singing in harmony, "Beautiful dreamer, wake unto me, Starlight and Moonlight are waiting for thee.'

Chapter 43

Mrs Rourke is Hatless

Soon after Robert's appearance in court, he banned Mrs Rourke from the house. This was another blow for Kitty as she'd greatly valued the friendship and acts of kindness of her former landlady. Robert maintained she was a bad influence, and was the one who'd persuaded Kitty's 'fancy man,' Trodden, to lay in wait for him. Of course she ridiculed the idea of Billy being her 'fancy man', adding that Mrs Rourke didn't even know him.

At this, Robert said with a sneer, "Listen thee, I knew t' first time I met that bugger, Trodden there was sumat goin' on between thee and 'im. And ever since, tha's bin tartin' thasel up to meet the bugger in secret - and we all know what for!"

Though finding the idea quite laughable, Kitty's response was sarcastic, "Ach, Robert, so ye've caught me out, have ye? Aye, I use all the money ye give me to buy myself the finest satin and lace from the market, then I make myself clothes like those worn by ladies who walk the streets at night. I'm sure *you* know the ones I mean! Then I put red razzle on my lips, leave the four children with Mrs Rourke, and set off to see Billy. Of course, I'd done the housework, shopping and meals before I left."

The sarcasm wasn't lost on Robert who glowered, saying "Tha thinks tha'rt so bloody clever! But tha can't fool me!"

Two more years 'ticked' away in this hostile fashion. And by 1892, Kitty was still relying mainly on letters from home to bring her moments of 'escape'. The latest one from Mam contained good news of her sister, Mary Anne, and husband, George. It seemed that George had done so well as a tailor in Wigtown that he'd been offered work in Belfast. Whilst there, George had recently been made a Master Tailor.

Also, there was a lovely surprise when she read on to find Mam had had a further visit from Pat. His latest news about Denis, now aged fourteen, was that he'd left school and was working on 'Miser Murray's' land until he obtained a job elsewhere. Also, the lad was already taking an interest in politics and, like his Dad, had been sorry that Parnell (popular leader of the 'Home Rule Party') had died so young the previous year. The two of them had had hopes of him being able to achieve 'Home Rule' for Ireland.

Kitty's 'escape' from the realities of her own life didn't last long. Soon, she again woke with a queasy feeling. She'd been hoping her attempts to avoid 'sexual encounters' with Robert might have reduced the risk of further pregnancies. But a few weeks later she was positive about her condition, and dreading telling Robert the news.

In fact, she decided not to say anything to Robert until it was absolutely necessary. However, Kitty felt she needed to confide in someone about her pregnancy. And, next to her Mam, Mrs Rourke was the person who could fulfil that need. So she lost no time in setting off to Walkers Yard, with toddler, Anne, trotting along beside her. As always, there was a warm welcome for them both, and soon, Kitty was drinking a mug of tea and explaining how apprehensive she was about coping with another baby in view of all the tension in their household. Of course, Mrs Rourke was immediately sympathetic and promised Kitty that she could stay with her when ready to give birth. She added, "And if there's any trouble with 'that bastard', my grandson and Pat will 'deal' with him."

It was only when Mrs Rourke got up to give Anne a small buttered crust that Kitty noticed how stooped she was, and how slowly and painfully she was walking.

Finally, it was time to leave, so blowing a kiss to Mrs Rourke, Kitty made her way to the door with Anne. Once outside, she found Mary was just about to enter the house carrying a bowl of broth. Kitty remarked on the changes in Mrs. Rourke.

A worried Mary explained, "Mam's rheumatism has suddenly become worse. She's suffered from it for some years now - but this is something else!"

With the promise of going round to Walkers Yard more frequently, Kitty eventually waved 'Goodbye' to Mary and, along with Anne, made her way home. It suddenly occurred to her that, for the first time ever, Mrs Rourke had been minus her 'rose-hat'. The observation disturbed her.

It was a month after her visit to Walkers Yard that Kitty felt she could put off her 'news' to Robert no longer. Angry and shocked at the prospect of another child to feed, he blamed *her* for the expected birth. "If tha hadn't kept crackin' on tha were tired or not feelin' well, this wouldn't 'ave 'appened. It were like bein' wed to a block o' wood."

Kitty's visits to Mrs Rourke were now more frequent. She was surprised when, on one such morning, Lizzie asked, "Are ye taking that tripe and milk to Mrs Rourke because she's ill? "Surprised that Lizzie had noticed her 'food expeditions', Kitty replied, "Yes I am Lizzie. Would ye like to come along with me and Anne?"

The girl's reply was immediate and made Kitty feel guilty.

"Yes I would! Mrs Rourke has *always* been kind to me."

These words also caused great remorse in Kitty. The girl had come to expect only verbal and physical abuse from her father. Now she had to admit that little affection had been shown by *her* to Lizzie. Though she occasionally thanked the young girl for her invaluable help around the house, their only conversations together had been during her early lessons in reading and writing. Kitty decided to try to remedy the situation. Yet, with the advent of another child, it wasn't going to be easy.

The three set off for Walkers Yard. Anne was holding Kitty's hand whilst Lizzie seemed pleased to carry the basket with tripe in it. On arrival, Lizzie actually gave a smile when Mrs Rourke exclaimed,"Well now, isn't it just grand to see ye again, Lizzie."

Soon all four were seated comfortably in the kitchen. After a while, despite Kitty's offer of help, Mrs Rourke rose in obvious pain to make tea for the two of them. She winced as she bent to lift the heavy, bubbling kettle from the hob and poured water into her 'ever-ready' teapot. Though Mrs Rourke was soon happily chatting about her own three grandchildren, Kitty noticed her former landlady seemed to be wheezing a great deal.

When it was time to go, instead of making her way straight back home, Kitty decided to make a brief call on Mary. The latter was in her kitchen, ironing a pile of clothes. Her face was strained as she placed her iron back by the fire saying, "The ironing can wait! It's so good to see ye Kitty, and you too, Anne and Lizzie. I've been meaning to let ye know about Mam. Just over a week ago, she had a fall. Luckily, our Molly had called in to see her Gran and came for me. We tried to get Mam to bed, but she was stubborn, saying she was 'fine'. Then the wheezing started and she seemed to be fighting to get her breath. Molly, bless her, walked the two miles to fetch Doctor Robinson. Anyway, he prescribed medicine, saying that if she rested, kept warm and took it regularly, her condition might improve." Mary paused, tears in her eyes.

"But last night the coughing never stopped and there was blood in what she was coughing up! Mary paused, tears falling freely now. She continued, "Kitty, love, I have the strongest premonition that Mam's illness is serious, and I can't bear the thought of losing her." Kitty, who was herself near tears, put her arms around the weeping Mary. Lizzie moved closer to the two women, and gently patted Mary's shoulder. Meanwhile, little Anne surveyed the scene for a few moments with a puzzled look. Then, joining in 'the spirit of the moment', put her hands to her eyes and forced out loud sobbing sounds.

Only one week later, on a warm mid-morning in June, young Pat was urgently knocking at the Gibbs' door. As soon as Kitty saw him, she feared the worst. And so it came as no surprise when told his Gran had died early that morning. At once, she asked if she could be of help. Pat replied,"We hoped ye'd ask that. Mam's with two neighbours, layin' Gran out. She looks lovely and peaceful. Granddad and me are organising the Wake. He's callin' on all our friends and neighbours and askin' them round later today. Also he'll organize the drink too. I'm plannin' the food, so I wondered if ye could make a big lob scouse for tonight? I know Gran showed ye how to make one just like hers."

"Of course, I'll be glad to do that." Then, as an afterthought, Kitty asked, "But don't ye think lob scouse is more of a winter's meal, Pat?"

"Well ye may be right! But it was Gran's favourite meal whatever the weather -so I thought we should include it for *her*. Mam and Molly will be makin' ham and brawn sandwiches as well."

With a knowing smile, Kitty said, "Aye, and I'm recollecting it's also *your* favourite too! Summer or winter. Now give my sympathy to your family, especially your Mam, Mary. I'll be round with the scouse as soon as everyone here's been fed."

Chapter 44

A Wake

It was almost eight o'clock when Kitty arrived at Walkers Yard accompanied by Lizzie, Mary, little Anne and, of course, two huge dishes of 'lob scouse'. Robert had no wish to attend the wake and certainly resented the time his wife and daughter spent on preparing for the occasion. Bob had chosen to stay behind with his father, the two having become quite close in recent years.

They entered via the already crowded and noisy kitchen. Here a barrel of ale was proving very popular with some of the guests. Small tables and stools held mountains of sandwiches which the three girls eyed with happy anticipation. Everyone was welcomed by Mary and Pat, the latter taking the dishes of scouse from Kitty and Lizzie, smiling as he did so.

Mary indicated they should make their way through to the front room where her mother had been laid out on a bed. Mrs Rourke had been dressed in a shift and also her old hat, its red rose replaced by her white one for this *very* special occasion. At the head of the bed were candles and, though it was June and still light, there were a few placed around the room since all curtains and windows were closed.

Kitty, tears in her eyes, stood by the bedside saying her prayers of farewell. Then she bent over and kissed the woman who had been like a second mother to her. In doing so, she felt the touch of the white rose on her face. It was like the wings of a beautiful butterfly gently caressing her cheeks, she whispered, "Ach, 'tis good to know you're still there to give me comfort." Then she blew a last kiss to her friend and left her side.

As she moved away from the bed, Kitty was surprised and moved as Lizzie, who'd been holding little Anne's hand, asked, "Am I allowed to give Mrs Rourke a kiss too?" "For sure ye are!" was Kitty's immediate reply.

She had no recollection of the girl kissing anyone except her Granddad. And again she experienced a feeling of guilt regarding Lizzie.

As all four returned to the busy kitchen, there was the sound of a tin whistle being played. It was a popular Irish jig, and Kitty's thoughts went straight to Pat and her first-born, Denis. She pictured the two of them playing their tin-whistles together.

However, these flights of fancy were interrupted by young Molly, granddaughter of Mrs Rourke who greeted her warmly,"Grand to see ye again, Miss Kitty - I know you're married now, but 'Miss Kitty' is how I remember ye." Smiling at the children, she asked, "Would ye like me to look after these three girls? There are other children here, and I'll soon be organizin' games for them, so the grown-ups can enjoy themselves. We need to give Gran the party she deserves!"

Of course Kitty was glad of the offer, and the two elder girls looked pleased at the thought of playing some games. However little Anne, who'd been awake since dawn, seemed quite weary. Noting the child's yawns, Molly had an alternative suggestion for her. "And before we start, I can give the toddler some bread and milk, then I'll tuck her up in one of the beds upstairs."

Once that was sorted out, Kitty joined the crowd in the kitchen. Many of them were listening to or humming the jig being played. It took only a moment to realise that the player was Seamus, one of the group of Irish 'regulars' from her days at the 'Packet'. As soon as he saw her, he gave her an enthusiastic wave which she returned with equal enthusiasm. Scarcely a moment later, a familiar voice said,"Would ye believe it? If it isn't the lass with the lovely green eyes!"

There at her side was Billy Trodden. His greeting was almost the same as the one he'd given her at their first meeting.

With a look of pleasure, Kitty turned to Billy and to his surprise threw her arms around him, saying, "Ach Billy, ye don't know how good it is to see ye again."

With a twinkle in his eye, he replied, "If I thought tha'd give me another 'welcome' like that, I'd pretend I'd only just seen thee, and we could do it all over again!"

"Ye old rogue! But I'll let ye off. Ye've always been a good and loyal friend to me. Besides, I'm truly grateful ye had a 'quiet' word with that husband of mine. He deserved it! For sure, it changed the look of his face for a week or two. Also, he kept his hands off me for some time."

Billy's face darkened at the implication that Robert's temper-control had been short-lived. Noting the change in his expression, Kitty cut in quickly with,"Come on now, Billy. Away with thoughts of Robert Gibbs - he's not worth it. Don't forget we're here to give Annie Rourke a great party?" Billy nodded. Then Kitty continued, "Talking of Mrs Rourke, I didn't know ye were a friend of hers."

"Well I'm not, but Seamus *is*, he used to lodge with her a while ago. And he told me of her passin' when he was walkin' round t'market. He said she were a fine woman and asked if I'd like to join him at t' wake."

It was then Kitty heard the familiar voice of Margaret, "Ach, Kitty, love, I was so looking forward to seeing ye again. I've only just arrived, but I spotted ye at once."In no time at all, Margaret and Kitty were exchanging hugs, and the latter was asking her friend about married life in Mesnes. Then Kitty realised Billy was looking 'left out' and introduced her two friends to each other. Billy had a question for them.

"I understand ye have a lot to chat about, but while Seamus is playing catchy Irish jigs, why don't ye both have a dance? That's if ye *can* dance a jig."

Kitty laughed, asking, "What kind of question might that be, Billy? Sure every colleen learns to do a jig almost before she can walk!" Then turning to her friend, asked," Shall we show him Margaret? Then we'll teach *him* the steps."

Not even bothering to wait for an answer, she took Margaret's hand, and, closely followed by Billy, they went over to Seamus, and began to dance. Soon several of the other mourners, both men and women, were happily joining in. And in no time at all there was a group of spectators clapping in time to the lively rhythm. Even the group of children with Molly, who'd been playing a sitting game of 'Queenie, Queenie', had stopped to watch.

And so the party continued until the early hours of the morning. By then, plates and bowls were empty and the barrel had been practically drained. Patrick Rourke stood up - it has to be said, a little unsteadily, and young Pat called for order. His Granddad then led the mourners through to where his wife lay.

Once everyone was inside her room, Patrick made his way up to the bed, kissed his wife's forehead, and said, "Codladh samn, Annie love". Kitty realised it was the first time she'd heard anyone call Mrs Rourke by her Christian name. Then he began to sing. 'The Last Rose of Summer.' His tenor voice rang out amid the hushed crowd, and as he reached the final words, the mourners quietly began to say their 'Farewells' to Annie Rourke.

Kitty carried young Anne in her arms as, along with Mary and Lizzie, she headed for home. Whilst walking, she imagined she could hear Annie Rourke speaking, her white rose bobbing along with her words, "That was a grand wake everyone gave me! Just Grand!"

Chapter 45

Desperate Times

Though Mrs Rourke's death and burial had been such sad occasions for her family and friends, her lively wake had brought comfort to them all. They felt Annie could rest in peace in the knowledge that she been given the best final party possible. And, despite the sudden loss of a dear friend, Kitty had experienced a rare period of happiness on meeting Billy and Margaret again, and also 'losing' herself in the Irish music and dancing.

Now, four months later, she must prepare herself for the imminent arrival of a fourth baby. Luckily, Mary, who, together with her mother, had helped at the birth of Kitty's three other babies, said she was now quite capable of delivering the baby on her own. So when labour began late one rainy Saturday afternoon, Robert set off to Walkers Yard on a familiar mission. Of course, he would have preferred to be getting help from someone other than one of the Rourkes.

In less than an hour, Mary, accompanied by daughter, Molly, was at Kitty's bedside. By then contractions had become rapidly stronger, almost time for the 'pushing' to begin. This was the first birth witnessed by seventeen year-old Molly, who was looking anxious as her mother gave the order, "Push *now*!" Noticing Molly's face, Mary said cheerfully, "Won't be long now. It's her fourth baby, so it's easy, just like shelling peas! Isn't that right, Kitty?"

Red in the face, and panting heavily between pushes, Kitty managed a faint nod, and then pulled hard with both hands on the rope tied to the head of the bed-stead, ready for another push. With it she let out a series of loud, 'Arrghs', as she strained, her face growing even redder. Molly wasn't at all sure it *was* as easy as shelling peas. However, when a baby boy slithered into the world, she felt she'd witnessed something wonderful.

Downstairs, Robert was showing Bobby a few boxing moves. He enjoyed these rare occasions with his son, though being a Saturday night he would have preferred to be with his friends in the pub. Mary and Anne were playing together, they were taking turns in putting their dolls in the cradle for the new baby. Then they would cover them with blankets, and rock them to sleep,

Some distance away, eleven year-old Lizzie was watching them as she cradled her rag doll by the fire. She'd never liked Mary much, and now resented her monopolizing Anne whilst leaving her out of their game. Also, Lizzie could hear her father and Bobby laughing together. She hated both of them. Her half-brother never missed a chance to tell tales about her to his Dad and her father was becoming more violent towards her. When Kitty tried to stop him, he'd turn his anger on her.

At last, there was a baby's cry followed quickly by a shout from Molly, "Ye have another fine son! Kitty is well but tired. In a few minutes ye can come up with the four children to see her and the baby.

In truth, Robert had been resigned to Kitty having another girl. Now he shouted upstairs, "I'm reet glad it's a lad!. We'll be up to see t' babby and Kitty in a minute or two." Bobby, Mary and Anne stood with Robert near the stairs, eager to see their new brother. Lizzie remained by the fire.

❧ ❧ ❧

The Gibbs' second son was christened in St Joseph's Church as were his siblings. He was named William. Kitty remained relatively weak for some time afterwards, so it was lucky that Billy was a good baby. Also Kitty was increasingly grateful for all Lizzie's help with the housework and for looking after Anne so well. She made a point of praising the girl more frequently. It was just a pity that, as with Bobby, Lizzie seemed very resentful of her second brother, Billy.

The relationship between Robert and Kitty remained cold, though since the arrival of a second son, he seemed to be drinking slightly less. But still, Kitty found it difficult to feed everyone in the house and clothe her family, despite the extra rent from the lodgers. And things were soon to become worse. That same year, 1893, brought further financial problems for most mining families. The price of coal had been falling dramatically for some time, and the owners were insisting on a twenty-five percent cut in wages. Naturally, the miners were angry at this and so, in September that year, they went on strike. With no money coming in, most miners' families were starving, and so soup kitchens were opened in parts of Wigan.

Of course, this hit the Gibbs' family very hard since a proportion of their income came from the wages of the two miners. Once again, Kitty began to supplement meals by scavenging vegetables left behind in the market. However, many miners. wives were on the same 'errand', resulting in Kitty often returning home with very little to show for her efforts.

Despite this dire time, Kitty still tried to ensure that everyone had some protein included in their meal. But on counting her money one morning, she was dismayed to realise she'd only enough money for five eggs, and if she were to have one herself, she needed eight. Reluctantly, she concluded there was only one thing to be done.

With young Billy in the pram, Kitty set off to Carrington's shop. Mr Carrington was always very pleasant with her. However, on this occasion, his eldest daughter was helping to serve. She wore the expression of someone who'd just sucked a lemon - and had a personality to match. However, Kitty gave her a disarming smile as she took six eggs from the tray on display, then paid the five pence for them. Unsmiling, 'lemon-face' took the money, and turned to serve another customer. As she did so, Kitty swiftly took three more eggs from the tray, placing them with the others in the paper at the bottom of the pram. Quickly, she left the shop.

Unfortunately, 'lemon face' had spotted the theft from the corner of her eye and rushed out of the shop shouting, "Stop! Tha's just stolen some eggs." Startled, Kitty stammered out," No, n-no. I paid ye for these eggs." In no time, a small crowd gathered, and 'lemon-face' called for the police constable who patrolled the area.

The outcome was that Kitty admitted she hadn't paid for three of the eggs. A charge was brought against her, and she later appeared in court pleading 'guilty'. Before a fine could be given by the magistrate, Mr Carrington spoke up saying he didn't want to press the charge. So Kitty only paid the two and a half pence for the stolen eggs and was discharged with a caution. But of course, the case still appeared in the local paper, albeit only a brief paragraph. Robert simply commented, "Tha should've stuck to tha story and made 'em *prove* three were pinched."

However, Kitty did receive sympathy and concern from two sources following the paragraph in the paper. Only one day after reading the news,

Mary called round carrying a basket and a large paper-bag. From the basket, she took out butter, flour, apples, and oatmeal biscuits for the children. As Kitty began to thank her friend, Mary said quickly, "Wait, there's more to come! Billy Trodden's sent these for ye." Then she handed the paper-bag to Kitty who took out a variety of fresh vegetables and baking apples from Billy's stall. These were followed by two large blade-ends of lamb. Apparently, he'd done a bit of 'horse trading' with the butcher to get the meat.

Overwhelmed by such kindness at a time when money was tight for many families, Kitty was near tears as she again thanked Mary for all the gifts.

Unfortunately, the miners' strike continued, with troops being sent to pits in some parts of the United Kingdom. Robert told their two lodgers, Arthur and Frank, he was sorry, but he couldn't go on like 'a bloody charity' and continue to feed them. So they moved out, relying on the soup kitchens for food, and sleeping wherever they could at night.

In fact, it was February of the following year before the strike was settled by the government. It was the first time a government had taken such an action. Miners could return to work on their original wages which were guaranteed for a year.

Unfortunately for Kitty, during the six months of the strike, she felt she'd no option but to steal again on several occasions. The winter months had brought both snow and icy winds, and despite her continually mending items of clothing, Robert and the four elder children still needed warm woollen stockings and scarves. So Kitty stole several of these items. At first, she was deeply shamed by being reduced to theft, reflecting on what her Dad would have thought about her. Later, she began to accept Robert's view of their situation. This being, "In bad times, every bugger must do what *has* to be done." And luckily for Kitty, some of her pilfering went undetected.

There were many times when a wistful Kitty would recall what her life in Sligo had once been. A life in which it seemed she was destined for a successful and happy future in the lovely countryside of Sligo Then she would return to the present. Bitterly, she thought to herself, "Would ye look at yourself now! Living in Wigan. A place blackened by smoke and full of poor people, many of them out of work. And here ye are, bringing four bairns into this sorry world, all fathered by a drunken bully. So what have I become now? A shadow of my former self. A poor, crafty, lying shoplifter!"

Chapter 46

Lizzie (1885)

Once the miners' strike had been resolved, the two lodgers, Arthur and Frank were able to return to the Gibbs' home. This increase in income ended Kitty's market 'expeditions'. Yet, she still had to endure Robert's frequent outbursts of temper.

Also, she was aware that, as Bobby grew older, he seemed to take pleasure in avenging himself for Lizzie's obvious dislike of him. Now a strong boy of eleven years, he would mock his fourteen year-old slightly built half-sister mercilessly.

"Just look at thee, wi' tha scrawny little stick- legs, and a face that could turn milk sour!" Of course, he soon realised that such remarks were better made out of earshot of Kitty - if he didn't want a clip round the ear. Lizzie seldom said anything in reply. She had learned long ago that any retaliation would be relayed to Robert.

Bobby's mockery sometimes continued at bed-time. The Gibbs' family all slept in one of the two bedrooms. Robert and Kitty were in the double bed with William in his cradle beside them. Bobby had his own single bed whilst Lizzie and Mary slept at the head of the other single bed and little Annie slept at its foot. Bobby knew that Lizzie always had her rag-doll in bed with her. So before their parents came upstairs, he would chant, "Softie Lizzie and her stinky, stupid doll!"

Silently, Lizzie would clutch her doll tightly and turn her face to the wall.

Some weeks later, Robert, as usual, returned home in a foul mood after a night drinking in the pub. The three younger children were all in bed, but Lizzie was still up ironing whilst Kitty was darning holes in the family's stockings. Bobby was up too, because his Dad had promised to do some boxing with him that night. As the door opened, Bobby looked up expectantly. However, after a row in the pub, Robert was in no mood to see two of his children still up.

Glaring at everyone, he asked Kitty, "What the 'ell are them two doin' up at this time o' neet?" Then turning to Bobby and Lizzie, he said sharply, "Get up to tha beds!" Bobby was about to speak but Robert spoke threateningly, "I said *now*!" They needed no more telling. Once inside the bedroom, Bobby seized Lizzie by the shoulders, his angry face close to hers as he hissed,"It's all tha fault! Dad would've boxed with me if I'd bin on my own!" Then he went over to the rag-doll sticking out from underneath her pillow, picked it up, and screwed its limp neck round, saying, "Tonight it keeps in bed wi' me. It goes in t' bin tomorrow." And putting it near his backside he let out a loud fart.

This time he'd gone too far. Lizzie made for the door, shouting angrily, "Right then! Now you and your Dad can watch your precious football burn on the fire!" She flew down the stairs to find a startled Robert drunkenly trying to kiss Kitty. Lizzie went straight to the cupboard where Bobby's football was kept, grabbed it, and made her way to the fire with it. A furious Bobby arrived calling urgently,"Stop her, Dad! Stop her! The wicked cow's goin' to burn our ball!"

Instantly, the words had a sobering effect on Robert. He intercepted Lizzie's dash to the fire and snatched the ball from her hands. The speed of his move caused Lizzie to lose her balance, and she fell down. Passing the ball to Bobby, Robert declared, "Get up tha nasty little bugger! Now get over to Bobby and say tha 's sorry." Still on the ground, filled with anger and resentment Lizzie replied, "I'll get up when I'm ready. And I'll never say 'sorry' to that bully. I hate both of you!"

Robert picked up a nearby wooden hair-brush. Yanking Lizzie from the floor, he began beating her repeatedly with the wooden end of it. In order to free herself from him, Lizzie bit the arm holding her. Enraged, Robert let go of his hold, but quickly seized her again. This time, he yanked her by the wrist, but it twisted as he did so. A piercing cry of pain emerged as Lizzie yelled, "Ye've broken my wrist!"Robert let go, then a furious Kitty grabbed the hot iron from the stand by the fire and ran towards him, screaming, "Right ye great brute, see how this feels…"

The sentence was never completed since Robert, having deduced her intent, knocked the iron to the ground, and almost simultaneously, punched her in the jaw.

At the same time, Arthur entered the room from upstairs. He surveyed the scene in amazement. Kitty had a swollen, bleeding lip, Robert was breathing heavily with a face of thunder, Lizzie, tears in her eyes, was holding her wrist in obvious pain, and Bobby, holding his foot ball tightly, was glaring at Lizzie. Angrily, Arthur asked, "What the 'ell's goin' on? I were fast sleep, then I hears a scream like a bloody banshee, yellin' fit to wakken t' dead!" He scowled at Robert as he spoke again, "I'm guessin' this is thy doin' Gibbs? It may be none o' my business, but this isn't first time I've sin Kitty wi' bruises. She's a fine woman and a good landlady. And if tha lays a finger on 'er agen, I'll be layin' my fist on *thee*! So think on!" Then he turned and headed for the stairs.

It was Kitty who spoke first. Ignoring Robert, she looked sternly at Bobby, "Right, put your ball in the cupboard, then straight up to bed with ye!" Next, she went over to Lizzie, saying gently, "Hush now, I'll find something to bandage that wrist with, then we'll soak it in my boiled comfrey." She addressed Robert with contempt, "As for *you*, ye need to sleep off that booze. But it won't be upstairs!"

The following morning, Kitty was relieved to see that Robert had already left for work. Arthur smiled sympathetically and enquired about her swollen lip. Kitty replied it wasn't too bad, and thanked him for his intervention the previous night.

However, that morning, she left the house accompanied by Lizzie and young Billy. Their destination was Walkers Yard. Here, she described all the events of the past night to Mary. As she concluded, she confessed, "I just don't know what to do for the best. We can't go on like this, and that's for sure! I fear for Lizzie's safety."

Mary was appalled. She feared for both Kitty's and Lizzie's safety. Then unexpectedly, she turned to Lizzie asking her if, discounting her father and Bobby, she was otherwise happy at home. Surprised, Lizzie was reluctant to answer at first. Quickly, Kitty reassured her, "Take your time. Don't be afraid to tell the truth."

Lizzie took a deep breath, then began, "From being a toddler, I'd only known the love of my Grandma and Granddad Pinnington. They'd talk to me and play with me. Such lovely times!" Lizzie's face lit up at her memories. A pause and her face clouded. "Anyway, I was about two when they told me about my mother dying. Then Granddad said I had a Dad too, but he didn't love me, and had left me with them when I was a baby. Of course I believed them. There was another pause. "Then later, as you know, Granddad took me on a train, telling me I was going to meet my Dad. I remember crying. Then I met you, Kitty. A woman I didn't know. Then a man came in and said he was my Dad. All I knew was my Dad didn't love me!" Tears filled her eyes as she continued, "I didn't understand when Granddad said I was going to live with *him*!" Another pause, then Lizzie managed a smile as she said,"But I quite liked *you* Kitty. Ye gave me biscuits and a cuddle. In fact ye were very kind to me, but once the babies came, ye seemed too busy for time with me."

"As for my Dad, he *never* showed me any *rea*l affection. I got used to him ignoring me or finding fault with me. But then came beatings - usually when drunk with ale. God! How I hate that gobshite!" At this point, Lizzie seemed unable to continue. Her fists turned white as she clenched them. At last she seemed calmer, saying as she looked at Kitty, "And besides all that Kitty, you and 'gobshite' always seemed to be concerned about your other children. I was left out and felt so jealous!"

Finally, Lizzie looked directly at Kitty and Mary in genuine affection, speaking to each in turn. "I thank ye for the kindness ye've shown me, Kitty, and for teaching me to read and write. And I thank you Mary, for the friendly way you always greeted me. Yet quite honestly, I've never known any lasting happiness since I left Grandma and Granddad's home!"

The outcome of the meeting was that Mary said she was prepared to report Robert to the NSPCC for child cruelty to bring matters to a head. Kitty agreed readily, thinking that the recently formed NSPCC would make sure Robert got the punishment he deserved. There followed a further suggestion from her friend which came as complete surprise to Kitty. Mary said she'd always liked Lizzie, and if the girl was agreeable, she would be pleased to have her living in Walkers Yard as a member of the family. Mary also wondered if Lizzie might want to assist her daughter,

Molly, in helping to run the lodging house there. She added that there were now *four* lodgers to cater for.

Lizzie's delighted face expressed her agreement more than any words could have done. And Kitty certainly had no problems with the suggestion.

The court case didn't proceed as had been anticipated. Robert had to appear before the Magistrate's court in Wigan - but so did Kitty. The NSPCC had concluded that she too must be guilty of cruelty since she had apparently done little to prevent her husband beating Lizzie. Moreover, it was also concluded that Kitty had agreed to Lizzie being kept at home to work instead of being allowed to attend school.

As the two 'prisoners' gave evidence, their trial became a noisy and rowdy affair. Robert, when accused, claimed it was Kitty who had ill-treated Lizzie whilst he was at work. An enraged Kitty had to be restrained when she got up and tried to attack her husband, declaring he was nothing but a liar, and that she had always done her best for the girl. She also referred back to the occasions when Robert had appeared in court for causing her bodily harm. Robert angrily maintained his innocence.

Lizzie had been asked to give evidence but refused, saying she was afraid to face her father. She remained in a room at the rear of the court with the matron of the children's home.

The final outcome was that both parents were found guilty of child-cruelty. The penalty being six months' imprisonment, but since Kitty had four other children who appeared to be well-cared for, only Robert served the sentence. Mary, who had not been called to give evidence, was allowed to take care of Lizzie and bring her up as one of the family.

Chapter 47

A Special Letter

The trial had proved to be a great ordeal for Kitty. Neither she nor Mary had foreseen the possibility of Robert involving her in the charge of cruelty. However, as Kitty had hoped, Robert's absence during his prison sentence did at least provide some respite for her from his drunken rages. On the other hand, she now had to cater for the family and the lodgers on a reduced income during this period.

Luckily, once again, Kitty was given help by her loyal and generous friends, Mary and Billy Trodden. Also, quite unexpectedly, Arthur, the lodger, volunteered to pay a slightly higher rent during Robert's time in prison. He added the proviso, "But it's only a loan. And when yon bugger's out o' clink, then he starts to repay me. Of course, Kitty accepted Arthur's offer and made sure that his meal portions were always generous.

It was six in the morning on a dark, bitterly cold day in December when Kitty and Bobby went to meet Robert at the prison on the day of his release. There was a light covering of snow on the ground so Kitty had taken along Robert's winter coat. As the prison door opened he stepped out, she saw at once that much of his old arrogant swagger had gone. Bobby, happy to see his father again, ran forward to greet him calling, "Dad, Dad!" Robert smiled and fondly put his hands on the lad's shoulders saying, "Good to see thee, lad! I've missed thee!"

Behind Bobby, Kitty moved forward to hand Robert his coat, then without any trace of emotion, remarked, "There's some tea and toast at home if ye want it."

Sheepishly, Robert took the coat from her, saying, "That's good Kitty, I'll be more than glad of a bit o' toast and tea." Bitterly, he then declared, "I've bin fair clemmed in that bloody, godforsaken hole!"

Without comment, Kitty simply turned to make for home. Robert, with Bobby walking contentedly beside him, followed her.

For some time in the Gibbs' household, life improved for everyone. Prison and hard labour had had a salutary effect on Robert. Firstly, he'd resolved to visit the pub only on Saturdays, and only for an hour or two. Moreover, he seemed to be keeping to his resolve. So, for the first time in years, Kitty was able to rely on a fairly consistent income. Secondly, his attitude towards Kitty had changed considerably.

And whilst never actually apologising for the actions of cruelty which had led to his prison sentence, he was a more tolerant man, and gradually getting back his sense of humour.

Yet, for Kitty, too much had happened in the past. There'd been too many lies and broken promises to make her change her opinion of him now. The best she could do was concede that this sober Robert was helping to keep the family on an 'even keel'.

Bobby now had no Lizzie to bully and remained close to his Dad. Also, since Robert's homecoming, had asked to be referred to as 'Bob'. Billy seemed to be getting on well with his big brother, whilst Mary and Anne were quite friendly most of the time. Sadly, nobody apart from Kitty, seemed to miss Lizzie.

As for Lizzie, at last, she was receiving the love and care she deserved. She was also a great asset as she worked along with Molly, helping with housework and meal preparation in the boarding house. Kitty was particularly pleased when Lizzie asked if she could now return to her baptismal name, Elizabeth. It seemed that, like Bobby, she was confident enough to begin establishing her own identity.

It was also a time of change in Wigan. Michael Marks, a Jewish immigrant from Poland, had established a 'Penny Bazaar' stall in the Market Hall. It had become quite a 'favourite' with Kitty and the younger members of the Gibbs' family. Everything cost one penny - just within their price range. (^{1})

The arrival of the twentieth century continued to see the Gibbs' family reasonably settled in terms of finance and family relationships. And though Kitty could never again feel any real warmth for Robert, she was able to 'jog along' with him.

Of course, the children were growing up. Anne, now aged eleven, and Billy, aged nine, were still at school, but Bob was already working for his father. Mary had recently left school, and due to her acuity in arithmetic, she'd been successful in obtaining work in the 'Penny Bazaar'. It was Kitty who'd made sure that all the children (including Elizabeth) were able to handle and calculate money well. When Mary began work, she also asked to be called by her second name, Catherine.

Letters from home remained a source of pleasure for Kitty, and she was especially glad to receive one which revealed how well her mother was keeping at the age of seventy-two. However, she was puzzled when a letter arrived addressed to 'Miss Kitty' in unfamiliar writing. She opened it to read,

"Dear Miss Kitty,

My name is Denis Dowd. I hope you don't mind me writing to you and calling you by that name. It was the one Dad always called you. I'm very sad to tell you he died last week, he was 67. He had been ill for some time and died in his sleep. He was a great Dad to me and I miss him so much! A year before his death, he told me you were my birth mother. A big surprise, though I'd already guessed you were someone very special. He loved to talk about you and used to say he wished I'd met you.

Your mother gave me your address when I visited her with news of Dad's death. She helped me with writing this letter. I would be so happy if you felt you could write back to me. When my Irish mother, Anne Dowd was dying she told Dad he could tell me about you when I was older. And of course, I'll always love her for the love and care she gave me.

My good wishes to you,

Denis Dowd."

Denis' letter was read and re-read by a very emotional Kitty. It was lucky that she was alone in the house, everyone else being either at work or school. Tears flowed freely as, once again she was filled with memories of her last bitter-sweet moments with Denis, and also her last meeting with his father. "Dearest Pat" she thought, "now you're gone forever. But at least our son is alive and knows I'm his mother - so that will be my consolation."

Once the tears had finally ceased Kitty was able to have a chuckle to herself as she realised Mam must have known beforehand about Denis' letter, yet had said nothing. Smiling, she addressed her mother, "Ach, ye crafty besom, Mam! Ye kept *that* quiet, didn't ye?"

Next, she carefully put the letter in a drawer where Robert couldn't find it, and began thinking how she'd word her reply. She waited until the children had had dinner and returned to school. Eventually, she began to write.

"Denis, my dear son,

How wonderful to hear from you. You've never been far from my thoughts since I left Ireland. That was just after your birth, twenty-two years ago. Luckily, due to letters from my own mother - 'Mam' - I have been able to picture the varying stages of your growth, right up to the fine, young man you are now. Yet I always feared that when Pat eventually told you about me, you would hate me."

Kitty continued the letter expressing sympathy for Denis' loss of a father who, in his own words had been, "A great Dad..." She went on to ask him about his siblings, then she told him of her marriage and subsequent births of Bob, Catherine, Anne and Billy. It seemed politic not to mention the years of trial and tribulation in her marriage.

Finally, she ended the letter,

"My love to you, my son,

Mam x"

Footnote[1]

Michael Marks, together with his partner, Thomas Spencer, planned to have a shop in Makinson Arcade, Wigan, by 1900.

Chapter 48

A Time of Changes

With the approach of the twentieth century, many changes were taking place. The British Empire had been growing steadily over the years. By the turn of the century, much of the world on the map appeared to be in red, the colour which marked British domination. Queen Victoria was still on the throne, and in 1897 had celebrated her Diamond Jubilee. (^{1})

When gold was discovered in areas of land ruled by Afrikaners, known as Boers (Dutch for farmers), Britain saw the chance to extend its empire still further. However the Boers refused to give up their independent republic to the British, and war broke out in 1899. It lasted until 1902, when victory was finally achieved by the British.

The war did not affect the Gibbs' family, though Kitty thought sadly of the young men who'd gone out fighting in a war started because the British government were out to seize land. However, on a Saturday afternoon visit to Walkers Yard, she was soon to realise that opinions about the war differed greatly. Whilst sitting in the kitchen chatting with Mary, raised voices were heard in the other room. Patrick and grandson, Pat, were arguing with Jack, one of the lodgers, about the latest fighting in Mafeking. Jack declared,"Them bloody Cloggies wants a reet good thrashin', an' if I was younger I'd be o'er there in quick sticks, fightin' for our Queen an' country!"

In a flash, young Pat retorted, "Fighting for the Queen and country? I'm thinking ye need to look more carefully at history. 'Them Cloggies' as ye call them, are the oldest European settlers in South Africa! Yet there go the bloody land-grabbing British government again! A sniff of gold and they want it!" Then he nodded towards his Granddad, continuing, "And the Irish know all about the British and land! Isn't that right Granddad?"

Patrick nodded circumspectly. For Mary's sake, they couldn't afford to offend lodgers too much. However, Pat had more to say,"And if I had to fight, I'd be fighting with the Boers for their rights. As for fighting for Queen Victoria, she may have reigned over sixty years, but she hasn't done much actively since Albert's death!"

The lodger looked angrily at this young upstart and was about to respond, but Patrick looked at his grandson warningly, saying firmly, "That's enough, Pat!" Turning to the lodger, he said, "I think it's time for some biscuits and a mug of tea."

However, it wasn't long after Patrick's comments about Victoria that the 'Grandmother of Europe' breathed her last in 1901.Crowds in London mourned her passing. Britain now had a king - Edward V11- second son of Queen Victoria.

Changes also occurred in the Gibbs' family. A year after Victoria's death, an eighteen year-old Bob was still working for his father. On a warm but windy day in early September, the two had just started work on the repair of a roof in Pemberton. Bob was busy mixing cement for his father who was now ready to put the roof's upper tiles in place. One of the young mill-girls who regularly passed that way, noticed the well-built young man bending over a bucket. She also noted his good looks as he walked over to the ladder with the bucket of cement. She called out, "Tha wants to be careful, goin' up yonder. There's a fair wind today."

Looking round in surprise, Bob took in the pretty, young girl with her blonde hair tied back. He was quick to respond, "Tha needn't bother about me! Bein' on a roof's easy fer Bob Gibbs. One of t' best lookin' an' t' fittest lads around!"

Sarcastically, the girl queried, "*Ses who?*" And turned to walk away, but then hesitated, calling over her shoulder, "My name's Ellen Marshall." And with a wave, she ran to catch up with the other mill girls as they clattered their way to work.

It wasn't long before the two were courting quite seriously. Both Kitty and Robert liked Ellen, but viewed her as only one of a series of his girl-friends. So they were surprised and concerned when Bob announced his intention of marrying Ellen the following January. Almost as an afterthought, Bob added,"We'll get wed in t' Register Office. I'll be a Dad soon."

Robert's reaction was angry, "Tha bloody, stupid bugger! Fancy fallin' into *that* trap! Now we'll lose thy wage!"

The baby, Ethel Marshall Gibbs, was born the following year. Bob and Ellen were living temporarily with Ellen's parents. A first grandchild for Robert and Kitty who were eager to visit the new family. Robert had mellowed somewhat, and greeted his granddaughter by observing she was "a bonny little babby." He then congratulated his son and Ellen with the words, "Well done! 'Appen t' next babby'll be a lad."

Ellen's expression clearly conveyed *her* opinion of Robert's comment.

Meanwhile, Catherine and Anne, now aged sixteen and fourteen years respectively, were wage-earners and had also become quite close friends. Catherine was enjoying her work in the 'Penny Bazaar', frequently regaling her family with tales of customers to the Arcade. One in particular, Lizzie 'Snurch', had everyone amused by Catherine's tales of her and her six year old son. She'd given birth to him in her late thirties. The nick-name, 'Snurch' had been given on account of her continually running nose which she stemmed by 'snurching' up her nasal fluid. A tall woman, with long straggly black hair, streaked with grey, she'd walk round the Arcade in her dark-green shawl, holding the hand of her son. It was the bright-red lipstick contrasting with her grey complexion and habit of suddenly breaking into songs from the Music Halls, which caught people's attention. Whenever she sang 'She's only a bird in a gilded cage' the lad would look up at her admiringly, asking passers-by, "Hasn't me Mam getten a luvely voice?"

Anne now worked as 'general help' in a large six-bed roomed house in Mesnes owned by Mrs Gresty, one of the ladies from the 'Temperance Campaign'. The cook, Alice, had 'taken Anne under her wing' having found her polite and hard working, though like her mother, she had a feisty side to her nature. During spare moments, Anne always loved it if Alice, a plump but very agile woman in her late twenties, showed her some of the dance-movements she'd seen at the ballet, 'Cleopatra'. Mrs Gresty, knowing of

Alice's interest in dance, had paid for her train-fare and ticket to see the ballet at the Palace Theatre in Manchester.

Soon Anne was passing on ballet routines to sister, Catherine. The sisters would go up to their bedroom to work out ballet sequences of their own. This involved delicate arm-movements accompanied by intricate spins on their toes. A far-cry from clog-dancing which was popular in Lancashire.

Billy and his Dad were quite amused by the sisters' 'Ballet productions'. Sometimes, having seen Catherine and Kitty disappear upstairs, they would sneak up after them, and peer round the partially closed door. "What the 'ell do those two daft fairies think they're doin'?" was Billy's question to his Dad as they twirled and floated round the room. Their white aprons were draped over one shoulder, then tied at their hips in the style of a Grecian tunic.

"God alone knows!" Robert answered. "They look like a pair of demented ducks!" Suddenly aware of spies, the door would be slammed by one of the 'ducks'.

Billy, now eleven years old, was eager to be leaving school the following year, and hoping he would be able to work with his Dad and big brother. However, Robert wasn't sure he could afford to take on another apprentice.

As for Elizabeth, she continued to be much happier living with and helping Mary. She also liked working alongside Molly. Kitty still made regular visits to Walkers Yard, and was always pleased to see the great changes in Elizabeth.

Of course, amid all these changes, one thing remained constant for Kitty, and that was letters from Ireland which still played a vital part in her life.

Denis had been addressing her as 'Mother' for some time now, and Kitty had felt quite privileged when he began to talk about a girl he'd met called Mary. His later letters described how his feeling for her were growing stronger, and how he was going to ask her to marry him. In his next letter, Kitty learned that Denis' marriage proposal was made on the day he took Mary to Sligo Town and the two of them were walking by the

River Garavogue. This brought back memories for Kitty as she recalled the peace she'd found there when working at Dooley's Drapery - a life-time ago.

Quite soon after his proposal, a happy Denis wrote to tell Kitty of the date of his forthcoming marriage to Mary Holmes. He also expressed the wish that she could be present see him married.

Sadly, both really knew it was never going to happen.

Footnote[1]

Queen Victoria (1837- 1901) brought together many royal European families through the marriages of her nine children. The queen became known as 'Matriarch of Europe.' After Prince Albert's death, Victoria wore black for the remainder of her reign so she was also given the name 'Widow of Windsor'.

Chapter 49

Suffragettes

The twentieth century also saw the spread of the Suffragette Movement.([1]) Women's suffrage had first been advocated by Mary Wollstonecraft in her book, 'A Vindication of the Rights of Women' (1792). But now it was no longer the 'peaceful protest' to obtain the right for women to vote which was started in 1897 under the leadership of Millicent Fawcette. Later leaders of active suffragettes were Manchester-born Emmeline Pankhurst and her daughters, Christabel and Sylvia. They were tired of the number of suffrage bills brought before Parliament then defeated by leading politicians of the day. Apart from personal oppositions, ministers did not want to affront Queen Victoria's implacable opposition to the women's movement.

It was Christabel who, in 1905, planned to interrupt a meeting of the Liberals to be held in Manchester. Groups of suffragette supporters, mainly liberal, well-educated and 'well-to-do women', had been invited to travel to Manchester that day. Amongst them was Margaret, Kitty's friend, who'd been living in Mesnes since her marriage.

The day after her return from the meeting, Margaret went round to tell Kitty and Mary about the exciting events. And so that morning, the three friends sat in the kitchen of Walkers Yard. Margaret lost little time in describing her 'adventure'.

"Well now, as ye probably know, we all met up at Wigan Station armed with banners. All of us eager to board the train to Manchester. It was grand to see so many women from Wigan and the surrounding districts there. Ye should've seen the banners in their bright colours, especially gold, white, and purple. All carrying messages such as,

'VOTES FOR WOMEN' or

'DEEDS NOT WORDS'.

And though it was October, the weather was fairly mild and so a few went without coats and wore their best long dresses for the occasion." Margaret paused for breath, then continued,

"Next we made our way down the stairs shouting, "Votes for Women!" We certainly woke up those dour-looking officials and the passengers on the platform."

In the kitchen, the audience of two had increased to four as Elizabeth and Molly stopped their work to move over to hear some of Margaret's account. Very impressed, Kitty remarked, "Aye, I can imagine the stir ye all caused!"

"We certainly did! Luckily we all managed to get on the train, though it was very packed. And of course we were trying to cope with banners as well. Anyway, it wasn't long before our train arrived at Victoria Station. We got out and marched to the meeting place, chanting loudly, 'Votes for Women'. Suddenly there was a hush, and out of a large car steps Christabel herself! The cheering and applause was deafening. Of course, booing came from men in the crowd, but we soon drowned out *their* noise!" Margaret laughed at the recollection, then continued, "The police made us wait outside the building, but we saw Christabel and her key-women go inside."

"It was some time before she came out. This time she was escorted by two police officers! But head held high, she waved triumphantly to the crowd. The cheers were deafening!" Margaret's audience smiled as they pictured the scene.

"Later, we were told about the events inside. It seemed that Christabel had waited quietly until things got underway, then she suddenly interrupted Churchill. She demanded to know what plans the Liberals had for women's suffrage. Wouldn't ye know? The bastard refused to answer her question! So together, all the women raised their banners, and shouted out, 'VOTES FOR WOMEN'

"Of course, all of them were forced outside and Christabel was put under arrest." Her audience looked disappointed. Impatiently, Margaret pointed out, "Don't ye see? *She* was the *winner*! *She* broke into a meeting of men. Men who are likely to win the next election. And *she* made the headline news in all the papers!" When put like that, the audience realised women's suffrage had made real progress.

Footnote[1]

After the war, all three major political parties acknowledged the need for the enfranchisement of women. An act in 1918 allowed all women of thirty years and over the right to vote. In 1928, this was lowered to twenty-one years.

It is interesting to note that women in New Zealand had the right to vote in 1893! In Australia, it was 1902, in Finland it was 1906, and, not long ahead of us, Norway gave women the right to vote in 1913.

Chapter 50

Llandudno

Also in 1905, Catherine, who was still working on the 'Penny Bazaar' stall, had attracted the attention of a young postman, James Carr, who lived in Scholes. On Saturday afternoons, he would pause at the stall and look round carefully at the variety of penny items for sale - and equally carefully at Catherine. Gradually, after a few such Saturdays, James bought a small pair of scissors - which he didn't need. Then he plucked up the courage to ask Catherine to see him after work.

After their first outing together, many more were to follow. Catherine soon learned that Jimmy too had connections with Ireland via both parents. It seemed his father, also called James, had been born in Ireland, and his maternal Great Grandma had been born in County Down. Besides this common bond, the two enjoyed each other's company, and fairly soon they were officially 'going out' together. Jimmy was regarded as 'quite a nice lad' by Kitty and Robert, and, as Robert observed, "Lad's getten a regular job, so he should be able to support our Catherine."

Catherine was particularly excited when, in September that year, Jimmy offered to pay three shillings and three pence each for them to go to Llandudno by train that Sunday. These day-trips were popular, with people going to seaside resorts such as Southport, Blackpool and, more recently, resorts in Wales. They were very busy in 'Wakes Week' when the mills closed down for a week in summer.

The couple met at the North Western Station at five-thirty on a sunny, though still quite cool June morning. They joined the crowd of lively laughing passengers, all eagerly awaiting the five-fifty-five train. Catherine wore her new blue dress with its fashionable 'sailor' collar. On her head 'sat' her summer straw-hat. Precisely, at five-fifty-five, the guard blew his whistle, waved his green flag, and the train slowly pulled away from the station like some great creature which had been roused from its slumber. A cloud of smoke emerged sending out flecks of soot. Excited passengers watched the platform, grey buildings, and chimneys of Wigan gradually disappear.

The train soon picked up speed and began roaring along to Warrington. Here, all passengers for Llandudno alighted and boarded the train which would take them to their final destination. Some people continued looking out of the windows, others had a doze after their early start, lulled by the steady, soporific rhythm of the train. However, by the time the train was passing through Rhyl and Colwyn Bay, all passengers were wide awake and watching out for Llandudno!

It was almost nine o'clock when everyone streamed out of the station chatting happily. Catherine and Jimmy followed the signs indicating, 'Promenade'.

Quite soon, along with most of the other passengers, they arrived at the crescent-shaped promenade with its row of large grand-looking hotels, many of them painted white. Ahead of them was the stunning view of the beach and the incoming tide. On the left towered the Great Orme, on the right was a smaller Orme. Certainly a far cry from the views they were accustomed to. Catherine stood spellbound, taking in the view and sea-air. Only the seagulls disturbed her peace with their raucous calls.

After a walk in the direction of the smaller Orme, they sat on one of the forms along the promenade. Here they hungrily ate their sandwiches whilst watching the now receding, but shimmering sea. The day was steadily getting hotter.

Their hunger satisfied, they strolled back along the promenade to the pier close to the Great Orme. At the pier's end they bought a bottle of lemonade and stood watching a crowd of men packing up their fishing tackle now the tide was low.

Catherine, who'd just taken a swig of lemonade was surprised when Jimmy suddenly turned to face her, saying earnestly, "I've loved thee since I first saw thee in t' Penny Arcade. And I think tha has feelin's for me too. So I'm askin' thee to marry me. What does tha say?"

Amused by this incongruous place for a proposal, Catherine burst out laughing as she listened to the remarks of the group of men examining their catches. "Well Jimmy," she declared, "you certainly chose a romantic spot to ask me!" Seeing his crestfallen face, she added, "However, if ye'll buy me a slap-up meal of fresh cockles and mussels, I might accept your proposal."

Relieved, he said, "Ye drive a hard bargain! But cockles and mussels it is!"

So later in the afternoon, the now 'engaged' couple shared sea-food, liberally sprinkled with pepper and vinegar - supplemented by a couple of uneaten sandwiches.

As they walked back to the promenade from the fresh-fish shop, they saw a crowd of holidaymakers standing round some kind of brightly-coloured canvas erection. The words, 'Richard Codman', was written in large letters on its side. Going closer, they heard a strange voice, not unlike that of a squawking parrot, coming from a puppet. It had a large, hooked, nose and gaudily painted face. In the puppet's arms was a stick with which it appeared to be beating a puppet-crocodile whilst squawking,

"That's the way to do it! That's the way to do it!". The audience, most of whom were children, roared with appreciative laughter. Neither Catherine nor Jimmy could follow the 'plot' to this drama which seemed to centre around a woman called Judy, a baby, a crocodile, a ghost, a string of sausages, and a policeman. But the laughter was infectious and soon both of them were joining in. Just before the performance ended, a woman in a long dress and mob-cap came around with a collecting tin. Some people moved away, but Jimmy ostentatiously put in *his* penny.

Realising they had now only two hours or so before it would be time to catch the return train at seven fifteen that evening, they made their way to the shopping centre. Here, Catherine bought sweets for her little niece, Ethel, and a rattle for brother Bob's second daughter, Mabel, born earlier that year.

From there, they discovered it was only a short walk to the beach at West Shore. It was smaller and quieter than the one on the promenade. The evening sun glinting on the calm waters contrasted with the dark Welsh mountains behind. Both sat quietly on the sand without speaking for some time.

Reluctantly, Jimmy whispered, "Time to get back to the station, love."

Chapter 51

Romance for Anne

The year 1906 saw James Carr being welcomed as a new member of the Gibbs' family after he and Catherine married in St Joseph's Church. It was a quiet affair attended only by their immediate families. Mary, Elizabeth, Margaret and her husband were invited to the 'wedding' meal after the ceremony. An added bonus for Kitty was that Catherine and Jimmy were living in a small house fairly near to Farrimond Close where she and Robert lived.

Soon after this event, Kitty received a letter from Dennis announcing the birth of his and Mary's first child, a son, John. As always, she read letters from Denis when alone, usually in the bedroom, and once again she was filled with a mixture of joy and regret. Regret that she hadn't been there to see her little Grandson, but joy that Denis and his family were part of her life, albeit a part which she had to keep locked away from her family in England.

One Sunday afternoon, a year after Catherine's wedding, Kitty and Anne called in to see her for a chat and cup of tea. Anne, now eighteen, was looking forward to telling her sister and mother a bit more about the new gardener who'd been taken on for two days a week by her employer, Mrs Gresty. The three were settled by the fire in the back kitchen whilst Jimmy was seated in the corner engrossed in reading the paper. Catherine took one look at Anne's eager face, blue eyes beaming behind rimless-spectacles, and said, "Now before I brew the tea, we want to know if anything's happened between you and that gardener lad." Excitedly, Anne began, "Well, last Friday afternoon, I had to pass by him to take the basket and pegs into the kitchen. As I drew level with him, he asks me my name and tells me his is Joe. So I just tell him my name and try to go past him into the house. But he blocks my way. Then he asks me if I'd like a ride out on one of the trams on Saturday afternoon." Anne paused and sniffed, continuing with, "So, of course I told him I wasn't so sure about going out with someone I don't really know! Anyway, he points out I'll never get to know him if I don't give him a chance. So in the end I agree. Next, he asks if I can meet him at two o'clock at the tram depot in Platt lane. I just nod and go back in the kitchen." Anne paused, expecting some comment.

Jimmy had stopped reading, hoping to hear a bit of juicy gossip. But after the lengthy mundane exchange between Anne and Joe, he stood up remarking, "Think I'll 'ave a walk round t' town. This tale of Annie's is gettin' a bit too excitin' fer me!" Putting down his paper, off he went.

Anne didn't like his sarcasm, and was cross because he'd called her 'Annie'.

Like Robert, Catherine too was getting impatient, and said,"Get to what happened when you got off the tram, Anne!"

"Well I was there on time and he was a real gentleman, taking my arm as he helped me on the tram. We chatted away and soon we arrived at Pemberton. He suggested we have a walk and we went past an old church there. We kept walking, and he pointed out the buds on some chest-nut trees which were starting to open." Anne stopped and thought a moment. Then abruptly said, "Anyway, it was a lovely afternoon. I really like him and he says he'd like to take me out again soon."

Both her mother and her sister were taken aback by the sudden conclusion.

"Is that it?" asked a disappointed Catherine. "Talk about an anti-climax!" Anne sniffed again and replied snappily, "Well it's all you're getting for the time being!"

For Kitty, Anne's account of the outing had brought back vivid memories of *her* tram ride to meet Robert all those years ago. Then she recalled that first kiss. But it was Pat Dowd who had held her, and kissed her.

She came back to reality with a start, suddenly realising her daughters were staring at her. A concerned Anne asked, "Are you feeling alright, Mam?"

"I'm fine thanks. Is he taking you out again?" Kitty asked, changing the subject.

"Oh yes!" declared Anne happily, "Just as soon he has a free Saturday."

A couple of weeks later, when Kitty next called in for a cup of tea and a chat with Catherine, she found her daughter looking pale, but clearly with news for her. "Well Mam, you'll soon be having another grandchild! Baby's due near the end of the year. Jimmy and I are both pleased, though I'll have to give up my job at the 'Bazaar', but since he has a regular job, we should be able to manage."

"As long as you're both happy about the news, then I'm delighted for ye, Catherine," said Kitty, giving her daughter a big smile. "Will I be warning Mary and Molly to stand by for action before the year's end?"

"Not just yet, Mam!" was her daughter's laughing reply. But I *will* be hoping they'll be the ones looking after me and baby when the time comes. Although the government has started training midwives to do the job, I prefer to have people I know and trust around me when I go into labour!"

A later letter from Kitty's mother, now eighty and relatively healthy, contained news of the progress of women's suffrage in Ireland. Clearly, she had been very impressed by Kitty's account of the suffragette's success at the meeting in Manchester. Apparently, an 'Irish Women's Franchise League' had been formed by two women, Margaret Skeffington and Margaret Cousins. Mrs Tooey thought it was about time women got together to protest about the rights of women and hoped they would become more active. "Just like those brave women you wrote to me about Kitty - especially that braw lass, Christabel Pankhurst!'

There was also news from Mam concerning the 'Home Rule' question. It seemed that, here too, Ireland was becoming more demanding. Though two bills concerning Home rule had been defeated by 'that damned House of Lords', it appeared the tide might be turning soon. This was because of increased pressure from Sinn Fein and the recently formed Nationalist Organization. There was now, as Mam wrote, 'At last a chance to take charge of our *own* land and our *own* laws!'

1907 saw the birth of *three* more Grandchildren for Kitty. Catherine and Jimmy had a daughter who was baptised Anne after her aunt. Bob and Ellen had another daughter, Beatrice. Over in Ireland, Denis and Mary had a second son, Pat.

Robert now had three grandchildren in total - all of them girls! And whilst he registered pleasure to the parents of his Granddaughters, his comments to Kitty when alone were, "Christ all bloody mighty, we're bein' overrun by bloody girl babbies! What's up wi' all t'women, I'd like to know? 'Ave they forgotten how to mek lads?"

Ironically for Robert, and also Jimmy Carr, Catherine did give birth to a son the year after Anne was born. However, the second birth had been a very difficult one, with the labour lasting forty-eight hours. The baby was small and sickly so was baptised a week after his birth. Poor little James lasted only two weeks more. Catherine, still weak from giving birth, mourned for her child. Robert was totally devastated to lose a much longed-for son.

Chapter 52

Anne and Catherine (1910)

The year after Catherine and Jimmy lost their son James, another child was born to them, Edna Agnes. Unlike her frail brother, she proved to be a healthy little girl, though having a third baby so soon, left Catherine feeling worn out for some time. Of course, Kitty was always ready to help her daughter with Anne and baby Edna. On one such occasion Catherine asked her mother,"How are things between Anne and Joe? She looked miserable last week."

Kitty frowned as she replied "Well now, I wasn't going to worry ye about it, but I've serious doubts about this Joe. They've been seeing each other on and off for over two years now, and he still only meets her at the tram depot. Then they travel to some place outside Wigan and just go for long walk." She shook her head as she went on, "He's a mean beggar with his brass too! Worse still, he keeps making arrangements then saying he's sorry but he can't make it!" Kitty sighed, "And yet Anne still thinks he'll marry her!" Then seeing Catherine's worried look, she advised, "Now don't *you* be troubling yourself about her! Ye've enough to worry about with your two young lassies!"

About two months after Kitty had voiced her doubts about Joe, an excited Anne announced that Joe had been paid well for some recent gardening, and intended taking her by train to Southport the following Sunday. Kitty merely replied, "I just hope it happens! Are you meeting at the depot?"

Disappointed, Anne retorted, "Mam! Don't spoil it just because *you* don't like him! Anyway, we're meeting on the platform at Wigan Station."

When Sunday arrived, Anne went to the early mass at St Joseph's. On her return home, she put on her best long blue skirt and white blouse. Over it she wore her short new summer-coat with its smart nipped-in waist. Her straw hat was fixed on her auburn hair with a hat-pin and, after a last glance in the mirror, she set off. Once at the station, she went down the steps to find a smiling Joe waiting on the platform.

The journey to Southport took less than an hour, and soon they were holding hands as they walked away from the station. Joe suggested, "First, we can walk up to Lord Street wi' all its famous shops - though o' course they'll all be shut today."

The street from the station was crowded, it seemed everyone was making their way to Lord Street. Anne enjoyed looking in the shops, especially those which displayed beautiful long dresses in their 'floaty' materials which narrowed at the ankle. She also liked the few daring ones which actually ended *above* the ankle.

An electric tram with an open top went past and some of the passengers on top waved to Anne. Cheerily, she waved back to them. It seemed to her that everyone in this famous street, with its lines of trees on both sides and its row of quality canopied shops, was in a happy mood that day. Then she felt Joe tugging her arm as he asked, "Does tha know yon woman across t' road?"

As she turned, Anne was surprised to see a magnificent statue of Queen Victoria near to an imposing building, which Joe later told her was Southport's Art Gallery. "It's the young Victoria!" replied an impressed Anne, "In newspaper pictures she always looked like a little old lady in black."

"Aye, it's one of 'er when she were young," Joe agreed. "I think it were ready a few years after she died. Anyway, changing t' subject Anne, let's find Neville Street now. It'll tek us to a shop that sells t' freshest fish tha's ever tasted!"

Soon they were sitting at a small street-table enjoying a meal of shrimps, cockles and oysters. All was accompanied by buttered bread and mugs of tea. Once they'd finished their *al fresco* meal, Joe announced, "Now Anne love, we'll mek our way to t' fairgound and I'll buy us ice-creams as we go."

So arm in arm again, they made their way up to the promenade and past Southport's long pier. Its theatre advertised performances of the 'Pier Pierrots' about to take place that afternoon and evening. Joe then turned down through King's gardens which gave a view of the tall Water Chute in the fairground. Anne could hear the shrieks and screams of laughter as people in small, rectangular 'boats' whooshed speedily down to the water. "Can we go on that one Joe?" Anne asked.

Emphatically Joe replied, "Certainly lass! And lots of other things too!"

After sampling many of the fair ground's attractions, they walked to the end of the pier. Joe told her it was thought to be the longest in the country at one thousand and sixty yards. He added, "Dad towd me they made it longer some years ago when t' sea started siltin up. It made things better fer steamers to Wales or Th' Isle o' Man."

At six o'clock Anne's wonderful day came to an unexpected end. Joe suddenly led her back to Lord Street and into the doorway of one of the shops. Here he put his arms round her and looked at her with a serious face. Anne sensed something was wrong. He seemed to be finding it difficult to speak. Eventually, he found his voice.

"I love thee Anne Gibbs - always have, ever since I first saw thee peggin' out washin'. But I've not been honest with thee! I were already goin' out wi' a lass! I kept tellin' myself I'd end things with 'er. But I kept puttin' it off. Now she tells me she's expectin' a babby..."His voice trailed off.

A stunned Anne just stared at him. Then with as much strength as she could muster, she hit him across the face, exploding, "You damn coward! You damn liar!" As an afterthought she demanded, "Then what in God's name was today all about?"

A shame-faced Joe replied, "Anne, love, I'll tell thee t' truth. I thowt I'd give us *one* special day together, one to remember. Then we'd travel back together and kiss 'goodnight'" Almost whispering, he said, "Tomorra I'd leave a note for thee."

Joe paused, looking wretched. "But seein' thee so happy and trustin' made me realise t' least I could do was tell thee everythin' *now* - and I'll hand in me notice at work tomorra."

With a cold look at Joe, Anne sneered, "Aye - it's the *very* least you could do! And, by the way, don't give up your job. You'll need money for your wife and child. I won't fret, I'll think of you like I think of any rat! Now give me my ticket!"

Leaving the doorway, Anne was soon making for the station, ticket in hand.

After finishing her house-hold chores, Kitty planned to visit the market for groceries. First she'd ask Catherine if she needed any shopping done as she'd been looking very tired recently. Her daughter was ironing when Kitty arrived, Annie was playing with pegs in a large wicker basket, and baby Edna lay sleeping in her cradle. Catherine managed a smile as her mother entered. Then Kitty saw that one eye was very badly bruised, and it was clear that any facial movement was causing pain.

"Ach, Catherine, love! Who in the Lord's name has done that to ye?"

Putting her iron back on its stand by the fire, Catherine went over to her mother, tears welling up in her eyes. She then told of how Jimmy had started meeting up with some of his army friends in the pub. He'd first met them when he'd been a reserve with the British Army. It seemed he'd been arriving home both late and drunk. When she'd asked him to stop, he'd made it clear that he wasn't prepared to let a woman try to tell *him* what to do. Matters had come to a head the previous night, when he'd staggered home drunk again. Catherine went on to describe the scene, "I was so furious, Mam, and I started yelling at him, then I threw my mug of tea over him. He swore at me and said if I wanted a fight, I'd get one. Next thing he'd punched me in the face." It all brought back bitter memories to Kitty. She asked, "Do ye want me to have a word with him?"

"No, Mam!" came Catherine's quick reply. "He apologised this morning and promised he'd drink less. So, I'm waiting to see if he keeps his word."

"Ach well, let's hope he does" was Kitty's doubtful reply. Then, after a few words with young Anne, and taking note of Catherine's grocery needs, she left.

As Kitty had surmised, it wasn't long before her younger daughter outlined the day she'd spent in Southport with Joe - and its shock ending. Not surprised, she asked, "So, tell me now, how are ye coping with work and having to see him each day?"

"Mam, I really loved that man, and so *wanted* to believe all he said. Now, after it's so blindingly obvious what a bastard he really is, seeing him doesn't affect me. So I'll work there until I find another job that suits me better."

Relieved that Anne *seemed* genuine in her assertion, Kitty replied, "That's grand news! And maybe a new start somewhere is what ye need now."

That same year, Denis's letter brought news that Mary had given birth to a third son, Francis. Kitty, of course, was pleased to hear of another grandson. But she couldn't help having a little smile as she thought of her son over in Ireland with his three sons and her son Bob here with his three daughters.

Chapter 53

Bolton Market

After the end of her 'romance', Anne began to look forward to chatting with Elizabeth whenever she visited Mam on Sundays. Her step-sister was now twenty-nine, and more or less running a newly purchased boarding house in Wallgate with Mary. On one visit, Elizabeth said to Anne, "I think *you* need a bit of a change and some fun after all that's happened recently. So how about having an afternoon out with me next Saturday?" Anne looked interested, but made no immediate reply. So Elizabeth continued, "I've heard Bolton has a very good indoor market, so you could treat yourself to something new. And it only takes about half-an-hour by train."

It didn't take long for Anne to answer. The thought of something new was tempting. "I think it's a great idea. Bolton's market's supposed to be one of the best!"

It was about one o'clock when Anne and Elizabeth walked into Bolton Market Hall the following Saturday afternoon. It was very busy. Shoppers were weaving expertly in and out of the various aisles like ants moving round highly-organized colonies. On looking up they saw a balcony running all round the building. Elizabeth had heard that when the market first opened sixty-odd years earlier, the balcony had been used to sell pets of a rather exotic nature, including snakes and monkeys. Both were amazed at the variety of stalls selling almost anything you could wish for. These included: curtains, toys, hats, household equipment, millinery, hosiery crockery, and jewellery. The aromas too were varied. The syrupy smell of homemade treacle toffee contrasted with the savoury smell of black peas simmering in large containers. But it was the millinery stalls which most attracted Anne. She had longed for one of the large and lavishly decorated hats of the Edwardian era, but the high prices in Wigan's 'class' shops had been an obstacle. Here the prices were considerably cheaper.

And so she led Elizabeth in and out of aisles. Hats were tried on and put down whilst stallholders patiently held up mirrors, exclaiming, "Just made for you."

At last, after an hour's non-stop perambulation, Anne decided on a large mid-blue hat with a wide brim and black feathers which cascaded down one side.

An exhausted Elizabeth, looking ready to drop, exclaimed, "In the time we've been traipsing round this market, we could have walked to Wigan and back!"

Anne, now resplendent in her new hat, looked disappointed at her friend's comment. Noting Anne's face, Elizabeth added, "But I must say you look a real 'smasher'. So let's go over to the little tea-shop, next to that herbal stall. Then you can impress these lot from Bolton!"

Anne, now feeling like 'the cat that got the cream', readily agreed.

Soon they were seated at a small table now holding a pot of tea for two and potted-beef sandwiches. As they sipped their welcome tea, they watched the crowd of people round the herbal stall. Two men who had been buying large yellow pills there, entered the tea-shop area and sat down at a nearby table.

One was quite slim and tall with greying hair. The second, smaller and stockier, seemed the younger of the two, They ordered large mugs of tea, the younger one calling loudly to the departing waitress, "Mek mine strong!" Meanwhile, the tall one was looking at his jar of pills dubiously, and enquired of his companion, "Are ye sure these sulphur tablets are safe, 'Arry? They look bloody big to me."

Harry was emphatic in his reassurance. "Tek no notice o' t' size! Just tek three every day for three weeks. Nowt like 'em for cleansin' t' stomach out." Then giving a chuckle, he added a proviso, "But mek sure tha's alone when tha teks 'em! Or, tha'll clear t' pub out before tha can say 'Jack Robinson'!"

At that point, the two men became aware of the two women near them, and wondered if they had heard Harry. So, trying to look casual, they hastily began stirring their mugs of tea. After a few minutes, Harry looked over at the two women, and in his 'best' voice enquired, "Excuse me ladies, does tha come from round 'ere? Only I've not sin thee 'ere afore."

The question led to a conversation amongst the four in which the two 'Wiganers' learned that their new acquaintances were Harry Holt and John Singleton, both from Bolton. Harry worked in one of the mills as a cotton-loom overseer, and John, together with his wife, managed 'The Grey Man', a public house in Great Moore Street. With a wink, John said Harry boosted the pub's takings with his visits. In turn, Anne and Elizabeth introduced themselves and gave some information regarding where they came from, and the jobs they did. On learning of the variety of general work which Anne undertook, John observed, "You're exactly the type of young woman we could do with at the pub. I don't suppose you'd consider changing jobs? We need someone as soon as possible. How settled are you there in Wigan?"

The question took Anne by surprise. A variety of thoughts flashed through her mind and she reasoned with herself, 'I'm not settled in my present position and certainly want a change. But Bolton? I know nothing about the place except this market. Do I want to work in a pub? Well it would give me the opportunity to meet more people. Also, Wigan isn't so far away - not like Aunt Sarah in New Zealand!' Her eventual reply was cautious, "Well, I have been thinking of a change, but moving to another town is a big step." She paused thoughtfully, then asked, "Would it be possible to see 'The Grey Man' today, and to meet your wife? Also could I see a bit more of the town?"

The outcome was that, before the return trip to Wigan, Anne had accepted the job offered. She was to start the following month after serving a few weeks' notice.

As the two friends boarded the train in Bolton, Harry and John waved them off. Harry remarked, "I were quite teken wi' Anne. But wot the hell 'ad she got on 'er 'ead?"

When Kitty was told Anne's news, her first thought was that Bolton was some distance away. Yet her daughter seemed so happy about it that she gave it her blessing Kitty's eldest daughter had only sad news for her mother. At the end of 1910, Catherine gave birth prematurely to a second son. He was baptised, Albert and lived only three weeks.

Chapter 54

Events up to 1914

By the beginning of 1911 Anne was working at 'The Grey Man' in Bolton. The Singletons were treating her well and had given her a bedroom to herself upstairs. It was small but very comfortable. Additionally, all her meals were provided

It was soon apparent that Harry Holt was indeed a very regular customer at 'The Grey Man' and Anne was pleased to have someone she knew during her early days at the pub. Most of the regulars, seeing a new face clearing glasses or wiping down tables, looked at her with some curiosity. Some asked where she was from, and having replied 'Wigan' she was regarded as an outsider, but nobody was unfriendly.

Kitty was relieved that her younger daughter had settled quite well in Bolton.

However, her other two children were giving her cause for worry. Firstly, there was Bob, who had never said much about his home-life. But for a while now his wife, Ellen, had looked rather strained whenever Kitty called to see her and her Granddaughters. Recently, Ellen had told her that Bob's attitude towards her had changed soon after the birth of Beatrice. He'd become morose and had lost the sense of humour he used to have. It seemed that a friend of his at the local pub had been celebrating the birth of a second son. On his return, Bob was in a bad mood, "I ask thee! Two lads! And what's tha given me? Three bloody girls! When Dad retires and I tek over, there'll be no son to work wi' *me*!"

Subsequently, many rows took place after Bob's pub outings, and went from bad to worse. It culminated with Ellen refusing to sleep with Bob. She told Kitty, "It's now got to a state where we just don't speak at all!"

The situation put Kitty in an invidious position. So she finally decided that all she could do was to offer Ellen sympathy and help her with her daughters.

Yet it was Catherine who gave her the most worry. Not only did she recall her daughter's bruised face some while ago, but since her marriage, she had been pregnant each year. Also, the loss of each of two sons soon after their births had left Catherine traumatized on each occasion. Moreover, Kitty wasn't at all convinced that Jimmy's late-night drinking bouts had ceased.

In a recent letter from Denis, Kitty learned that Mary had given birth to a fourth son who was to take his father's name, Denis. Though the couple had hoped for a daughter, they were both happy to have four healthy children. Kitty was grateful that they, at least, seemed content in their marriage and the children 'given' to them.

By Spring that year, Anne was nicely settled in her work at 'The Grey Man'. When she returned home for visits, she enjoyed telling her mother, and often Elizabeth too, tales of life in Bolton. Usually, Harry Holt featured in her accounts. He apparently contrived to have little chats with her before the pub became too busy. Recently, he'd asked if she was from a big family, and she'd replied, "Not really, there are just four of us." Harry's response was, "Is that all?" So thinking she'd tell him something impressive, she'd added, "But Grandma had *ten* children."

Still unimpressed Harry retorted,"Only ten childer? I'm one o' thirteen - not countin' two what died as young babbies!"

The conversation then turned to marriage. After discovering Anne wasn't married, Harry informed her that he'd no interest in gettin' wed. Anne then learned he'd lived with his Dad and younger sister, Florrie, since his mother's death sixteen years earlier. He explained, "Florrie cooks fer us, while me and Dad go out to work in t' mill. Mind you, Florrie's gettin' wed next month, so me an' Dad'll 'ave to start cookin' fer oursels."

In a later visit from Anne, Kitty discovered that her daughter was also enjoying some lively nights when a pianist visited the 'Grey Man' to play songs from the Music Halls. Anne described how, as the night wore on, the group of men singing along to the piano, would be silenced by John, the landlord, saying, "That's enough, lads. Time for 'Arry to give us a turn." Anne laughed as she told how funny it was to see how Harry *always* refused at first. But then would get to his feet, and begin singing - minus piano accompaniment. She said one of his songs began, "Oh it's Angelina, anybody seen her throw her legs about? Skirts so short, the very best sort, the gallery boys did shout …"

With a smile Kitty chipped in with, "Aye certainly not the kind of song we Irish colleens were used to, Anne!"

"Well, he always gets whistles and calls for 'More!'" was Anne's quick reply.

After Anne's departure, Kitty observed to Elizabeth, "I'm glad she's settled well in Bolton. And it seems she's taken quite a liking to that Harry Holt."

A few months later that same year, Kitty was dismayed to find Catherine's face was badly bruised - though this time it looked much worse than on the first occasion. Also, she was now quite definite about going to court to get a separation order. Bitterly she said, "Mam, I've had all I can take! A child every year, and two of them dying as babies!" Tears now poured freely down Catherine's swollen cheeks. "I'm putting up with it no more."

"And I'll be at your side, and I'll speak for ye in court." was Kitty's reply.

When Robert was told the news later that night, his first reaction was to go round and 'Give that bugger what he deserves'. Inwardly, Kitty thought, "Ach, ye've a short memory, Robert!" Aloud, she suggested their daughter and Grandchildren moved in with them. They had space as only Billy lived with them now.

The court case took place a few months later. James pleaded 'Not Guilty', saying he'd been angry because his wife had been out all one night, returning only the following morning. Catherine told the court, she'd been at her wit's end and had gone to talk to her sister, Anne in Bolton. Then she'd spent the night there.

Finally, the court granted a separation order, and Jimmy was ordered to pay his wife ten shillings each week. Catherine, Annie and Edna stayed with Kitty and Robert.

About two months later, Jimmy saw Kitty in the town and told her he was sorry about everything. He said he loved Catherine and his children and wondered if he might be allowed to see Anne and Edna occasionally. Kitty found it hard to have any sympathy for Jimmy. He'd been a bastard towards Catherine, but she had to admit that he'd never laid a hand on his daughters. Eventually, both Catherine and Robert agreed to Jimmy seeing his daughters from time to time.

The end of 1912 and the year 1913 brought many changes in political events and also a change in family relationships.

It had been a great relief to Kitty when Bob and Ellen had become reconciled. Their three daughters, aged nine, seven and five years, seemed much happier now that the constant angry remarks between their mother and father had ceased.

Meanwhile, the suffrage movement had gained considerable momentum. Having made no progress in their aims, the women had become more militant and violent. The government retaliated by having many such women imprisoned. Here many of them went on 'hunger-strike' in protest. These women were brutally force-fed by means of long rubber-tubing being pushed down their throats.

Kitty, knowing of her mother's support for women's suffrage, wrote to tell her of all the latest developments in Westminster. In return Mam, who was now no longer able to see well enough to write, asked Denis to send Kitty the recent suffrage news. Accordingly, he described how, that year, Meg Connery, a leading member of the Irish Women's Franchise League, had broken into a press conference on 'Home Rule' held on the steps of Iveagh House in Dublin. She'd pushed through to Edward Carson and the Westminster spokesman, Andrew Bonar Law, and given leaflets to the crowd there. Denis concluded the account with his Grandma's actual words on the subject. "Aye, a fine one in the eye for Carson and Law. And grand publicity for women!"

However, the final part of Denis' letter, added as a post script, made Kitty both worried and sad. He wrote that her mother was now bed-bound and unable to walk unaided. She didn't seem to be in pain, but repeatedly talked about being ready to meet her final peace. Despite her mother, now aged eighty-five, having lived beyond her 'allotted' three score years and ten, Kitty couldn't imagine life without her Mam.

It was only two months later that Denis' letter informed Kitty of her mother's death. Mercifully she had gone peacefully in her sleep. Mary Anne had travelled from Scotland to be near her mother that very day. This made Kitty feel heartbroken to think that circumstances had prevented her being with Mam along with her sister.

A second letter from Denis arrived soon after the first. He wrote that her mother's Wake had been a lively affair with music, singing and dancing. The house had been filled with neighbours and as many of her children as were able to make the journey. Kitty was glad that her mother's Wake had been such a happy occasion - but the news also renewed her sadness at not being there herself. The Sunday after her mother's death, Kitty and her four children attended early Mass where they said prayers for a Mother and a Grandma. Each one lit a candle in her memory.

Near the end of the year, Denis' letter contained news of his and Mary's first daughter - a sister for their four sons. Both were delighted to have a daughter at last, and, not unexpectedly, she was baptised, Mary. There was even more good news from Denis. He and Mary had been living in his father's old thatched cottage and now, after many years of fighting for the compulsory sale of land by landlords, this had actually started in Riverstown. In a few months they would be able to rent one of the newly-built council houses. Kitty could sense the excitement in his letter as she read, "...and it will have a detached, *slate* roof. What about that, Mam!"

There was also news of another birth in the family, this time the parents were Bob and Ellen. It seemed their reconciliation had produced another child - a fourth girl! On first hearing the news, Kitty was apprehensive. However, when Bob called round, his words reassured her, "Mam, I'm happy about little babby, Elsie!"

On New Year's eve, the Gibbs' household welcomed neighbours and all members of the family to share food and drink with them. It made Kitty so happy to have her children together. There was Bob and his family,

Catherine and her girls, and also her two unmarried children, Anne and Billy. At midnight, everyone welcomed in 1914 with hugs and handshakes, and the usual exchanges of, 'Happy New Year'.

Nobody seemed aware that 1914 would bring dramatic and horrifying changes. This was despite the fact that some of the adults had heard of the growing tension amongst the great imperial powers.

Russia, Germany and France had one common aim. All were eager for expansion.

Chapter 55

Anne and Harry

Anne had to work in the evening of New Year's day, so she left her home at midday to catch the train to Bolton. It had been a great evening and she'd enjoyed being with her family and seeing her five young nieces. But she greatly regretted having had a bit too much to drink. Since waking, she'd had a splitting headache.

Once on board the train, her headache became even more severe. Also the queasy feeling she'd been experiencing recently had returned. On arrival at Trinity Street Station she hurriedly made her way to 'The Grey Man', anxious to rest before starting work - and also before seeing Harry again.

By six o'clock Anne was back at work, the headache had gone. Yet she hadn't been able to face the meal Mrs. Singleton had provided for her. It wasn't long before Harry entered the pub, though tonight he was with a tall, thin man with a moustache. She'd really hoped to have a quiet word with Harry on his own.

Harry gave her one of his cheeky grins as soon as he saw her. Then he and the tall stranger made a point of passing close to her as they made their way to the bar. Already, several men were gathered there, some waiting to be served, some already drinking and discussing events of New Year's Eve.

As they neared, both men wished her, 'Happy New Year' and Anne returned their greeting. Needing to move on to another table, Anne whispered urgently to Harry,

"Can we meet after I finish work? I'd like to speak to you - but without your friend." Pleasantly surprised by her request, Harry replied, "Course we can. I can easily get rid of 'im. He's me brother-in-law, Dick Holden, wed to our Alice. I only browt 'im to give thee a 'look over'. Tha must know I've teken a real likin' to thee."

Not keen on the idea of being 'looked over', but anxious to get on with her job, Anne simply replied, "Right then, I'll expect you about quarter past twelve, just round the corner from the pub." Then she swiftly moved on to the next table. Admiringly Harry watched her go, asking, "Well, Dick, what does tha think?"

Dick hesitated before answering, "Aye, she seems a nice enough lass." Inwardly, he wasn't so sure that Anne was as keen on Harry as Harry was on her.

As the evening wore on there was the usual singing by the boozy customers. This time, Harry wasn't called on to sing. Instead, one of the 'regulars' called, "Come on 'Arry. Tell us that tale about what thee and Dick got up to last neet."

So amid more calls of, "Come on, 'Arry! Let's be knowin' what tha did!", Harry began the account of his latest escapade. He told of how he and Dick had decided to spend the early part of New Year's Eve at Bolton's annual fair. They were more interested in the side-shows, piping hot 'jacket' potatoes, and black peas rather than all the rides. He'd started to tell of the boxer in one of the shows who was challenging men to last three rounds with him for a shilling, when Dick called, "For Christ's sake, 'Arry, get to t' part where we went into t' waxworks." Harry glared, but did as 'requested'. "Anyroad, we sees they've getten a new side-show o' waxworks in a big long tent. We goes in and sees lots o' famous folk like Victoria an' Albert, King George wi' Queen Mary, an' so on. But when we comes to t' top end, we sees ordinary folk like miners, sweeps, tradesmen and the like. Then we notices a man and a woman come in. After payin', this man tells 'er to go round by 'erself as he can't stand bloody wax dolls. Me an' Dick keeps quiet, watchin' as she walks along t' row. Then seein' as nobody's watchin' us, I nods to Dick, and we both stands in t' row o' traders. We keeps still wi' out movin', just lookin' straight in front of us."

At this point, Harry illustrated his words by standing absolutely still, head up, and arms hanging motionless by his side. Then he continued, "As she reaches me, she stares at me. Suddenly, I winks at 'er. Well, she just stands there, screamin' like a bloody banshee. And when Dick raises his cap to 'er - well, that was it! She'd seen enough! And she's off, yellin', "They're alive, Jim! They're bloody alive!"

"The fella at t' other end, rushes over, gets 'old of 'er arm, and drags 'er out!"

There was loud laughter from the audience, and also Anne. She thought to herself, 'I can't help liking him. Though I wonder what he'll say about my news?'

Whilst carrying on with her job, Anne recalled when it had all happened.

It had been an evening at the beginning of November the previous year. Harry had asked if she'd like to go to his home that night after work. He'd said he'd cook a special meal for her. Previously, she and Harry had only had the occasional walk round Bolton on Saturday afternoons, but though surprised, she accepted his offer.

And she had to admit she'd enjoyed the evening. The meal of roast beef and vegetables followed by rice-pudding and glasses of stout had been quite a treat. And that, together with the warmth of the fire, had given her a feeling of contentment. So when Harry later indicated he'd like to take things further, she was happy to end the night in a way which brought both of them pleasure. She'd never *honestly* considered that their 'one night' of intimacy might have consequences!

Harry was already waiting when Anne arrived. He gave her a warm smile saying,"Tha looks reet bonny Annie! And our Dick thinks so too!" Brushing aside his greeting, Anne told Harry her news. She concluded with, "Now before you say anything, just listen to me. I'm not asking for marriage or anything. I've told you this because soon it'll be apparent that I'm pregnant, and I'll probably have to stop work later on. It's then I'll be needing some money to tide me over until I'm working again." Anne paused, "So I'm wondering if you could lend…" She got no further, as Harry quickly said, "No Annie. I won't lend thee money. I'd be only too 'appy to marry thee. I may not be much of a 'catch', but I *can* offer thee an t' babby a home as well as love."

Surprised by Harry's immediate and unexpected offer of marriage, Anne thanked him, saying she needed time to think about it. But she had a twinkle in her eye as she added, "Whatever my decision is, I'll thank ye to stop calling me 'Annie'!

Seeing the twinkle, Harry's hopeful reply was, "Reet Anne! I'll try to think on.

Naturally, Kitty was the next person to be told Anne's news. There were no pointless recriminations from her - what was done, was done. Her daughter had admitted she enjoyed Harry's company but did *not* love him. Now Anne wanted her opinion about marrying him. Kitty stared thoughtfully into the fire before answering.

"On the plus side, ye like Harry, and he seems quite pleased about the prospect of being a Dad. He already has a house, and he's quite a bit older which may mean his 'wild' days are behind him". Kitty gazed into the fire again. Then she continued,"But on the other hand, ye don't love him. Ye know, I'm not sure that 'love' is any guarantee of a happy marriage! However, ye like Harry and say he's a very popular man. But remember *where* it is he's so popular. In a pub whilst drinking!"

Kitty paused, letting everything sink in. Anne pondered her mother's words.

Eventually she spoke, "Thanks Mam! That's helped. Now let's have a cup of tea."

After Anne's departure, Kitty then began thinking about her elder daughter, Catherine. Two years had passed since the separation from Jimmy Carr, and Kitty had been happy to observe Catherine gradually returning to her cheerful and confident former self. However, over the past year Catherine had started going out some nights to see a 'friend' she'd made when working at the 'Penny Bazaar'. Of course Kitty had been delighted at first, but recently the 'nights out' frequently meant Catherine returning home in the early hours of the morning. Admittedly, her daughter was up early to tend to Annie and Edna, and she was certainly a great help in the house. But Bob's disclosure about his sister had her worried.

Apparently, he'd seen her several times with a man called Danny. He was reputed to 'have a bob or two' - and also a wife living somewhere down south. It seemed he was a comedian who often spent a few weeks travelling round various theatres in the Lancashire. On such occasions, he would make his 'base' in Wigan.

To Kitty, this information spelled potential heartache as well as big trouble for her daughter - especially if Jimmy got to hear of it. Cautiously, she'd approached Catherine regarding Danny, mentioning she believed he had a wife. There had been a smile and a shake of the head as her daughter responded, "Oh Mam,! I *know* he has a wife. But she lives miles away. He's a kind and generous man who treats me well. Don't I deserve a bit of happiness? And besides that, he always returns home to his wife. So I'm no threat to his marriage."

With a sigh Kitty said, "For what it's worth, I think you're playing with fire."

The youngest member of the family, Billy, had never been a cause for concern for Kitty. He'd always seemed quite content working alongside his Dad and brother, and going out for the occasional drink. Often, he'd stated that going out with girls wasn't for him, though he was a tall, well-built and good looking young man. Then 'out of the blue', he'd casually mentioned that one of the girls from Victoria Mill had started chatting with him on her way to and from work.

"Aye, she's a nice lass, her parents are from Wales," Billy informed them, "she's called Jane Thomas and I'm thinkin' of takin' her out this week-end."

Billy's news was a surprise to both parents. Kitty was quite pleased that he'd met a girl he liked. Bob merely remarked, "Well lad, your Mam's from Irish and Scottish parents, so we might as well mek up the set with someone from Wales!"

In fact, Billy had an even bigger surprise for his whole family. Only three months after mentioning Jane Thomas, he announced that the two were to be married the following week in St.Thomas' Church. Afterwards, they'd be living with Jane's parents in Wigan for a while.

Of course, everyone was amazed at the suddenness of the proposed marriage, but even more by the choice of church. In disbelief Kitty asked her son, "Why on God's earth are you marrying in an Anglican church?"

Defiantly, her son replied, "That's nobody's business but ours. At least I've told thee about t' weddin' Mam. All we want now is tha blessin'."

With many misgivings, Kitty, Robert, Bob, Catherine and Anne went to watch Billy and Jane enter St Thomas' Church on their wedding day.

They waited outside until the pair came out as a married couple. There followed embraces and wishes for the couple's future happiness.

Certainly not the wedding Kitty had wanted for her son. But *maybe* the marriage would work out well.

Chapter 56

1914

As June arrived, so did another grandchild for Kitty. Jane gave birth to a baby boy at the end of the month and named him William after his father. Since the couple were still living with Jane's parents, Kitty and Robert were not directly involved in the birth, though they were invited to his christening at St Thomas' Church. He was a contented baby and slept throughout the ceremony.

However, an event was shortly to take place which would affect many lives in European countries - as well as those in the Gibbs' family.

For some years, governments had been aware of underlying tensions amongst the great imperial powers. Whilst Turkey and Austria-Hungary were in decline, others were in ascendancy, namely Russia, France and, more recently, Germany. In fact, outside Europe, Germany's expansion in Africa was rivalling the imperial power of Britain. Yet despite these tensions it was generally considered that none of these powers wanted war. So nobody would have believed that, on June 28th, the shooting of Franz Ferdinand, Emperor of Austria-Hungary, would lead to Britain being at war by August 4th, 1914.([1])

By that date, Anne and Harry had a son, named Harry after his father. Coincidentally he'd been born on the day of the assassination. The couple didn't marry before young Harry's birth since the priest in Wigan was adamant that Anne's chosen husband must adopt the catholic faith before any church marriage. Typically, Harry had vehemently declared that such an event would be, "O'er my dead body!"

Anne was hoping that, if they waited a little while, either the priest or Harry would relent. In the meantime, she called herself Mrs Holt. However, once Britain was at war, there was the danger that Harry might be called on to enlist at any time, so she decided it would be best to postpone any ideas of marriage until the war ended. Like most people, she was sure the end would come before Christmas that same year.

Naturally, Kitty had hoped her daughter would be married before the arrival of young Harry, but she'd lived in Ireland long enough to know how religion could tear families apart. So she accepted Anne's philosophical view of the situation.

In any case, there were other, more important, worries for Kitty. Jimmy Carr, having signed on for nine years as a reserve in the British Army in 1905, had already been given a posting in France. He'd called round to see his daughters and Catherine before leaving in September, saying he'd been sent out for twelve months' active service. After embracing his daughters, he'd looked up at Catherine, saying quietly, "And when this bloody war's o'er, I hope you and me can try to mek a new start together." Without waiting for a reply, Jimmy had turned, and stepped out purposefully down the road. Two tearful young girls and a sad-faced, thoughtful woman gazed after him.

By October, there'd been news of men in the British Expeditionary Force being slaughtered by the Germans in Ypres. They'd been making their way through Belgium to France. The thought of her sons, Bob and Billy, aged thirty and twenty- two, being called to fight in deep and muddy rat-infested trenches filled Kitty with dread. And, of course, though her eldest son, Denis, was now aged thirty-six, there was still the chance that he might be called to fight. She had heard that both Irish Nationalists and Ulster Unionists were supporting the war.

Although the British Cabinet was not in favour of conscription, voluntary recruitment was accelerated by the many posters which appeared everywhere with their very persuasive exhortations. One showed a long 'crocodile' of uniformed soldiers marching at the front. Following the soldiers marched men of all ages and occupations, clearly about to enlist to fight in the war. The caption read:

STEP INTO YOUR PLACE.

Another poster showed two women and a child, looking out of a window and watching men in uniform marching along the road. A caption in large lettering read,

WOMEN OF BRITAIN SAY - "GO!"

The result of such posters was a wave of patriotic enthusiasm and within the first month, five hundred thousand men had volunteered to serve their King and Country.

Soon after the war's outbreak, Kitty had received a letter from Denis asking how she and her family were coping. He confirmed that John Redmond, an Irish Nationalist parliamentarian, had agreed to Nationalist controlled Irish volunteers being used to help defend Ireland against enemy action. In return Redmond wanted a positive stand by the British government in support of claims for Home Rule. Denis had also written he'd been glad when the British Prime Minister, Asquith, had put the Irish Home Rule Bill on the statute book. However, Asquith had made it clear that no further action on the bill would be taken until the end of the war. Though Denis thought the war would soon be over, he wrote that many people were not happy about the delay.

Of course, Kitty was relieved that her first-born had made no mention of enlisting to fight in the war. Also, since Denis was now thirty-six, she felt he would not be conscripted to fight. She hoped the same would apply to Harry, Anne's 'husband' who was only two years younger than Denis.

On the whole, Kitty kept cheerful. She repeatedly told herself that the war would be over quite quickly - so all her worries were pointless.

Footnote[1]

A brief outline of the events which so suddenly led to the start of the 'World War'.

1. June 28th. Franz Ferdinand, Emperor of Austria-Hungary, was shot in Sarajevo by Gavrillo Princep,
2. July 28th. Austria-Hungary declared war on Serbia encouraged by Germany. (Kaiser, Wilhelm ll was Grandson of Victoria).
3. July 30th. Russia, with the Tsar's approval, began mobilisation against Austria-Hungary. They felt they should support Serbia.

3b. Germany ordered Russia to stop mobilisation. They also ordered France to maintain neutrality in case of war in the East.

3c. Russia and France refused to obey these orders.

4. August 1st. Germany joined Austria-Hungary and declared war on Russia.

5a. August 2nd. Germany demanded that Belgium should allow German troops to cross Belgium into France.

5b. August 3rd. Germany declared war on France.

6. Belgium refused Germany's demand and asked for Britain's support.

7. August 4th. Britain declared war on Germany since we had made a treaty with Belgium in 1839 to preserve their neutrality. (Britain's King, George V, was also a grandson of Victoria.)

Chapter 57

War Years (1915)

Christmas 1914 had come and gone without the hoped for end of war. In fact it had been a war of deadlock, battering, suffering and loss of life on all sides. In the early months, the generals had made it clear that new recruits should be taught to believe bayonets were the best and most decisive weapons in warfare. It wasn't until 1915 before it was questioned by people such as Lloyd George, minister of munitions, and Winston Churchill, first lord of the Admiralty. This resulted in the use of machine guns and large guns. Yet it was clearly a war destined to go on for some time.

Kitty was busy baking bread, some of which she would take round to Bob's wife, Ellen, to give to her daughters. As she kneaded the dough, she felt relieved that the war had not yet seriously affected the importation of supplies of food stuffs, particularly wheat. Her thoughts then went on to her eldest daughter.

Now that Catherine's estranged husband was away fighting in France, she was receiving only fourteen shillings each week from the army. So it was a blessing that she and her girls were living with her. Yet Kitty was *not* happy about her daughter's continued relationship with the mysterious Danny, the comedian.

"For sure, that Danny's more of a threat to Catherine and her family than the bloody Germans!" she thought as she gave the dough an angry and unnecessary thump. There was a tap at the open kitchen door and there stood her friend, Margaret.

Her greeting was, "Good morning to ye Kitty! But what's the cross face about?"

Wiping the flour from her hands, but disregarding the question, Kitty returned the smile, saying, "Ach, come in, Margaret! 'Tis good to see ye! It was Christmas when we last met, so sit down, and I'll make us a cup of tea." Then she added, But don't mention that bloody war!"

Making her way to her 'usual' chair, Margaret replied, "Well Kitty, I'm afraid it's the war I've come to talk about! Our branch of suffragettes has formed a working group to support our men fighting at the front. Kitty's response was immediate, "Do ye mean to say the suffragettes are supporting this bloody war?"

"Not at all, Kitty! But since war became inevitable, we *are* supporting the men fighting on our behalf. As ye know, unmarried women are taking on jobs usually done by men, such as working on the land or in ammunition factories or delivering post. A great way of proving women can do men's work. Also, we married women will be helping by knitting socks, scarves and suchlike. Of course, the wool will be provided for them - we know that many women are struggling financially. Anyway, I'm co-ordinating it all." Margaret paused pointedly. Kitty thought a while, then said,

"Now ye've put it like that, I understand. Aye, if we show men we're able to do our bit in the war, it should benefit the suffragettes. Ye can include me and Catherine in the knitting group."

A week later, a letter from Anne in Bolton caused Kitty some concern. Although Anne had regularly travelled from Bolton to see her mother and family in her early days, such journeys had become more difficult after the birth of young Harry in June. So letters kept mother and daughter in regular contact.

Basically, her daughter was just wanting some sympathy on discovering she was pregnant with her second child, due in early September, only thirteen months after young Harry's birth. Additionally, Anne complained that though Harry was always kind to her in his own way, he'd lived so long with his Dad and sister that he'd become very 'set' in what he ate. He was used to asking for meals which suited *his* taste and also being cooked in just the way that *he* wanted it.

Despite understanding how depressed her daughter must be feeling at the present time, Kitty had a chuckle to herself as she recalled Anne's first attempt to make one of Harry's favourite meals. It had occurred when

Anne left work, six months pregnant with her first baby, and had recently moved in to live with Harry. She had explained to Kitty what happened one morning.

"Well Mam, just as Harry was about to set off for the mill, he told me he'd left a rabbit in the larder so I could make rabbit stew for our tea. I wasn't too worried about that as I thought it would have been skinned. But what a shock I had when I got it out of the larder and found it had all its fur on. Head and everything!" Anne sniffed and continued, "Anyway, I looked at this dead rabbit with its dull, dead eyes. Then I looked at its two big teeth wondering where to start. Then I decided I'd better get rid of the teeth. So I found Harry's pliers and I pulled the beggars out." Amused by this pointless action, Kitty asked Anne what she did next.

"Nothing!" was Anne's reply. I just put it back in the larder, went to the butcher's, bought some neck of mutton, and made him an Irish Stew."

Luckily Harry had seen the funny side of it all - but he soon made sure that Anne learned how to skin a rabbit properly.

The next months of 1915 passed without the war ministry calling for compulsory enlistment, meaning Kitty's three sons were still at home with their families. However, there had been news that Jimmy, who'd been in France since the start of the war, had received a bullet wound in his right thigh in May. After convalescing in Wales at Llandrindod Wells, he was sent home to Wigan. Though having some sympathy regarding his wound, Kitty was concerned when he called at the house, begging to see his children and also his wife. Catherine let him take the children out for the afternoon. But she rejected his idea of living again with him and their children as a family. There was no indication of how long his leave would last, so Kitty's main fear was that 'Damned Danny' might appear on the scene again.

Luckily for Anne, Harry, had not been conscripted when she gave birth to their second child, also named Anne. Luckily the birth had gone fairly well since Kitty had been there to help her whilst Harry had looked after their young son. Kitty had been pleased to see how caring and helpful Harry was towards Anne and the new baby - and had even thanked her for her help. It was an unexpected gesture since, on previous meetings, he'd made it obvious he'd no love for Catholics. But her great disappointment, and Anne's too, was that neither of the children had been baptised in the Catholic Church. The priest's many calls to remind Anne of her duty were futile.

Two weeks after baby Anne's birth, Kitty had taken the train to Bolton carrying a beautifully knitted shawl for her granddaughter. Being a Saturday afternoon, Harry was at home. His greeting was polite but cool. Soon after Kitty's arrival, there was a knock on the door so Harry went to open it. There stood Father Michael - clearly taken aback at seeing Anne's 'husband' at home. Harry spoke first, "Oh it's thee, is it? I hear tha's bin threatenin' my Missus wi' 'ell and damnation. Well listen to me. If tha ever comes anywhere near this 'ouse again, I'll punce thee all t' way from 'ere to bloody Timbuktu!"

Harry then stepped menacingly forward, adding, "So Bugger off!"

Hastily, the priest complied with the order.

The latter part of 1915 also saw an increase in the new weapons of war which Germany had begun to use. U-boats were now frequently blocking our merchant ships with their food supplies. Also, Zeppelins or airships had started to bomb England, though these first ones were big and clumsy and made easy targets for our fighter planes. The use of poison gas was to have long-lasting effects on many allied soldiers in the form of blindness and lung diseases. Gas masks were quickly supplied though they were cumbersome to wear and to carry around.

To boost public morale, our newspapers wrote about engineers working on a weapon which was described as 'a large armoured tractor' (later to be known as a 'tank'). Though it was acknowledged as being heavy and slow-moving, it was also claimed to be impervious to machine gun-fire.

So the year ended with the same hopes. Namely that the following year would mark the end of the war.

Chapter 58

A Tragic Fall (1916)

There were still no signs of the war's end. In fact February of that year saw the mandatory blacking-out or dimming of all bright lights both indoors and out. Up until then, the dimming of exterior lights and street lamps had been mainly optional, usually done by partially painting them in black. In London however, blacking-out had been much stricter for some time.

For the Gibbs' family, a further blow came a few weeks later when Bob was called-up to join the machine gun corps. Fairly soon he was in France. Of course, both Kitty and Ellen were devastated at the thought of Bob being in the front line of the fighting. There was also the additional worry of a reduced income for both families, Ellen was now receiving only fifteen shillings each week to pay for rent and food. The soldiers received a shilling each day, unless, like Bob, they were married. In this case, pay was cut to sixpence, their contribution to the money paid to their wives.

Similarly, Kitty was having to manage on significantly less money from Robert who was now minus his best worker, and so not able to take on as much business as usual. Luckily, Robert still had his younger son, Billy to work alongside him. The latter had been exempted from service.

Jane, Billy's wife, had never hidden her extreme dislike of anything connected with Catholicism. But despite this, Kitty had to admire her daughter-in-law for the way she was coping during the war. Jane, aware of how food prices were rising almost monthly, soon realised that as the war continued, fresh food including wheat was likely to become even scarcer. This was especially likely since German U-Boats were attacking American merchant ships. Then Jane had an idea. As she was able to afford to buy more flour than most families, she thought she could make a reasonable profit by starting a small bread business. After all, it should be easy to convert a room into a small shop in their terraced house. Luckily, two-year old Billy was a very good baby.

By April that year, with food prices ever higher, many families relied on bread to help feed their children. So Jane's business was doing well. She rose early to do all the baking and was able to sell it at a slightly lower price than the larger bakery shops. "Well Jane," said Kitty, putting the loaf she'd just bought into her bag, "You and I may not always see 'eye to eye', but ye've a canny eye for business!"

Near the end of April, the papers were full of worrying news about Ireland. It seemed there had been an uprising in Dublin, caused by a small group who were fighting for a free and independent Ireland. They called themselves, 'Irish Volunteers'. It was reported that these Irish rebels, totally ignoring the world war, had seized Dublin's General Post Office. Though taken by surprise, Irish soldiers, armed police, and some British soldiers had managed to get to the scene. Heavy shelling had followed in which the Post Office was set ablaze, and the outnumbered rebels fled. But there were many deaths and injuries on both sides. This became known as 'The Easter Rising' since it took place on Easter Monday. ([1])

"Dear God!" Kitty exploded to Catherine on hearing the news, "Why on earth did those eejits have to make their demands *now* - in the middle of a world war?"

Of course, Kitty lost no time in asking her son, Denis for his view of the event. In reply, he wrote she was correct in thinking it had been pointless, and hadn't helped the fight for independence. However, he stressed it had involved only a small 'splinter' of an anti-war group. Denis further wrote that his main worry was Prime Minister, Asquith. He guessed he would soon send in more British soldiers to capture and 'deal' with the rebels.

There was no surprise about Harry Holt's reaction to the news when Kitty next visited her daughter in Bolton. Anne was nursing baby Anne, whilst blonde-haired young Harry played with his mother's washing-pegs. Mother and daughter were chatting about the children when Harry burst in from the back-kitchen, glared accusingly at Kitty, and said, "A fine lot of 'elp thy lot are givin' us! I thowt tha reckoned they were on our side? Now there's bin 'undreds of our men killed in Dublin! His parting remark was, "They're nowt but bloody traitors!"

Before Kitty could respond, Harry left as suddenly as he'd arrived, farting as he went.

Yet more bad news was to follow, but this time, closer to home. Kitty's elder son, Bob had been in France only four months when Ellen rushed round to Kitty with the news that Bob had been shot in his right leg. He was being allowed time to convalesce and would then be sent home for a week's leave. Though both women comforted each other with the thought that the news might have been worse, they were also fearful of what *could* happen when Bob had to return to the front.

Admittedly, when she saw him, Kitty found her son to be quite cheerful, glad to be with his family, and able to enjoy outings to the pub with his Dad. Yet Robert remarked to Kitty after his first night out with Bob, "Lad's a lot thinner. He's tryin' to mek jokes about what it's like out yonder, but underneath, I know t' lad's dreadin' bein' sent to France again. I'm fair worried."

Kitty nodded. "Me too, Robert. Me too."

When Bob's week at home ended, he was ordered to return to France via a ship sailing from Dover. On the afternoon of his departure, Ellen and three-year old Elsie stood at the doorway of their house. Little Elsie waved enthusiastically, calling out, "Bye bye Daddy, see you tomorrow." Ellen also waved. Whilst holding back tears, she called, "God be with you. Take care."

Bob, kit-bag plus gas mask on his back, turned to reply, "I'll be fine, lass. Just remember, 'Keep the home fires burnin' …"

Then he set off to his former home where Robert, Kitty and Catherine were waiting for him. After a big hug from his sister, Bob left the house with his parents. They'd decided to 'see him off' at the station on the first stage of his journey to Dover. Once her son was on board standing by an open window, Kitty forced a smile as she blew him a kiss saying, "Take care, son. And may the Good Lord keep ye safe."

Robert raised both thumbs, saying, "Aye lad, tek care of thasel!"

Both watched and waved until the train had moved out of sight. Robert then patted Kitty's arm, and soon they were walking in their opposite directions. Robert making his way towards the house in Walmer Street where he was repairing a roof. Kitty making for home.

Deep in thought, Robert eventually arrived at Walmer Street. Billy, who had said his 'Goodbyes' to his brother the previous night, was working on a house some distance away. He waved as he saw his father walk past, calling, "Did our Bob get off alright, Dad?"

"Aye Billy. Me and Mam waved him off."

Two houses away from the one where Robert was working, a woman looked up as she swept leaves from her path, and exchanged a few pleasantries about the weather with him. Soon Robert set about mixing himself a bucket of cement and had climbed up the ladder to the roof. But for once, his mind wasn't fully on his job. He kept thinking of his son who would soon be in those lice-ridden, mud-filled trenches. He pictured all those young men, wondering when the next gas-attack would come…

A second later Robert lay on his back at the foot of the ladder.

The woman he'd spoken to just minutes earlier dashed round. Only to find what she considered to be his lifeless body. Immediately she went inside and told her son to run to the nearby surgery of the local doctor and tell him to come quickly to Walmer Street. Within about ten minutes, the doctor arrived. It didn't take long for him to pronounce Robert dead.

Of course, from there, the body was taken to the mortuary to await the inquest which would have to take place before the body could be buried. Billy was devastated. He'd been so close, yet hadn't even been able to see his Dad in the ambulance before his body was driven away.

Both Kitty and the lady who'd witnessed the fall, Mrs Edith Dickinson, were called to give evidence to the Coroner at the inquest.

Kitty described how she and Robert had been waving off their son at the station. She told the Coroner her husband was in good health, but had been worried about their son returning to France again.

Mrs Dickinson told of how she'd spoken briefly with the deceased before he began work on the nearby house. She then described how she'd been in her garden and had actually seen the fall in which he'd "turned a somersault before landing on his back." Her account went on to describe the doctor's arrival and subsequent removal of the body.

A verdict of 'Accidental Death' was given.

Robert's family and friends were naturally shocked at his sudden death and also at the manner in which it had happened. They all knew how skilled he'd been at his job and how he never took chances when working at the top of a ladder. There were tears from Catherine and Anne at the loss of their father, but it was Billy who grieved the most. He constantly thought that if only he'd known about his father's fall, he might have been able to get to his Dad in time to save his life.

Of course, a telegram had been sent to Bob immediately, but as yet, there'd been no confirmation that he'd received it.

Naturally, Kitty too had been shocked by the death of her husband. After all, they'd been married for thirty-two years, and despite all the trials and tribulations in their marriage, their four children had given them a common bond. Yet, she couldn't say that she'd ever regained the affection she'd had for Robert in the very early years of marriage. She mused to herself, "No Robert. You were simply the father of my children. You were never my soul-mate." Unbidden, a vision of Pat's face appeared. He was looking at her just as he had all those years ago at Sligo station, saying, "Somehow, someday, we'll be together with our son."

"Aye Pat, *you* would have been my soul-mate. But that was never to be, was it my love? "

Breaking off from her reverie, Kitty addressed herself sternly, "Now then, Kitty, ye need to be organising a decent wake for Robert. He deserves that!"

Footnote[1]

Easter Rising. 24TH -29TH April 1916

Some of the British newspapers wrote that the consequences of the 'Easter Rising' might have been worse if a German ship load of armaments for the rebels had not been intercepted by the British Navy on April 20th. However, many Irish people disputed this version of events, claiming it was propaganda by the British. They maintained it was Irish Americans, reluctant to be involved in the world war, who had tried to send over weapons for the rebels.

After the Easter Rising, Asquith left the British Army to deal with its aftermath. There followed a draconian policy of wholesale arrests followed by imprisonment, internment and executions. The latter applied to most of the main conspirators. Feelings between the Irish and the British hardened. And though the uprising failed, participants became regarded as heroes and/or martyrs.

Chapter 59

Robert's Wake

Billy proved to be a great support to his mother, both in helping her with the necessary documentation required after a death, and also in inviting his father's work-mates and drinking friends to the wake. Additionally, he said he'd order and pay for all the drink. Of course, Kitty, Catherine and Ellen would be preparing the food for the occasion, with Jane supplying all the bread for the sandwiches.

It was a great relief for Kitty to have her family providing a large chunk of the costs of Robert's wake. Widows' pensions did not go very far, especially as prices continued to rise. But despite all the financial help, Kitty couldn't afford the cost of a headstone for Robert. Sadly, he would have to be buried in a public grave. The funeral service was to be held at St Mary's Church, Lower Ince - a church Robert had always admired when he'd worked there in the past.

A letter soon arrived from Denis after he'd been informed about Robert's death. During their correspondences, Kitty had occasionally hinted at the fact that her marriage to Robert had been far from ideal - though she'd never gone into details. So, along with his condolences, he asked a question he'd often wanted to ask previously. Namely, to enquire if she'd ever considered a return to Ireland now that her four children were married. There were assurances of a big welcome from him and his wife, Mary, who had always supported his regular contacts with her.

As Kitty read about the possibility of being welcomed back to Ireland, her thoughts were filled with a yearning for the lovely countryside of Sligo as well as being with her son and his family. But then she came back to earth as she realised that this was impossible whilst her children in England needed her. Although Ellen seemed to be managing fairly well whilst Bob was away, there was always the fear that he might not return home from the war. Similarly, Billy and Jane were doing quite well at the moment - but Jane was expecting another baby in August, and was wondering how she could keep up with all her baking then. Moreover, Kitty's two daughters were giving her *immediate* cause for concern. Catherine and her children were still living with her - but 'mystery man', Danny was still on the scene.

Then there was Anne over in Bolton with two very young children and the strong possibility that Harry could be called to enlist at any time She would certainly need some help with young Harry and Anne if that occurred. And apart from that, there had been some recent concern about Harry's drinking. Only a few weeks before Robert's death, he and brother-in-law, Dick, had appeared before Bolton Magistrates' Court, charged with disturbing the peace by fighting near 'The Grey Man'. They were subsequently each fined twenty-five shillings. Apparently, Harry and Dick had challenged two Irishmen to a fight - the cause being differing attitudes to the war. Kitty's worry was that a man who turned to fight when drunk could easily transfer his anger to his family.

No! The idea of going over to Ireland just now was not feasible.

It was six o'clock in the evening of Robert's wake, and already quite a crowd had gathered in the back kitchen. To Kitty's surprise, Harry was there sitting alongside Anne. He was dressed in a smart black suit and wearing a black bowler hat. Apparently, Harry's sister, Alice, had offered to look after the children. Kitty couldn't understand why a man who disliked Catholics so much would be attending the wake. She concluded his liking for drink was greater than his prejudice.

Just then a group of Robert's friends from 'The Bear's Paw' arrived, they'd 'clubbed' together and brought along flowers to be placed on the coffin next day. They were red and white, Robert's favourite colours. The men had firstly gone into the front room to say 'Farewell' prayers to their friend who lay in his best suit in the candle-lit room with its closed curtains. Next, they went through to the back kitchen. where Billy was serving drinks from a barrel of ale.

Recalling that a large pan of 'scouse' had proved popular at Mrs Rourke's wake, Kitty had provided one for Robert's 'Last farewell'. She was standing by the gently simmering pan, ready to ladle out helpings to hungry guests. Chatting together nearby were Mary, young Pat, Molly and Lizzie. She had certainly no reason to mourn her biological father. She simply wanted to be there for Kitty who was holding the 'scouse' ladle in her hand, 'at the ready.' However Kitty was so engrossed in listening to her family and friends talking together that she didn't notice the man waiting to be served. Then a familiar voice asked impatiently, "What's a man got to do to get a plateful of 'scouse' from thee, Kitty? Are tha too busy to notice an 'old lodger'?"

Immediately she turned as she recognised the voice, "Ach, if it isn't Arthur Wilson! Holy Mother, what an age since I last saw ye, it's so good of ye come. I'll never forget how ye gave Robert a piece of your mind on my behalf all those years ago!" Then Kitty ordered him briskly, "Now give me your plate, and let's be filling your belly!"

With a cheery smile, Arthur took the plateful of steaming 'scouse' from Kitty saying, "Thanks Kitty, ye allus made sure I got good helpin's! Tha were a good landlady, but I won't pretend I came for Robert's sake." He added, "Though I hope he rests in peace. Anyway, maybe we can have a chat later, Kitty?" There was a smile and nod from Kitty. Then Arthur, with his plate piled high, began to chat with Lizzie.

As the night wore on, bellies filled with food and drink, the entertainment was well underway. Seamus, from the 'Packet,' was another man who had attended the wake for Kitty's sake rather than to mourn for Robert. Having brought his penny whistle, he was soon asked to play a selection of popular jigs. Gradually, many mourners joined in the dancing, even those with no links to Ireland. One exception was Harry Holt, who remarked contemptuously, "Does that lot think that's dancin'? It looks as if they've all getten St Vitus Dance!" Anne, who was jigging alongside Catherine, gave him a glare. As the music came to an end, Kitty called out to him, "Right Harry, *you* can entertain us now!"

Harry's reply was immediate. "Oh aye. I can sing a bit. Anne towd me 'er Dad were once a sailor. So I'll gi' thee all one he'd like." He then rose somewhat unsteadily and began his 'entertainment'.

"Oh there was a jolly sailor, in the days of Hipperoo

He went ashore, and met a ..."

"That's enough Harry!" came Anne's sharp voice as she stood up and gave his arm a tug. "Time you were getting the train back to Bolton to pick up the children from your Alice."

Some of Harry's audience looked a little disappointed that the jolly sailor's experiences had been so abruptly cut short.

Next day, the funeral mass took place in St Mary's Church. Here, family and friends gathered to pay their respects and give their blessings to Robert. Missing from the service inside the church were Jane Gibbs and Harry Holt, though Jane did join the mourners for the burial.

Chapter 60
Kitty In Bolton (1916-17)

In August, 1916, not long after Robert's death, Kitty received the dreaded news from Anne that Harry had been called up to enlist. More men were desperately needed in northern France where fierce and bloody trench warfare had been taking place since July 1st near the River Somme. Britain, and France were trying to advance and regain territory taken by the Germans in Verdun.

The same month Kitty also heard from Denis. He and Mary had given her a sixth Irish grandchild, a boy who was to be baptised James. Denis was also greatly concerned about how she was coping during the privations of the war. He'd realised she must be so worried, having a son fighting in France as well as her two sons-in law, Jimmy and Harry.

It comforted Kitty to know he and Mary were regularly lighting candles on behalf of her and her English family.

It was still August when Kitty had further news of a new grandchild. This time it was Billy and Jane who were the parents. They now had a second son, this one was to be named Robert after his Granddad. Although feeling quite well after his birth, Jane decided to cease her little business until the boys were a bit older.

September brought more news, but of a different, yet welcome nature. Catherine informed Kitty that she could stop worrying about her and 'Damned Danny.' Apparently, he too had been conscripted, so they'd said their 'Goodbyes.'

"Well Catherine, I can't say I'm sorry to hear about that - though I feel sympathy for any man sent out to those trenches." Kitty then looked anxiously at her daughter, saying, "I'm hoping ye won't waste any tears on him."

"No Mam! No fear of that. I liked Danny and he brought a bit of laughter and affection into my life when I needed it. It's about time I gave all my attention to my girls."

In January 1917, Catherine had a letter from husband, Jimmy, now a Lance Corporal. Apparently, he'd received another wound, this time it was gunshot in his left leg. He explained that after convalescing he would be going back to their first home in Great George Street, and moreover, was being discharged from active service in February of that year. Jimmy then pointed out that he would most likely qualify for a pension, and once he'd recovered from his wound, he'd been offered his job back as a postman. However, the main thrust of the letter was to ask Catherine to give him another chance. Jimmy maintained he'd become a changed man whilst fighting for his country, and still loved her and his daughters.

After giving the matter a great deal of thought, and with many reservations, Catherine decided to give him another chance. She reflected that she was a much stronger person now and the girls were older, more able to cope with any outbursts of temper. Besides, it would be good to have a home of her own again. She also decided a new start deserved a new name. Having always liked the name Kathleen, a variant of Catherine, she adopted that name.

So in mid-February, Kathleen, Anne and Edna bade their tearful 'Farewells' to Kitty, and set out for Great George Street.

As wounded soldiers returned home from the front, some kept silent about their experiences in France, but Jimmy Carr was certainly not amongst them. After work one night, he gave Kathleen his view of the war and its leaders, "That bloody so called 'Battle of the Somme' was nowt but a farce right from t' start! And Haig just went along wi' Joffre's barmy ideas. I tell thee, Kathleen, though they *called* it an alliance, there was no real plannin' went into it. There was bugger all co-operation between t' froggy leaders and ours. And not much news got passed among t' trenches!"

Kathleen shook her head in amazement. She knew the war wasn't going well for the allies, but she'd no idea about the leaders' incompetence. Jimmy continued, "They should've known that Jerries would bring out their strappin' great tanks when t' trenches got bogged down in t' mud. And what did our lot bring out? Clumsy useless things that crawled along like boozed-up snails! It were nowt but a bloody fuck-up, Kathleen, so …"

"Yes, Jimmy." interrupted Kathleen. "A total shambles. Just watch your language, the girls may be awake!"

From the bedroom came stifled giggling.

For several months after Kathleen's move back with Jimmy, Kitty made regular trips to Bolton to help her daughter as much as she could, often staying there overnight. Harry's sister, Alice, also became quite friendly with Anne and would often drop in to ask if any shopping was needed. She and Dick had three children, two daughters, Florrie and Bertha, both in their twenties, and a son, Dick who was eight years old.

A major worry for all families was the ever-increasing price of food and its decreasing availability in the shops. Alice, along with young Dick, had called round to Anne's on her way to the market. The two were invited in for a cup of tea and Alice was soon seated in a chair by the fire, telling of her disgust at the latest trick of shopkeepers. It emerged she'd discovered some shops had been injecting brine into boiled ham to make it weigh heavier.

Anne shook her head at this latest news, adding, "And the way this war's going, I can see food being rationed before long. God know how we'll cope then!" Then deciding to turn the conversation away from doom and gloom, she observed, "One thing we can be glad about is the King changing his Jerry surname of Saxe-Coburg-Gotha to Windsor, yesterday."

Alice wasn't impressed by this revelation, simply commenting, "Good God! Wi' a name like that, I'd have changed it long ago! Anyroad, I only dropped in to see if tha wanted owt from t' market."

"I think we need spuds, carrots and …" Anne never finished the list. It was only then she'd noticed what had been happening whilst they'd been talking.

Bored by the conversation, young Dick and Harry had quietly crept over to little Anne who had awakened from her sleep in her pram. The bold Dick had 'devised' a great game whereby one would hand Anne pegs which she would happily drop over the side of her pram. Meanwhile, the other would put his hand in the nearby coal-bucket, smear it with coal-dust, and then gently wipe his hand over Anne's hair and face. Both took turns at being 'peg-giver' and 'coal-dust getter.' The little girl, enjoying 'peg-dropping', seemed oblivious to the 'darker' side of the game. Then came a yell from Anne. "Stop that Harry!"

Startled, the lad froze, caught in the act of coal-dust smearing.

"Tha little buggers!" said Alice as she went over and administered a sharp slap on Dick's legs. "Just look at t' babby, 'er looks like a little chimney sweep!"

Despite themselves, Anne and Alice couldn't help but smile at little Anne's black face.

Letters from Denis were still very much treasured. He and Mary had had a sixth child, James, at the end of the previous year, and his latest letter described how the new addition to their family was now sitting up and saying his first word, 'Mama'. Denis also wrote that their eldest, John, was now eleven and growing tall. His skill on the tin-whistle had even surpassed that of his Granddad, Pat.

He went on to comment that, since the good news of America having entered the war in April, the end might not be too far off.[1] Denis concluded by writing, "And if that does happen, Mam, and you feel your families there are settled, don't forget you have a family here, longing to have you stay with us. I love you Mam."

Denis' final paragraph now filled Kitty with hopes of possibly seeing her son, his family and Ireland in the not too distant future. "After all," she thought, "if it doesn't work out, I can always come back here."

Footnote[1]
1917

Woodrow Wilson, president of the US, had been very reluctant to join in the war against Germany. However, in January, 1917, Germany announced unrestricted submarine warfare on all shipping in the war zone of the Eastern Atlantic, including any neutral vessels. They had previously pledged to suspend submarine warfare in the North Atlantic and the Mediterranean. Therefore, when Wilson cited this violation of Germany's pledge to the US Senate, war was declared on Germany on April 14th.

Though the US had a very strong navy, they had no army ready to fight. It would take some time before they had trained enough men to be ready and capable of fighting in the war. And, in fact, America's entry to the war proved not to be so advantageous until much later in the year.

Moreover, for some time our ally, Russia, had been concerned with economic problems, shortages of food, inflation of prices, lack of weapons and heavy losses. Tsar Nicholas ll was regarded as weak and unfit to rule, and plans were made to overthrow the Tsarist regime in order to establish the Soviet Union. Leaders, such as Lenin, were not interested in the war, only socialism. In 1917, Nicholas was forced to abdicate. In July 1918, he, his wife Alexandra and their five children were assassinated.

Chapter 61

Kitty in Bolton (1917 – 1918)

Despite the help of our new ally, America, the war continued without either side having seemed to gain the upper-hand. Lives continued to be lost and general discontent spread. In many countries, some people were beginning to think that victory was not possible, or even necessary. Such ideas led to the call for peace by negotiation. Those who held these views included: opposition leaders, socialist leaders, shop stewards, and also Woodrow Wilson and Lenin. But these ideas were not welcomed by other allied leaders, who basically believed that a defeated Germany was the 'correct' outcome of the war.

Meanwhile, Anne wrote to Harry with news of the children whenever she had the time, and Harry wrote whenever he was able. Both were frustrated by the long though necessary delays between the sending of, and arrival of their letters. One letter received in September contained news of Harry's promotion to Lance Corporal. Anne was pleased for him and decided to share the news with young Harry, now aged three, and Anne, aged two. She interrupted them playing with a ball to tell them their Daddy was now a special soldier with a white stripe on his arm. "Isn't that good?" she asked. Both thought they ought to agree, and nodded. Then young Harry asked, "So can we have bacon and potatoes for dinner?"

Just before Christmas, 1917, Kitty thought things would be easier if she went to live with Anne in Bolton, possibly until the end of the war when, God willing, Harry would return home. After all, Kathleen seemed to be reasonably content with Jimmy now. Also, Ellen was coping quite well with her four daughters as well as looking forward to the return of Bob from France.

When Kitty's proposal was put to Anne, she was only too happy to have her mother live with her whilst Harry was away. So in late December that year, Kitty gave up her tenancy of Farrimond's Row and, by January 1918, was living on Tonge Moor Road in Bolton. Since the war had reached a 'stalemate', both Kitty and her daughter were amongst the growing group of people who thought it would be better for everyone if some sort of compromise with Germany were to be reached.

However, the trials of daily life were now of more immediate concern to them both. In February of that year, the introduction of food rationing was introduced, but like many others, they considered it quite unnecessary. Every family was issued with National Ration Books for the purchase of meat, sugar and butter. Moreover, each family had to register with the same butcher and grocer for all their rations. Kitty was quick to share her feelings with Anne and Alice, who was there with young Dick.

"Sure I see no reason for the government to do this now! For the last six months or so haven't the Americans been blowing up the German subs that were stopping our food supplies getting through? So there's been a lot *more* food in the shops!" Alice nodded, "Tha's reet Kitty, lass. Anyroad, I popped round to tell thee that Dick'll tek the two lads fishin' in Burscough canal on Sunday morn, if that's alright wi' thee Anne. Young 'Arry'll need to be ready at six o'clock, if they're to catch t' train fra' Wigan."

Anne accepted Alice's suggestion immediately. Young Harry and Dick, whose ears had pricked up at the words 'fishing' and 'train', gave shouts of delight.

❧ ❧ ❧

In May that year, Anne received a letter from Harry saying he'd been wounded in his left ankle and was being sent to Llandrindod Wells to convalesce. He was looking forward to being allowed home for five days' leave once his wound had healed. Though worried about his injury, she was eager to see Harry again. Kitty decided it was politic to sleep overnight at Ellen's on the first day of his leave.

On the day of his arrival, Anne stood on the platform at Trinity Street Station holding her children's hands, ready to greet her husband. Young Harry was eager to see his soldier Dad, though he'd only vague memories of him.

Eventually, a grinning Harry stepped down from the train. It was cold for May and he was wearing his great-coat over his uniform, helmet strapped to the kit-bag on his back. Immediately, the bag was put down on the platform, and his arms were clasped tightly around his wife. "Eeh Annie, luv, I thowt I'd never see thee again!" Then he planted a huge kiss on Anne's smiling mouth.

She asked, "And what do you think of your son and daughter, Harry?"

Looking down at his children, an emotional Harry placed his hat on young Harry's head, and gently patted Anne's auburn hair. Bending down he asked her,"'Ow about a kiss for tha Dad?" Anne looked at the stranger, burst into tears, and buried her head in her mother's coat. Meanwhile young Harry, his father's hat covering his ears, began marching smartly round the platform, giving salutes to everyone. Skills he'd learned from his Uncle Dick.

Harry watched his son proudly and, giving a chuckle, observed to Anne, "At least one o' my childer seems glad I'm back!"

After a tram-ride to Tonge Moor, the family were soon home. Here, Alice and Dick were waiting to welcome Harry. They'd managed to obtain a leg of mutton from the butcher, so the welcome smell of roasting meat greeted Harry as the door was opened by Alice, eager to see her brother again.

After more hugs and brief family chatter, Dick reassured his brother-in-law, "Now don't thee be thinkin' we're stoppin'". Winking, he added, "We know thee an' Anne 'll want time to be alone. But afore we go, we want to see tha Lance Corporal's stripe. Tha sister were so proud of thee when tha got promoted."

There was a rather awkward silence before Harry said anything. He looked hesitantly round his 'audience,' aware that everyone - except young Anne - was waiting for him to take off his great-coat. At last he explained, "Aye, well there's a bit of a tale about that. Tha all knows, I were made a Lance Corporal last September. Then we comes to January this year. After a day's non-stop fighting, we'd managed to push on, an' tek another Jerry trench. So we were tekin' turns in gettin' a bit o' kip. We slept standin' up, all caked wi' mud. I were well away, I can tell thee!" Harry stood with closed eyes to illustrate the point. "Then I feels some bugger shakin' me, an' sayin somat. It were a while afore I could open mi eyes. Then I sees it's one o' them bloody Tads tryin' to get at mi cigs in mi top pocket!" ()

"'Bugger off!' I ses. 'Get a cig off one of tha lot!' But th' impudent bugger stands there, sayin' 'Me friend. Give pliz, friend.'

"Well, I'd 'ad enough. So I ses, 'If tha doesn't bugger off, I'll throw thee o'er t' top!' Beggar doesn't shift. So I gives 'im a reet good pastin'." Harry paused to reflect on the fight, then continued, "It were only then I sees t' bloody Sergeant's bin watchin' all t' time!" Harry sighed. "Anyroad, mi stripe were soon teken away."

Anne and Alice were silent, but Dick let out a roar of laughter as he observed, "Eeh, I don't know! Only thee could get demoted fer fighting wi' one of our allies! A poor, war-weary Pole, just wantin' a cig! No wonder we're not winnin'!"

Young Harry couldn't quite make out whether the story he'd heard was good news or not. So to be on the safe side, he gave his father a smart salute and was rewarded with an impeccable salute from his father.

❦ ❦ ❦

During the remaining four days of Harry's leave, Kitty was careful to be out of the house as much as she could to give Anne and Harry time together. Often, she would take young Harry and Nancy out with her to visit places such as the nearby park, or Bolton Market, or Alice's home.

In fact, Kitty's main encounters with Harry and Anne occurred at family meal-times. After a light tea, little Anne was taken upstairs by Kitty and put in the cot in her parent's bedroom. Young Harry was allowed to stay up a little while longer, and his face would light up in anticipation when his Grandma came down again, knowing his father would then begin to tell stories of his adventures in some place called France.

Typical of Harry, his versions of life and events in the trenches were probably exaggerated. But though Kitty didn't think the young lad should be hearing about rats, lice, and men blinded after gas attacks, she had to admit that Harry was a good story-teller. He had a way of describing things vividly, but was always aware that his son was listening to him with wide-eyes. So he would mix his accounts with humour which seemed to reduce their horror for his lad.

When young Harry went up to bed about an hour later, he was certain he would grow up to be like his father. Afraid of nothing - neither Jerries nor rats!

The relationship between Kitty and Harry didn't change. On the face of it they were generally quite civil towards each other, but when his five days' leave came to an end she wasn't sorry to see him go.

Footnote[1]

'Tad' was a name used by some soldiers when referring to Polish men. It was a nickname based on the word Tad*pole*.

Chapter 62

The War's End – 'Spanish' Flu (1918)

The early months of the year showed few signs of the war ending. However, spirits were raised when, in April 1918, the 'Royal Air Force' was formed and by May, German raids on England had ceased. There were also many discussions and arguments amongst people regarding the efforts Woodrow Wilson had been making earlier that year. His aim had been to get Germany and the Allies to agree to fourteen points of what he considered to be a basis for peace. But, at that time, neither side wanted a compromise after so much bloodshed.

Meanwhile, in Bolton, the beginning of July brought the tell-tale symptoms of pregnancy to Anne. Mornings, were accompanied by sickly feelings plus a general lack of energy. So, for a couple of months, Kitty's life became very busy as she looked after young Harry and Anne, coped with housework, and tried to keep her daughter cheerful. Luckily, by mid-August, Anne was feeling 'herself' again, and beginning to feel quite positive about the arrival of what she called her 'war-baby'.

But August brought yet another blow for the British people - it was the arrival of the worldwide outbreak of the so-called 'Spanish Flu'. This particular strain was especially virulent causing many deaths, though Kitty and her family somehow managed to escape the disease.

Yet despite this potential 'killer', the mood of people in general became more hopeful. News gradually came through that the Allies and America had combined to work out a strategy against the Germans.

The British were to concentrate their efforts around Ypres in northern France, the French were to 'deal' with mid-France, and America was to attack near Verdun in the south. Thus the Germans would be encircled. By September, the strategy had been successful in parts, but it did not secure an outright 'win'. However, Germany had become disheartened, and General Ludendorff was beginning to think an armistice would, at least, avoid defeat. Also, there was growing political unrest in Germany. There had been many lost lives; food was short, and soon the government was urging Emperor Wilhelm ll to abdicate. (He was known as 'Kaiser Bill' to the British.) At last, in November 1918, Wilhelm reluctantly abdicated. He went to Holland and remained there until his death in 1941. On November 11th at five in the morning, the new Republican Government of Germany signed the Armistice in a railroad car in France. That same morning, at eleven o'clock, fighting ceased. The war was over. But with the loss of what was later found to be a total of about eight million lives which included all countries involved in the war. Britain had suffered a loss of over one million.

In Bolton on November 11th, streets were crowded with happy people. There was shouting, cheering, waving of flags; neighbours and strangers greeting and hugging each other. Many workers had been given (or taken) the day off. Kitty, Anne, young Harry and Anne, stood outside their house, joining in with the general excitement. They shouted to the people on crowded Tonge Moor trams as they passed by, their passengers blowing kisses and shouting back. Later that day, Alice, Dick and their children went round to celebrate with them. Everyone sat down to a meal of Kitty's famous 'scouse', and afterwards young Harry and Anne were sucking away happily on 'Uncle Joe's Mint Balls' provided by Grandma.

Once celebrations were over, people returned to the realities of post-war life. One of which was the continued, and increasing shortage of food imports. Though there was now no threat from German U-Boats, priorities were given to taking supplies to the many people involved in the war who had been left in near-starvation. This applied particularly to Germany and Russia where civil unrest and Revolution had taken their toll.

Soon after the armistice had been signed, Kitty had a welcome letter from Denis. Naturally, he was greatly relieved that the war was finally over, and that his mother and family had survived most of its horrors. He also included the latest news regarding Irish politics. "I'm thinking that power here will soon be going to Sinn Fein with de Valera as leader - then we should soon be free from English rule! I hope you're as happy as we are about that, Mam."

Kitty was indeed very happy about the prospect of self-government for Ireland. Despite living more than half her life in England, she had remained an Irish girl at heart.

There was more good news in a letter from Margaret. Now, having fully recovered from a dose of 'Spanish Flu', she was soon active with the Suffragette Movement again. It seemed that Prime Minister Gladstone had finally put the subject in the statute book for immediate discussion.

During the second week in December, there were more celebrations when both Bob and Harry returned to their respective homes within two days of each other.

Harry was delighted to be with his wife and children again. However, after a long embrace, he held Anne at arms length, and looking at her with some concern, said, "Eeh lass, tha looks pale." Anne was quick to try to allay his concern, though in all truth, she had been suffering from aching joints for the past two days. Harry looked down at the 'bump' showing beneath his wife's pinafore and spoke apologetically, "Aye Annie luv, I gave thee two babbies in a short time - then I gives thee a third - and buggers off to France! O'course tha Mam's bin a big 'elp, but it'll be good when we can be on our own agen. Once I've 'settled in', would tha like me to go t' Register Office and book us a Christmas weddin'?"

Anne smiled at her him, replying simply, "Yes Harry, I'd like that."

Meanwhile Kitty was busy in the back kitchen, preparing the special 'Welcome Home' meal for Harry. Young Harry and Anne were already eating their early tea which to their delight would be followed by little bags of 'Jelly Babies'. These bags had been specially designed by Bassett's to celebrate the end of the war and were named, 'Peace Babies'. Three babies were shown on each bag. One wearing a small tin helmet!

Once the children had been taken up to bed by Harry, he and Anne shared their special meal of roast chicken with all the trimmings. He ate ravenously, having had nothing but tinned bully beef for nearly two years. Anne had little appetite, her joints were aching and, despite her woollen shawl, she was beginning to feel quite chilly.

Later that evening, Alice and Dick called round to welcome Harry back home. Everyone was sitting round the fire chatting, and Dick was laughing at one of Harry's war tales. Yet, when Kitty looked at Anne, she realised her daughter had started shivering quite uncontrollably. Immediately she put her own shawl around Anne's shoulders, felt her hot forehead, and said quietly, "Don't worry my lassie. We'll soon have ye warm and in bed."

To Harry, who'd now realised something was wrong, she said urgently, "Get two hot water bottles ready and we'll get Anne in bed. I suspect 'Spanish Flu'."

All that night, Harry sat watchful and anxious, by his wife's bedside.

In bed that evening,, Kitty's rosary never left her hands as she prayed to the Holy Mother to take care of her daughter. It seemed so ironic that Anne should catch 'flu' just when it seemed the pandemic was over.

By six o'clock next morning Anne's temperature had suddenly risen, and she was coughing up sputum in addition to finding difficulty in breathing. Harry called out to Kitty who came immediately. She took one look at her daughter, and asked, "Shall I go for the doctor, Harry?" He nodded immediately, tears in his clear blue eyes whilst stroking Anne's hand.

The subsequent visit of Dr Overton was far from reassuring. After a thorough examination of Anne, he followed Harry and Kitty downstairs and gave his opinion. "I'm afraid your wife is seriously ill. Influenza has developed into pneumonia. And of course, the situation is made even more serious since she is almost seven months pregnant. So the welfare of the child must also be considered." Then looking firstly at Harry and then at Kitty, he advised,"Now it is essential that one of you is by Mrs Holt's bedside all the time. In any case, I will come tomorrow morning, but in the meantime let me know immediately if there is any blueness of her lips. In that case she will need to be given oxygen as soon as possible." Both Harry and Kitty assured him that a close watch would be kept on

Anne. The doctor continued, "There'll be medicine ready for Mrs. Holt at the surgery. Keep her propped up, and free from draughts."

Then Dr Overton put away his stethoscope and left.

Unfortunately, poor Anne was in need of oxygen the same night. It was given via a nasal catheter. Her lips had turned blue and there was greatly increased breathlessness. For days her health steadily deteriorated, but both Harry and Kitty were adamant that, at all costs, a transfer to hospital must be avoided. He'd often declared, "I don't trust bloody 'ospitals! I've paid enough into t' bloody health insurance club to afford as many doctors' visits as Annie needs!"

Meanwhile, Alice was also proving to be a godsend. Not only did she have the children to stay with her, but she took meals round for Kitty and Harry.

Dr Overton now visited twice a day to check on Anne. Harry and Kitty could only watch, and continue their vigils, though now both were fearing the worst. In fact, the usually indomitable Harry broke down one evening and, looking at Kitty, cried accusingly, "If thy God's so good, why's 'e doin' this to my bonny Annie?"

The days of December dragged on without change. Suddenly, on the twenty-first of the month, Anne's condition amazingly began to improve. Her periods of delirium eased and she was able to breathe without oxygen. A smiling Dr Overton announced that Anne was out of danger. He continued, "Now we need to get back her strength for the sake of the baby that's due in early March."

That same day, Anne ate a full bowl of broth prepared for her by Kitty, though it had to be made, on Harry's insistence, with a sheep's head, peas and barley. Things were 'looking up'. Then two days later Anne began to experience pains in the lower part of her back. These quickly became much more severe, and when a show of blood appeared along with the pains, it seemed the baby 'planned' an early arrival.

Immediately, Kitty began preparations for the birth as well as tending to Anne. Meanwhile, Harry dashed out to get the midwife who lived on Tonge Moor Road.

It was late on Christmas Eve before the midwife, assisted by Kitty, delivered Anne's baby. It didn't breathe immediately, but just seemed to be gasping. Finally, a feeble cry was heard - much to everyone's relief. Yet relief was short-lived as they looked down at a diminutive baby girl. Kitty gazed at the child in silence. An exhausted Anne shook her head sadly as she looked at her child, saying, "I'm so sorry I didn't give you the chance to grow stronger." Her voice trailed off as she mumbled, "Poor, poor little mite." Then she turned her face to the wall.

After cleansing the baby with great care, and swaddling it in a 'blanket' of cotton-wool, the midwife handed Kitty her granddaughter. Then she left the room and went down to tell Harry the news.

He was pacing the room, ashen-faced. His first words were,"'Ow's my Annie? I've 'eard nowt for a while. I 'eard a little cry fra t' babby, but nowt fra Annie. What's 'appenin'?"

The midwife tried to reassure him, saying, "Now don't worry Mr Holt. Your wife's had a bad time but she's resting now. With care, rest and good food, she'll soon be as right as rain. But your daughter is very premature and weighs only three pounds. She's well-wrapped up and will be sleeping in a drawer in the bedroom. But I'm afraid she won't live until Christmas Day. So let Anne be your first concern now."

Chapter 63

Post-War Developments (1919)

Christmas day arrived. And to everyone's surprise, the tiny girl born the evening before was still alive. Lying in a drawer near her mother, wrapped in her 'blanket' of cotton-wool and enclosed by two hot-water bottles, she awoke from a blessed sleep. At once there came feeble, yet persistent, crying from the child. Undoubtedly, this was a cry of hunger - a hopeful sign.

As she was too small to suckle properly, the midwife fed her sugar dissolved in boiled water from a small teaspoon. The child took every drop. Regarding this as another positive sign, the midwife told Anne to express some of the thin milky liquid, colostrum, from her breasts. And this time the little girl took her feed from the teaspoon whilst nestling in her *mother's* arms.

Harry and Kitty were sent upstairs to witness the scene.

"Didn't doctor tell thee tha'd be fine, Annie?" Was Harry's overjoyed remark to his relieved, though still pale, wife.

At Harry's request, Kitty went round to give Alice news of the birth of the 'miracle' baby. She found Harry's sister busy clearing away the breakfast dishes, helped by her two daughters. Young Harry and Anne, along with young Dick, were waiting to leave the table to play outside. Naturally, Alice was delighted and relieved to know that her sister-in-law's baby, though premature, had survived. Wiping her hands on her apron, she said to the children, "Aunty Annie's just 'ad a little girl."

The two elder girls, Florrie and Bertha looked pleased, young Anne and Dick seemed unmoved. Harry pulled a face, exclaiming, "Not another bloody sister!"

Later that morning Alice and all the children went round to her brother's house carrying holly and countless paper-chains. These had been made by them on the days leading up to Christmas. Kitty welcomed them all in as Alice explained,"We've bin saving these for thee till we got good news about Annie - now tha can mek evrythin' look Christmassy and celebrate t' babby's fight fer life. Also, Dick's bringin' round a nice roast chicken for tha Christmas dinner in an hour."

Quite overwhelmed by the kindness and thoughtfulness of the Holden family, Kitty thanked Alice profusely. It seemed to her that, after all, they could celebrate Christmas properly. Everything might just turn out fine.

The year 1919 arrived holding promise for everyone. The dreadful war was over and people realised that, though it might take some time, things should eventually get back to normal. For the Holts, the early months proved to be very busy but quite settled. The baby and Anne were growing stronger each day, and there was good news for Harry. The owner of Dart mill where he had worked as a loom-overseer was able to let him resume his job there. Harry was very lucky since many men had lost their jobs to women because of the war. They had to train for other jobs or, more often, 'go on the dole'.

Kathleen was the first visitor of the year from Wigan. She arrived in Bolton by train, bringing a beautiful hand-knitted blue bed-jacket for her sister, and an equally beautiful hand-knitted white shawl for the baby. For young Harry and Anne there were belated Christmas gifts of tangerines and chocolate. She had left her own daughters at home, thinking Anne wouldn't want the fuss of more children in the house. After much happy chatting together, Anne said, as she looked at her baby, "By the way, Kathleen, I've eventually got Harry to agree to her name. He wanted 'Alice' after his sister and his Mam. But I've insisted on her being called 'Edna', so that our two daughters have identical names. Also, he's agreed to have a little ceremony soon, and he's letting Mam say a little prayer of blessing for her!"

Kathleen was about to reply to the good news, but Anne had more to tell, "And there's also another ceremony to tell you about. When Harry came home at the end of last year, he said he wanted to make our being together as man and wife, official. So just before Edna's 'naming', Harry and I will be married at Bolton's Register Office." Then with a smile Anne added, "So, at least, I'll have one child who isn't a bastard!"

Smiling, Kathleen replied, "About time he made an honest woman of you!"

Anne laughed, Then apologetically continued, "But I'm afraid Harry insists the only guests will be Mam, plus Dick Holden and Alice. Just hope you understand."

Kathleen, *did* understand. She was sure Harry loved her sister but like Jimmy he wanted to take control of all the important decisions. So she just took Anne's hand, saying, "Of course, I understand, Anne, love. Just now you're having to make compromises." Then her tone became more serious, "Just make sure that when you're stronger, Harry doesn't get *all* his own way!"

Of course, regular letters to and from Ireland continued to give Kitty much pleasure. Her reply to Denis' Christmas letter omitted any reference to Anne's sudden attack of 'flu'. There seemed no point in including any negative news at the festive period. She decided that her next letter could contain news about the Christmas drama of Edna's birth. However, her letter did contain a query about the political situation in Ireland since the rise of Sinn Fein. There had been reports that Lloyd George had declared Sinn Fein, and the recently formed Irish Republican Army, illegal. He and his government were condemning them as murderers and thugs.

Denis's reply was, "I must admit that the so-called Irish Republican Army (not a *real* army), have been carrying out a campaign of murder and various attacks. It's mainly against the police and the British solders here. (I recall you told me your Dad, my Granddad, was in the RIC.) The British Government is trying to stamp it out with arrests, imprisonment and use of arms. So I'm afraid there's hatred between the two nations at the moment. But don't you be worrying yourself about it Mam! I'm thinking there'll soon be a settlement between us and the British."

Reassured by her son's words, Kitty turned her thoughts to enjoying a more settled life with her two young grandchildren, Harry and Anne. They were approaching the ages of five and four and were now developing their own distinct personalities. Harry was the 'joker' of the two, loving to play tricks on his sister, but always quick to defend her if any older children tried to bully her when they played outside. Young Anne loved to sing and dance, and was always ready to try to copy the cartwheels and gymnastics of the older girls.

Kitty was always pleased to see that Harry, Anne, and the children enjoyed the meals she had waiting for them at tea-time - but she couldn't help resenting the fact that, recently, Harry never expressed a word of appreciation for all her help.

At least he wasn't hostile towards her now, as he had been when she'd first moved to Bolton. The only time he showed any real irritation was when she bowed her head before eating, giving silent thanks for her food. She recalled how, in the early days, he'd put a stop to her saying prayers aloud at the table by ordering, "I'll 'ave none o' that mumbo jumbo In my 'ouse! I wants young 'Arry and Anne brought up proper! And no more o' that barmy crossin' thasel. Just think on!"

Despite 'hiccups' like that, 1919 moved on reasonably happily for Kitty and all her family, both in Wigan and in Bolton.

Just as long as she remembered to 'think on' and tried to keep her faith more or less hidden, Harry tolerated her presence in his house.

Chapter 64

Time to Leave

It was quite early on a chilly March morning in 1920 when Kitty received the letter from Kathleen in Wigan. It seemed that Jimmy had, for some time, reverted to his former habit of going out almost nightly and drinking heavily. Moreover he'd recently tried to use his fists again - but this time on thirteen year old Anne. It was because she'd dared to confront her Dad as he arrived home drunk. She told him in no uncertain terms that all his wages were going into the pub landlord's pockets whilst Mam was scrimping just to put food on the table. He'd fixed Anne with an angry glare and tried to punch her with his fist, but the blow missed because she ducked, and Jimmy over-balanced, falling against the door. Whilst he struggled to get up, Kathleen had given him a swift kick and quickly dashed upstairs with Anne.

The letter continued with Kathleen telling Kitty how, on the following day, there were the usual pointless apologies and excuses made by Jimmy. They fell on deaf ears. The outcome was that her daughter had had enough and would be leaving him as soon as she could find somewhere she could afford.

Naturally, Kitty was worried - especially regarding the shortage of money. But she also thought Kathleen was now able to start a new life without Jimmy Carr. She was proud too of Anne's courage in speaking up on her mother's behalf.

Unfortunately, Kitty's, worries didn't end there. In Bolton, both she and Anne had noted that Harry's visits to the 'Man and Scythe' in Churchgate had increased. For the first two years of baby Edna's life, Harry had cut back drastically on his visits to the pub. Yet since the turn of the year - and with encouragement from brother-in-law, Dick - the visits had become regular again.

Though neither women feared violence from Harry on his return home, there were other repercussions from his actions. All too often his drinking was followed by court appearances. Here, both Harry and Dick would be charged with 'breaching the peace', or worse still, causing bodily harm to someone during a fight. Their 'guilty' pleas were followed by fines and subsequent press reports, albeit brief, in 'Bolton Evening News'. So, not only was precious money being wasted on drink and fines, but also the press accounts were a great source of embarrassment to both wives. And Anne's confrontations with Harry only ended in apologies.

Kitty had tried for months not to interfere in her daughter's affairs, but after another drunken fight, she felt she just had to say something to Harry. So the very next evening, when her son-in-law was alone in the kitchen about to have a shave prior to another 'Scythe' visit, she went into action.

Calmly, but coldly, she spoke as he brushed lather on his face."I'll be brief Harry. There's no point in repeating all that Anne's said time after time. I truly believe ye love her, so for that reason, I'm giving you a chance to do something before it's too late. Her sister is leaving her husband in a week or two because he's behaving in the same thoughtless and cruel way as you. She's found an affordable house near Wigan and will be asking Anne to join her. And I've no doubt Anne will jump at the chance to leave ye if things don't change - and quickly!"

Harry, chin filled with foam, paused, looking taken aback by Kitty's words. She added, "If I were you, I'd think very carefully before going out tonight!"

❦ ❦ ❦

Kitty's words clearly gave Harry the shock he needed. Not only did he stay at home on the evening of the warning, but the next day he told Anne he'd now realised what effect his actions were having on her and his family. He blamed much of his behaviour on Dick and made a point of going round to the Holden's house and explaining that Anne was about to leave him if he didn't give up his drinking.

From then, life for Anne and Harry moved on fairly peacefully. However the atmosphere between Kitty and her son-in-law was unpredictable.

At times, he seemed to tolerate her presence reasonably well. At others, especially when she was talking to, or playing with his two elder children, he would look at her resentfully.

In Autumn that year matters came to a head. Five-year old Anne had started school in September, and one morning before setting off there with her brother, she went upstairs to say 'Bye' to her Grandma. As Anne entered the bedroom which she, her brother, and Grandma shared, she saw Kitty quietly speaking whilst running a long necklace of brown beads through her hands. She knew Grandma often said prayers but she'd never seen the necklace before. It seemed quite pretty with its silver chain connecting all the beads.

Seeing Anne, Kitty hastily put her rosary into the small cupboard by her bed. She asked brightly, "Morning darlin', are ye off to school now?"

"Yes, Harry's waiting for me Granny. Just wanted to say, 'Bye'. See you soon." Kitty replied, "'Bye' darlin'. See ye at dinner-time."

But all day at school Anne kept thinking about the pretty necklace. When school finished Harry left her and ran off to play with his cousin Dick, so Anne walked home on her own. Here, she found everyone busy. Mam was ironing, Granny was busy preparing the meal, and little Edna was sitting on the floor, happily chewing on a raw carrot. Noticing one of Granny's white aprons amongst the pile of items not yet ironed, Anne thought it would make a lovely cape for her to play 'dressing up' in. She worked out that she could wear it for a little while, then replace it at the bottom of the mountain of un-ironed clothes. Swiftly, she picked up the apron unnoticed, and made her way to the stairs, calling out "I'm just going up to play in my in my room, Mam."

"Alright, I'll call you when we're ready to eat," Anne replied.

Once in the bedroom, Anne went over to the drawer where Grandma had put the necklace. Carefully she took it out, and placed it round her neck. Then she draped the white apron over her head like a hood, letting it fall round her shoulders like a cape, while its two white 'ties' hung loosely down on either side. Of course, the 'cape' almost reached her ankles, and the 'necklace' hung well past her waist. Yet in Anne's imagination, she was a rich lady in her fine hooded cape and jewellery.

But, lost in her new world as a lady, young Anne lost track of time.

The next thing she heard was her father's voice at the bedroom door asking, "What's tha doin' in tha bedroom? Ma's called up twice an' 'er's ready to put t' tea on t' table!" Next moment, he'd flung open the bedroom door and was looking at his daughter dressed in what seemed to be a nun's outfit. Furiously, he demanded of her, "Wot's tha Granma bin tellin' thee abaht nuns? Come on! Tell me t' truth!"

In tears, the child didn't answer as she wondered what nuns were. She guessed they must be something her Dad didn't like.

Harry had had enough. He took her by the arm, and pushed her towards the stairs, shouting angrily, "Get down to tha Mam, an' show 'er what tha Granma's bin teachin' thee!"

Downstairs, Anne, Kitty and young Harry were all wondering what on earth young Anne had done. Then the tearful child appeared in her 'fine lady' outfit, closely followed by her Dad whose face had the expression of an angry bulldog.

Kitty let out a startled cry, "Oh Anne, love! How did ye find my rosary beads?"

Harry glared at Kitty. "Aye, I thowt tha'd pretend it were all little Anne's fault! Tha's bin poisonin' t' child's mind wi' all tha rubbish! And all t' while pretendin' tha's keepin' it to thasel! Tha'rt nobbut a bloody liar!" He paused to get his breath back. But before Kitty could make any reply, he declared,"Tha leaves this 'ouse now! Tha can go an' live wi' Kathleen. An' if *she* doesn't want thee, then bugger off back to bloody Ireland! That's weer tha belongs!"

Kitty strode over to her son-in-law, "Well now Harry Holt, let me tell ye this. I'm only too ready to leave this house and *you*. Ye bigoted old bugger. I've given Anne and everyone of your children all my love and care. And always will. But now I'm ready to be where I'm wanted by *everyone*." Then, waving her forefinger threateningly in his face she added the warning, "But I'll be watching ye every minute. So you think on that Harry Holt!"

Of course, there followed tears and pleadings from Anne as well as from young Anne and also young Harry. But both Harry and Kitty had made their decisions.

No longer would he tolerate the prospect of his mother-in-law 'poisoning' his children's minds with Catholicism.

And Kitty wanted to be free to practise her religion freely. In any case, now that Harry was showing signs of trying to curtail his drinking habits, Anne and her children had the chance of a fairly comfortable life.

Chapter 65

Bottling Wood

Having received her 'marching orders,' Kitty decided she might as well 'march' straightaway. Her elder daughter, Kathleen, had recently found and moved to a small affordable house in Whelley near Wigan. Fortuitously, she had asked her mother to visit as soon as she was able - so that was where Kitty decided to head for. She certainly couldn't face the thought of another meal, or another night, in Harry Holt's home. All she had to do was go upstairs and pack her scant possessions in the same old travelling bag that had accompanied her journey from Ireland to England all those years ago. Of course, when Kitty was actually ready to leave, there were heart-breaking scenes. Her two elder grandchildren were clinging to her coat, begging her not to leave, and between sobs, little Anne kept repeating, "I'm sorry I took your beads Granny."

As for Kitty's daughter, she was in the invidious position of wanting to tell her mother she didn't want her to go. But despite knowing that Harry had been incorrect in his assumptions about Kitty's supposed influence on young Anne, she knew life with her Mother *and* Harry would be intolerable for everyone. She hugged her Mam tightly for some time. That night, she wept bitter tears.

It was still early evening so Kitty decided to take the train from Bolton to Wigan and then walk the mile or so to Kathleen's home. She was sure her daughter wouldn't mind her spending the night there. From there she could plan her next move.

It wasn't long before Kitty was back in Wigan. She stood outside the station hoping to see someone who could direct her to Whelley near Bottling Wood, Kathleen's new home. By chance, the first passer-by was Arthur Wilson, the miner who'd once lodged with her and Robert. As well as being able to direct Kitty to Whelley, he wanted to know how life was treating her. For some reason, the life-changing events of the day caused her to break down, and Kitty began pouring out a 'potted' account of life in Harry Holt's house. A concerned Arthur wanted to know if she now intended living in Bottling Wood with her elder daughter, observing, "O' course ye'll soon be seeing it fer yoursel', but I reckon ye'll find it a bit of a ramshackle place." He thought for a moment, then continued, "Now don't tek this t' wrong way, but if tha wanted, tha could move in wi' me as a lodger. I never married, and my last lodger left a couple o' month ago, so it would help me wi' t' rent. Cross Street is where I live, number ten. Not a palace, but it's near where tha used to live so tha'll know it well." He paused again, adding, "If tha changes tha mind about Bottlin' Wood, come round about sixish, any day, and we can sort summat out."

Thanking him for the directions and the offer, Kitty said she'd better be on her way as it would be dark within the hour.

In fact, it didn't take Kitty long to find her daughter's house. Yet as she looked round at the surrounding area before knocking on the door, she was reminded of her first arrival in Wigan all those years ago. But this was far worse! Here, she saw coal-blackened, run-down houses with Alexandra Colliery and its huge slag heaps as their background. Arthur's opinion of the area had been quite correct.

Whilst knocking at the rickety door, Kitty muttered, "Dear God! Is this *really* the place you've chosen to live, Kathleen?"

The door was opened by her surprised daughter, Anne, and Edna stood close behind. Of course, Kitty was welcomed into the house immediately and offered something to eat and drink. Gladly she accepted, aware she'd not eaten that night.

During the course of the meal Kitty explained the reason for her unexpected appearance. Immediately, Kathleen was ready to go to Bolton next day and confront Anne and Harry, her sister and brother in law. Harry for his cruel and ungrateful treatment of Mam who'd been a godsend for his family. Anne for doing nothing to prevent Harry from ordering her Mam to leave.

Kitty pointed out that Harry had understandably grown resentful of having to share his home and children's love with *her*, 'A bloody Catholic'. She also explained the difficult position Anne was in. Not wanting her to go, but aware that without her Mother in the house there might be less tension in the family.

Kathleen remained doubtful, "Maybe you're right, Mam. Time will tell. Anyway, you know you're welcome to stay with *us* as long as you want. And there's good news about living *here*. In a couple of years, they're going to build brand new houses as they gradually pull down all these old ones. And anyone already renting a house has first choice in either renting or buying one of the new ones!"

"Well now, Kathleen, I won't lie to ye. It's a big relief to know ye won't be spending long in this place. However I won't be staying long, but I'd appreciate being able to have a few days with ye. I just need time to sort out where I'm living next - then in a year or so, I'm hoping to return to Sligo."

Three shocked faces gazed at Kitty in disbelief. There followed a moment of palpable silence before Kathleen spoke. "Sligo? But who will you know there? Your mother's dead, your brothers and sisters have moved away, or are dead too!"

An enigmatic smile appeared on Kitty's face as she answered, "Well now, that just shows ye don't know everything about my past life!" Then she told them about the young Kitty who'd been befriended by an older man in Ireland. How they'd kept in contact during her early days in Wigan and how, after his death, his son, Denis, had carried on the correspondence with her. Kitty continued by saying he had later married and had children. She ended her 'adapted information' by saying how often Denis had written to say that, once her children were settled in England, there'd always be a big welcome for her in his home in Sligo.

A long stunned silence followed.

It was broken by Kitty's speaking again. "So now that my four children here seem fairly settled, I'm thinking it's time to see my homeland once more. Not right away though, I'll be staying with a man your Dad and I knew for a while, Arthur Wilson. I bumped into him tonight and he's looking for a lodger. That would suit me fine. I'd be independent again, near my family, but not living with them."

In vain, Kathleen tried to dissuade her mother from her plans, but seeing that all her arguments 'fell on stony ground', she gave up, saying, "But remember, Mam, you'll always have a home with us if things don't work out as you'd hoped."

And so, after five days with Kathleen and the girls, Kitty moved to Cross Street to lodge with Arthur Wilson. Things worked out quite well. She got on with the miner and they had a similar sense of humour though his long hours down the pit meant they only saw each other from late afternoon. Staying there also gave Kitty the chance to see her sons, Bob, Billy and their families in Wigan more frequently. However, their reactions to her intention of visiting Sligo again were similar to Kathleen's.

After a few months with Arthur, Kitty wrote to Denis telling him of what had happened in Bolton, ending with Harry ordering her out of his home. She didn't want him to feel *obliged* to renew his invitation to join him and his family, so she stressed she was finding life as a lodger preferable to living in Bolton - at Harry's home.

Denis soon replied, expressing his shock at what had happened but pleased that Kitty felt 'easier' now she was not under Harry's roof. Then he again asked the question, "But isn't it time ye gave yourself some real peace and happiness and came over to Ireland to spend time with your family here?"

Consequently, it wasn't long before she and Denis were planning her journey to Ireland. Winter was approaching so it was decided that the summer months of the following year would be the best time for a journey by boat. Also, in the intervening months, Kitty would be able to prepare herself and her families in England for her forthcoming departure.

Chapter 66

Riverstown

It was six o'clock on a morning in late August when Kitty left Arthur's home to begin her long journey to Ireland. First, there had been the fairly short journey from Wigan's station to Lime Street in Liverpool. From there, she'd walked to where the packet steamer to Dublin was waiting. As she climbed aboard, she felt a flutter of excitement at this confirmation that she was now *really* heading for her homeland.

Downstairs with the steerage passengers she managed to find a seat. Soon she was hungrily eating the boiled ham sandwiches which Jane had made for her. She then began to recall how surprised and shocked her family had been when the news reached everyone. They all seemed to think it was a mistake to be travelling all that distance at the age of sixty - especially since she seemed to be joining a family she'd never met before. Gradually, though reluctantly, her children had come to terms with her decision. Next Kitty's thoughts turned to the ceilidh 'farewell' party provided by her family. It had been held in Billy's home since, as Billy had observed, "We might as well hold it where there's plenty grub on hand."

It had been good to have all her children and grandchildren gathered under one roof. And of course, Ellen and Jane had also been there to wish her well in her new life in Ireland. Only missing were sons-in-law, Harry and Jimmy - but then she hadn't expected *them*. Her friends included Lizzie, Mary and Margaret, and also Arthur, her recent landlord and erstwhile lodger.

As she thought of Lizzie, Kitty remembered the wretched life the young child had experienced whilst under the 'care' of her father, Robert. She was happy to see her now, both she and Mary were doing well in their boarding house. Along with them came memories of Mrs Rourke, her first landlady. She could see her clearly, the well-worn, shabby hat with its faded red rose on its long stem, bobbing about as she shared the latest gossip with them. Smiling, Kitty took a last bite of her ham sandwich.

During the eight-hour journey, Kitty passed the time by standing to stretch her legs, eating more of Jane's carefully wrapped sandwiches, and observing the other passengers. The majority of them seemed to be from different parts of Ireland. And before long she got into conversation with a friendly Irish woman who was travelling with her two sons to see her mother in County Wicklow. This would be the first time her mother had seen her grandsons, now aged ten and eight years. They were naturally very excited about their first journey abroad. When the steamer eventually arrived in Dublin, Kitty and the woman parted company, wishing each other well.

It was almost nine-thirty in the evening when Kitty's train left for Sligo. With a bit of luck, the train would reach its destination just before midnight. Physically tired, she'd planned to have a little nap before her arrival but she was so mentally alert that sleep eluded her. It was just before twelve when Kitty stepped excitedly but nervously from the train. Conflicting thoughts were now criss-crossing her mind. At last she was about to meet her first-born son. Yet what if he wasn't there to meet her? And if he was, would his family resent her? She walked somewhat apprehensively past the ticket-collector, and through to the station's entrance. Her doubts disappeared.

Across the road stood a tallish man grinning from ear to ear. It was so like the face and grin of Pat's - a face she'd known so well. Behind him was a pony and cart. This too brought back memories of her first encounter with Pat in the 'Coaching House' yard. Though no longer young, Kitty was still able to manage to run towards him with outstretched arms. At the same time, Denis ran to greet his mother.

As they embraced, Denis murmured "Ach, mother mine! D' ye know how long I've waited for this?"

Kitty looked into her son's dark green eyes and replied emphatically, "Not as long as *me* son! I had to part with ye only a few minutes after ye were born. Now, I can hardly believe I'm here, and with your arms around me. The Good Lord has truly smiled on me!"

Both were silent for some time. Just standing there, holding each other.

Suddenly aware of the lateness of the hour, Denis, put his arm round his mother's shoulders and led her towards the cart with its patiently waiting pony.

"Right now Mam! We've plenty of time ahead to enjoy each other's company. It's goin' to be nearly one o'clock by the time we're back home, and Mary's waiting up to meet you, along with our four older children."

As the pony and cart progressed through Ardkeerin, Denis suddenly gave a long, low whistle through his fingers. Almost immediately, Kitty saw a woman, whom she took to be Mary, coming out of one of the houses. It was, as Denis had described, single-storied, with a slate roof. Smoke was rising from its two chimneys and there was a fairly big garden with a bench at the front.

When they drew level, the pony was brought to a stop. A smiling Mary walked forward and gave Kitty a wave. Close behind her came four young boys. On seeing her, they too began waving eagerly. One boy, considerably taller than the other three, stepped forward to help Kitty as she climbed down from the cart. Politely, he shook hands with her, saying, "Failte! And welcome to our home Mrs. Gibbs. I'm Sean, and these three are my brothers, Pat, Francis and Denis." As he said their names, each boy stepped forward and shook Kitty's hand, also adding friendly words of welcome.

Each grandchild was given a heartfelt smile, followed by, "Thank ye," along with his name. Lastly, it was Mary's turn to approach Kitty, saying, "And the warmest of welcomes from me. Mary and James, our younger children, are in bed but are eager to welcome ye at breakfast time."

Overcome by the wonderful reception, Kitty looked fondly at Mary, replying "Thank ye. Ye 'll never know how much all this means to me."

Taking Kitty's arm, Mary ushered everyone inside, remarking, "Ach ye must be starving after your long journey! Being late, it's only a light supper, but I hope it'll keep ye going till breakfast."

Once inside, the four children who'd already eaten, were told by Mary to say 'Goodnight' to Kitty, then get themselves off to bed. Somewhat reluctantly, they bade Kitty "Beannaht." To this, she responded," Slanagus

Beannaht" (God bless Goodnight). Then they went along to their three, shared beds in the bigger bedroom.

It wasn't long before Kitty, Denis and Mary were sitting in the kitchen sharing a meal of freshly-baked yeast bread which they spread liberally with home-made blackberry jelly. The conversation was mainly about Kitty's journey, though she would have preferred to talk to her son and his wife about themselves and their children. The meal ended with a mug of hot milk. Denis raised his to Kitty, saying "To my dear mother. May your days here in Ireland be happy ones."

With a warm smile, Mary added, "Amen to that."

Whilst Mary cleared away the pots and mugs from the kitchen table and dampened down the fire, Denis opened a wooden door in an alcove at one side of the fireplace and beckoned to Kitty. Inside was a bed covered with newly washed sheets and a blanket. Denis said, "I hope ye'll be alright here, Mam"

"This'll be fine for me, son. Don't be forgetting, I was one of *ten* children!"

Then mother and son bade each other, "Slanagus Beannaht"

❧ ❧ ❧

But Kitty couldn't sleep for some time. Firstly, she went over every detail of this first meeting with her son after forty-two years apart.

But quite unbidden, thoughts of the people she'd left behind in England came into her mind - especially her grandchildren. She pictured young Harry with his blonde hair and impish but lovable ways. Then there was young Anne. The two had become very close, sharing little 'secrets' and stories of Kitty's early life. And, of course, there was little 'miracle baby,' Edna, the child they thought wouldn't live.

Similarly, her elder daughter, Kathleen and her children, had lived with her for two years after her first separation from Jimmy. Increasingly, Kitty had grown to know and love the two girls. Anne the quiet one, always wanting to help, and Edna, full of spirit, and afraid of nothing.

Of course, her sons had provided her with grandchildren too. Bob and Ellen had had four daughters, Ethel, Mabel, Beatrice and Mary. And, as though to balance, 'a surplus of lassies' as Bob had occasionally called his children, Billy and Jane had had three sons, William, Robert and Ronald.

Although Kitty had seen much less of these seven grandchildren, she loved each one of them.

Realising it would soon be time to get up, Kitty addressed herself pragmatically, "Right me girl! It's now time to enjoy being back in Ireland with the son ye thought never to see again." Then she murmured drowsily, "Ye'd better get some sleep now, or ye'll be fit for nothing come the morning!"

And indeed, the following days and year brought contentment for Kitty. From the start, she and Mary understood each other's 'position' in a household which held a wife and a mother-in-law. Past experience had taught Kitty the difference between helping and interfering - and for that, Mary was grateful.

Also, she got to know the children individually. The two elder boys, Sean and Pat, aged fourteen and thirteen, were eager to become independent. Sean had already left school and was working as a labourer along with his Dad. It gave Kitty great pleasure to hear him and Pat with their father at night, entertaining the family by playing on their tin-whistles. Bitter-sweet memories for Kitty.

Sons, Franny and Denny, aged eleven and ten years were still at school. Like many 'middle' children, they lived somewhat in the 'shadow' of their elder brothers.

Young Mary, aged seven and the only girl, was spoiled and teased in turn by her elder brothers. She reminded Kitty of Edna, being clever and rather precocious. And unlike many young Irish children, she was not afraid to ask questions if something 'sparked off' her curiosity. Shay (James), her younger brother was a shy little boy.

One day after her arrival, she was feeding the family's dozen or so hens with Mary and Shay. It gave her the chance to be with her grandchildren, and it reminded her of Cloonacool where she and Mam had fed the hens. Whilst she carried the bucket of peelings, boiled potatoes and egg shells, Mary and Shay had made their way to the expectant, clucking hens. Whilst watching them feed, Mary regarded Kitty quizzically, saying, "Mam told us ye used to know Grandma Dowd."

Cautiously, Kitty replied, "Yes, Mam was right, I knew your Grandma."

"So ye were her friend then?" pursued Mary. Kitty gave a slight nod, and Mary continued, "So ye must have walked to school together."

Kitty hesitated, then said, "No. Because we didn't go to the same school."

A puzzled Mary continued, "But I'm thinkin' ye must have played together?"

Wondering where this was leading, Kitty said, "No. We just knew each other."

Mary pondered awhile. Then she gave her opinion. "Well, Mrs Gibbs, I think it was a funny sort of a friendship. Maybe Grandma didn't always know what you were saying. Ye sound a bit different from most Irish folk, and use some funny words." Seeing Kitty looking worried, she added, "But I like your funny talk!"

Relieved, Kitty replied, "*That's* good. But maybe no more questions, Mary?"

One evening, some months after Kitty's arrival, Denis put forward a suggestion to her. He thought that since Kitty had now become an accepted member of the family, she might like to be addressed less formally by everyone. Denis went on to explain, "Mary and I could tell the children it would have been Grandma Dowd's wish for ye to be called 'Aunt Kitty'. Also, we could tell them she wouldn't have minded me and Mary callin' ye 'Ma'.

"I'd love that *son*. I think it's a grand idea."

Though everything in the Dowd household was running smoothly, the political scene between England and Ireland was a different matter. After 1918, the British coalition government (Lloyd George, Conservative, and Asquith, Liberal), had proposed a new Home Rule Bill for Ireland. One which didn't please all the Irish people, and by 1920 the IRA campaign became more widespread and brutal. Consequently, the British government responded by sending troops to Ireland and introducing martial law in the south.

It was a grim war, consisting of terror, counter terror and atrocities on both sides. One of the worst episodes took place in November 1920 in Dublin and became known as 'Bloody Sunday'. Luckily, Sligo was relatively less affected by the terrors of this period since IRA activities there were largely limited to harassment. This was due to Sligo Town being heavily garrisoned by members off the British army. Denis had commented, "Well now, for once, I'm glad to have Brits here, just as long as they keep the IRA under control, and out of our way."

By early 1921, it was clear that neither side were going to be 'winners' but it took until July eleventh before both sides signed a truce. The Anglo-Irish Treaty of 1921 established the Irish Free State (now the republic of Ireland) but excluded the six counties of Northern Ireland. Though the treaty ended the war with Britain, bitter feelings still existed within Ireland between those who supported the treaty and those against it. And these were destined to be long lasting.

As the time passed, Kitty grew increasingly close to her son, Mary, and her grandchildren - especially the three younger ones, Denis, known as Denny, Mary and Shay.

February of 1922 had brought several falls of snow, so it was a relief when March arrived, bringing some chilly, but fine, sunny days. Soon, the bright, yellow colours of colt's foot and celandine flowers were popping up in all the hedgerows It made Kitty long to see 'Caw Wood' again, named by Master Thomas long years ago.

So one Saturday afternoon, she and the three younger grandchildren set off for Ardkeerin's churchyard in search of nearby 'Caw Wood'. The noisy rooks were the first birds they saw and heard, and soon all three were trying to imitate their harsh calls - and laughing at each other's attempts. Mary was also interested in the wild flowers, and considered she'd found something special when she spotted a small, wild daffodil, just about to open. But it was a small, cheeky little robin which caught the attention of Shay. The bird was perched on the lower branch of a holly tree, seeming to cock its head towards the young boy in friendly greeting. Kitty warned them all to keep still and just quietly observe the little bird.

"It's called a robin," whispered Mary, proud of her knowledge. "A robin red-breast, because of its red chest." A thoughtful Shay pondered this information. Then he turned to Kitty; also speaking in a whisper, "But its chest isn't red, it's orange! So why isn't it called 'Robin orange-breast', Aunt Kitty?" A pause, then, "Or is Mary wrong?" Kitty explained, "Not at all Shay. Mary's quite correct." Mary beamed, then pulled a face at her brother. "But your question was a good one, Shay." He, in turn, pulled a face at his sister. "My mother told me that the robin was first described as 'red-breast' about five hundred years ago. There was *no* colour orange until about fifty years later when we first got the fruit we call orange. But by then we had already named the bird, Robin red breast!"

"So ye see, ye were both right! But nobody bothered to change the name."

Mary and Shay both looked pleased with themselves. Denny had been drawing a sketch of the robin in a small notebook but suddenly the object of the discussion, decided to fly off. Denny stood up, gazing after his 'model' in some disappointment.

Kitty observed, "He must have a wife to get back to. Anyroad he's better things to do than sit around whilst children blather on about the colour of his chest!"

This made Denny laugh. Then they continued their walk through the wood.

That night in bed, Kitty realised how much she'd missed the countryside, and being able to observe its wonders in the company of children.

❧ ❧ ❧

Of course, since leaving Bolton and Wigan, Kitty had kept in regular contact with her four children. As is often the case, it was her two daughters and daughters-in-law who sent her their news most regularly.

Anne seemed reasonably contented with life. Young Harry and Anne were quite happy at school, Anne more so than her brother. Both had good brains, but whereas Anne was eager to learn, Harry's favourite times at school were, in his words, 'Playtimes, dinner-time and home-time'. Also, husband Harry was going to the pub less frequently.

Billy and family seemed to be faring well. The building business was doing well so he and brother Bob had decided to go into partnership.

Sons William and Bob now aged seven and five, were fine, though William didn't seem as active or talkative as Bob.

The news from Kathleen had been optimistic. Her name was already on the list for renting one of the new houses to be built that year. The other good news was that young Anne had settled well in her domestic work for the Tarbuck family in Whelley.

Ellen wrote to Kitty on behalf of Bob and the girls. She mentioned him going into partnership with Billy, though her main news was about a fifth baby due that year. This time Bob had promised that, whatever its sex, it would be welcome.

So, all in all, the news back in England was positive. Naturally, her family had been worried about the 'situation' between England and Ireland, but Kitty had reassured them that the north-west of Ireland was being protected by the British Army.

※ ※ ※

Months passed, and on a mild evening in early September when the main work of the day was finished, Kitty and Denis were taking a rare opportunity to chat together. They sat outside on the bench made by Denis, expressing their relief at the truce which had been signed with England two months earlier. Denis was hoping the British Army who'd been sent over to garrison Sligo Town would soon be leaving.

"Aye, they've done their job, time for them to beggar off back now, and leave things to the RIC" Denis gave a long sigh, then said, "But I'll be honest, Ma, I'm none too fussed about policemen either! In fact, some of them can be real shites!"

Kitty paused. Though Denis had met his Scottish maternal Grandma on many occasions, she had never mentioned her husband's occupation. Smiling, she said, "Ach well, son, you're not the first Irishman with *that* view. But I have to tell ye that your Granddad, Edward Tooey, was with the RIC from 1842, before the days of the 'Potato Famine' until retirement. He died in 1878, the same year as your birth.

Denis looked at his mother incredulously, then laughed before saying,"Well Ma, they do say we can't choose our relations! Who'd have thought I had a Granddad who was a 'peeler!" Then he went on, "By the way Ma, ye said ye'd like to see Sligo Town again. Well the next time I'm going to Ballymote, I'll take ye with me, so ye can catch the train from there. The British Army may be still in the town, but there shouldn't be any trouble these days."

So on a cloudy but fine Saturday morning in mid September, Kitty alighted from Denis' cart and boarded the train for Sligo Town. The journey took less than thirty minutes, and Kitty was soon making her way from the station to the town centre. She was eager to see if the drapery shop, once owned by Edna Dooley, was still there.

It was very busy since Saturday was a market day. Kitty was struck by how many buildings seemed to have either been replaced, renovated or even demolished. When she eventually found the place where 'Dooley's Drapery and High-class Dressmaking' establishment had been, she discovered that it was now a very modern shop. Its double-fronted windows held models displaying all manner of ready-made women's outfits. The higher hemlines of many of the dresses would certainly have met with Edna Dooley's disapproval Yes, it was a far cry from the days of hand-made dresses when part of her work had been to carry rolls of material from the back room to the front of the shop.

A walk along the River Garavogue was her next 'port of call'. The first thing she noticed was how much work had been done on the pathway beside the river. A big improvement, for sure. The relaxing sound of water continually moving over stones and shells once again filled her with a feeling of calm. As Kitty continued her walk, she encountered several people also enjoying the chance to take a leisurely stroll there. Many gave her a cheery nod. A mile or so further on, she was pleased to see that many more trees of varying kinds had been planted on the far side of the path.

Before retracing her steps back to the town, Kitty stood quite still, just enjoying the 'music' of the river. Suddenly, a kingfisher with its brilliant blue, emerald and green markings flew from its perch on an alder tree some distance away, plunged into the water, emerged with some small fish, and flew off into the distance.

It was Kitty's first sighting of this unmistakeable bird. Years ago, Mam had described them to her, adding that seeing one was a good omen. Kitty smiled, saying softly, "So there ye are, Mam! Still watching out for your wayward daughter!"

Chapter 67

World events. Kathleen's New 'Friend'

For some time, the neighbours of the Dowd family had been rather puzzled by the sudden arrival of this stranger from England. Firstly, though she spoke with a Sligo brogue, it was often intermingled with an accent and expressions which seemed to suggest the north of England. Secondly, though she appeared to have settled in well with the Dowds, nobody could recall how she was connected with the family.

In fact it had taken over a year before Kitty was 'half-accepted' by them. It was about that time Kitty decided she wanted to make a full confession of her past sins to Father John in St Joseph's church. Though very apprehensive as she approached the confessional, she felt her burden of guilt had been greatly reduced once she'd received her penance. Yet she also considered her penance did not fully atone for her actions all those years ago. So it seemed her thoughts had been read when only a week later, Father John asked her to stay behind after the congregation had left. Once alone, he said,"Now, Kitty, I have a proposal for ye. The lady who scrubs the stone floors and polishes the pews in church is unable to continue due to ill-health. So I'm wondering if you would be willing to take over her work? The payment is small," he paused significantly, "but then it's God's work after all! Think about it for a while."

But Kitty made up her mind to accept the job that same day. She reasoned that this would serve two purposes. Firstly, hard work for little pay would be further atonement for her sins, and secondly, it would give her a bit of money of her own. She had a little smile as she thought to herself, "I bet that wily old Father John had it all planned once I'd made my confession to him."

❧ ❧ ❧

Of course, letters from England kept Kitty up-to-date with news about her family. She was particularly pleased to receive one from son, Bob, telling her proudly that Ellen had given birth to twins, a son and a daughter, to be baptised Robert and Joan. He wrote that when Ellie told him she was having twins, he thought it was sure to be two lassies. So they'd both been delighted to have a healthy son and daughter.

As people grow older, it seems that the years pass by at an alarming rate. And Kitty was no exception to this phenomenon. It seemed scarcely credible that she'd been in Riverstown for two years. She'd settled in well with her son and new family - despite the 'Anglo-Irish War' which was going on. Like many others in Sligo, Kitty and the Dowds just 'kept their heads down' and got on with their lives.

The signing of the Anglo-Irish Treaty in December 1921 should have put an end to the 'war'. But it didn't please everyone in Ireland. The treaty recognised the independence of the Irish Free State (later to become the Irish Republic), whilst the six counties of Ulster remained as Northern Ireland within the United Kingdom. It was this 'partition' of Ulster which was the main cause of contention in Ireland, and, at the end of 1922, there began a brutal civil war which lasted until 1923. Luckily, being pro treaty, Sligo escaped most of the horrors, but naturally everyone was relieved when it finally ended. But bitterness between factions endured. ([1])

Some time after the end of the civil war when Kitty and Denis were having one of their 'bench chats', he asked "Are ye still hopin' to see Cloonacool, the place ye were born, Ma? It should be safe to go there now, and I'd come with ye."

"Well I was, son," Kitty said doubtfully, "I have such lovely memories of the countryside there, but I also wanted to see Dad's barracks again. So once we heard the bloody IRA had burned them down, it made me think again. Perhaps it's best I keep memories of Cloonacool in my head." Denis nodded in agreement.

Another two years flew by before Kitty received news from Kathleen regarding their move to one of the new council houses in Bottling Wood. All were pleased with their new house, especially their address of 35,

Rosemary Crescent. Also, Anne and Edna had jobs working as 'general helps' for the Tarbuck family.

Yet less than a year later, Kathleen's letter revealed that the economic situation had caught up with the Tarbuck family. Now they were having to 'let go' of some of their staff, including Anne and Edna. The outcome was that Anne and Edna saw this as a chance to move up in the world. Both obtained jobs as waitresses in the prestigious Adelphi Hotel in Liverpool. It was thriving due to the increased number of guests staying there before emigrating - especially to America.

As the months passed, Kathleen's letters reported that the girls had settled well in their new work though women's pay was poor. However, pay for nineteen year old Anne increased when she was chosen to be trained as a silver-waitress in the main restaurant. But Kathleen was not pleased when, soon after promotion, Anne started mentioning a young man called Joe Ashton. He was one of the workers on the railway sidings at Edge Hill Station in Liverpool. In her next letter, Kathleen's displeasure had become strong disapproval when she'd discovered his religion. She now referred to him as 'That damned proddy'.

There was another surprise for Kitty when, at the end of that year, Kathleen's letter bore a different address. It was no longer Rosemary Crescent in Bottling Wood, but Cantsfield Street in Liverpool. "Holy Mother!" exclaimed Kitty. "What's she up to now?" Reading on, she discovered Kathleen had been missing the company of her daughters, so having heard that a council house was up for sale in Cantsfield Street near the Adelphi, she'd left Bottling Wood. and moved there.

"That girl has me in a tizzy!" was Kitty's final comment on the news.

By May the following year, Kathleen wrote to say that Anne and Joe were now married - and the ceremony had taken place in St Dunstan's Church of England. It seemed the wedding had caused a big row between her and Anne, and also between Joe and his parents. However, all three had attended the ceremony and kept their thoughts to themselves. After the ceremony, the couple went to their council house in Mason Street, not far from her mother's home in Cantsfield Street.

In that same year, news reached Ireland of the miners' strike in Britain and it appeared to be getting very serious. Bob wrote about it to Kitty.

"Aye Mam, the price of coal's been dropping for some while. So what do ye think the bloody bosses did? Only asked the men to work more hours for lower wages! Course, the lads did what any bugger would do. They threatened to strike. There's bad feelings everywhere, and the bloody strike affects everyone here!" (²)

A year after Anne's marriage to Joe, a baby son was born. Kitty's first Great Grandchild. Young Joe had fairish hair and large, cornflower blue eyes like his mother . Of course, the arrival of a first Grandchild mellowed Kathleen's opinion of the 'mixed marriage.' But the end of the letter had Kitty worried. It seemed Edna had banked on getting Anne's job as a silver-service waitress when she married, but it never happened. So now Edna was thinking of seeking work elsewhere. In a time of unemployment, it seemed foolish to Kitty. "What an eejit," she said to herself.

By 1929, life for many people world-wide was to become even bleaker with the onset of what became known as the 'Great Depression' (³). It was commonly thought to have started with the New York Stock Exchange crash in October of that year, and affected all capitalist countries. So for Britain and Labour Prime Minister, MacDonald, it was a truly disastrous time. A worried Kitty feared that it would hit her family in England very hard. Though Ireland was affected by the Depression, the Irish Free State, being mainly agrarian, was luckier than industrial countries.

Denis was fully aware of Kitty's worries, and tried to give her some comfort. During one of their 'bench talks' he said, "Ye must remember Ma, ye have two resourceful sons and they're in the buildin' trade. So though workin' for less money, they're not without work." Kitty replied, "Aye! But it's Kathleen and Anne I'm worrying about most. They may not be faring so well." Denis had no ready words of comfort regarding his half-sisters.

In fact Kathleen wrote that Anne, Joe and their baby were just about coping. But Edna was still thinking of leaving the Adelphi to find work near London.

Daughter Anne's news was more or less as expected. Since Harry held a good position as a cotton-loom overseer, he *had* a job - but on reduced pay and longer hours. Now he was being asked to work seven days a week.

Anne wrote, "You can guess Harry's reaction to this, Mam. I won't repeat what he calls the mill owners, but last night, coming home worn out as usual, he greeted me with, "Time of bloody depression Annie? More like a time fer slittin' bloody throats!"

Anne went on to write that Harry and Anne, being now fifteen and fourteen, were at least earning a bit of money in any way they could. Harry, encouraged by his Dad, had kept fit by going for boxing lessons to 'Bolton's Lads' Club. So now a strong, fit lad, he did gardening for people who lived in some of the big houses on Chorley Old Road. Young Anne had also found work as a servant there.

Anne concluded, "So though times are hard, we're managing. And that's more than can be said for many others. In fact, in some parts of Bolton folk have been organising protest marches against MacDonald's government. But they get nowhere. I've had to stop Harry from joining them - you know how he likes a punch-up!

And somehow, most people in Britain *did* manage to 'get through' those dire days of unemployment, reduced wages and hunger marches.(⁴) In fact, a letter from Kathleen written in 1930, contained some surprising, and potentially good news about Edna. Apparently, she'd 'taken the plunge' and moved south to Brentford, travelling on a discount railway ticket, courtesy of Joe Ashton. Here, due to a recommendation from the head-waiter, she had obtained work with the wealthy Bunting family. It seemed they'd bought shares in two companies in the early 1900s, these being the Ealing Studios and the Firestone Tyre Company. Both had been extremely successful and still continued to thrive despite the Depression.

Edna was back to being a general help, but Ken Bunting, her employer, was certainly giving her better pay than she'd received at the Adelphi. Also, her bright manner and experience as a waitress soon caught the attention of Rose Bunting, who asked for her help when they'd held dinner parties for their wealthy friends.

In a letter just a few months later, Kathleen wrote of Edna's friendship with the Buntings' gardener, a young man called Robert. And only three months after that, Kathleen's next letter informed her Mother that Edna and Robert Whiteland had married the previous week.

Kitty sighed, it seemed Edna was just like her mother - doing what she wanted, when she wanted!.

Kathleen then explained that, due to the Depression, Edna and Robert were keeping things simple with only the immediate family present, which included his parents and herself. She also went on to describe travelling down by train for the wedding and the feeling of excitement on arriving in London for the first time. From there it was only a short train-ride to Brentford.

Further letters from Kathleen informed Kitty of Edna's pregnancy, and her pleasure at being asked to be present at the baby's birth. So once more she'd travelled south, arriving in time to help the midwife deliver baby Kenneth into the world. Kathleen's second Grandchild. As she read of Kenneth's birth, Kitty, now aged seventy-two, felt quite privileged to have lived long enough to hear of the birth of a second Great Grandchild - even though she would probably never see either of them.

However another letter from Kathleen contained news which caused Kitty some concern. Apparently her daughter had travelled south again to see her little Grandson. But he wasn't the only person she'd seen when her visit ended! Kathleen wrote of how she had been waiting in London, ready to catch the train to Liverpool. An unexpected delay of an hour meant she'd begun looking for a seat on the crowded platform. Suddenly a bespectacled well-dressed man sitting at the end of one of the station-benches stood up to offer her his seat.

The letter continued, "So I thanked him, and sat down. He just stood by the side of me. I could tell he was weighing me up. Perhaps it was my polka-dot dress that caught his eye? Anyway, I didn't want to let on I knew he was looking at me, so I pretended to be looking at a mark on dress. Then he spoke to me in a deep posh voice, asking how far I was travelling. When I told l him I was going to Liverpool, he said he was going there too to attend a meeting. He was quiet for a bit. Then he says he's a clerk with 'Railway Clearing House'. Sounds like a good job to me."

"Anyway, the top and bottom of it all is that we carried on talking all the way to Liverpool. He was a real gentleman and said he'd like to see me again. And Mam, he lives on his own in a big house in Twickenham! He asked for my address and he's sending me a return ticket from Liverpool!"

"Oh Mam! I know you'll think I'm well past all this sort of thing. But I've never been as happy as this for a long time. Am I being a fool? I do like him!"

But Kitty *did* think her daughter was being a fool - and too old for all this nonsense. "Holy Mary, Kathleen!" she thought, "How could ye let yourself fall for his lies? He'll be married with a family, and you're just his 'bit on the side'."

However, all she wrote in reply was, "Just be careful, lass. Don't rush into anything. Remember ye've two young grandsons now to fill your life."

Footnote[1]

In Ireland during this same period, Fianna Fail (the republican political party, founded by de Valera) was gaining in popularity (helped by some questionable canvassing on their behalf by the illegal IRA). In January 1933 however, their 'methods' were scarcely required since de Valera and his party were returned to power with an even greater number of seats. The Dowd family were hopeful that this Republican Government might see the beginning of a new, independent Ireland- as promised by de Valera.

Michael Collins, leader of those who supported the treaty, accepted it along with the partition clause relating to northern Ireland. He thought it would eventually lead to a republic. The anti-treaty faction, led by Eamon de Valera, rejected it, wanting a republic which included the whole of Ireland. He was also opposed to the taking of an oath of loyalty to King George V. There followed a civil war in Ireland in 1922 which was more brutal and destructive than the Anglo-Irish war. It was 1923 before matters were resolved. The pro-treaty party (now led by William Cosgrove) had won. Two states existed in Ireland, the Irish Free State and Northern Ireland.

Footnote[2]

The General Strike involved over three million people from transport, and all the main industries. The mine owners were then offered a compromise which the TUC thought was reasonable. So after nine days, the government stepped in and 'kept them quiet' by giving them a temporary subsidy. But when this ended, the situation was as before, and the mine owners ordered a lock- out. In turn, this led to the Trades Union Congress calling a general strike during which the strike was called off. However, the miners wouldn't accept the new terms and remained on strike for a further five months. At this point, out of necessity, they reluctantly re-commenced working for reduced wages and longer hours.

Footnote[3]

Along with other industrial countries, Germany had suffered greatly during the 'Great Depression' and Adolf Hitler (who had formed the National Socialist Party, Nazi, in 1921), steadily gained mass support. This was mainly due to his ideas for making Germany a powerful country again and creating jobs for the unemployed. By 1932, the Nazis were the largest party in the Reichstag, and in January 1933 he was appointed chancellor.

Footnote[4]

There were 'Hunger Marches' all over the country. The march from Jarrow's shipyard to the House of Commons in 1936 perhaps being the most famous. Here, as in many places, there had been steep declines in production and prices, accompanied by a steep rise in unemployment.

Chapter 68

Visitors for Kitty

Ironically, it was rumours of a second war with Germany which began a slight upturn in industrial production in Britain between 1932-3. The government began to plan for rearmament. And with that came cautious hopes of the economic situation improving.

Indeed, Anne's letters were *definitely* sounding more positive. All three children were now working for increased wages. These, together with Harry's wage, had given Anne hopes of being able to afford one of the new corporation houses being built on Crompton Way, on the outskirts of Bolton. Harry soon had his name down for one.

In the next letter from Bolton, Kitty could sense her daughter's excitement as she described the one they'd been allocated. It was a two storeyed, three bed-roomed, semi-detached house with a room upstairs containing washbasin, bath, and flush-toilet. Downstairs was a large living-room with large windows at either end, a smaller room at the front, referred to by Anne as a parlour, and quite a large kitchen at the rear. In addition to having a fair-sized gardens at back and front, the house was reached by walking up a slope. Views of playing fields could be seen from the front windows. Besides all that, Anne wrote proudly of the area's important connections, "Crompton-Way get its name from Samuel Crompton, inventor of the spinning-mule. He was born quite near here.

So it seems, Mam, we're really starting to move up in the world. Oh, and before I forget, Anne's changed her name to 'Nancy'. More 'refined' she says. Harry says, she getting 'Too bloody big for her boots'!"

Kitty was certainly delighted by the news, thinking to herself, "All those rooms plus parlour, *and* a flush-toilet. And also Anne has a refined daughter!"

There was more good news regarding Kitty's sons, Bob and Billy and their families. It was Jane, Billy's wife who wrote to Kitty telling her that the brothers' business in the building trade had started to improve again. She also explained that she and Billy had decided to move to Bolton and would be renting a house on Halliwell Road. Here, Billy would deal with the actual work, whilst Bob, in Wigan, looked after the books and orders. So the partnership would still be retained.

Jane also wrote that their sons, young Bob and Ronnie, were fine though William, their eldest son, now nineteen, still seemed to be 'in his own world'. She continued, "Bless him. He's no trouble, but not able to hold down a job. Luckily, Bob's managed to get a seven-year indentured apprenticeship as a master joiner."

Kitty was pleased about the move to Bolton. It meant they could keep contact with Anne and Harry more easily. She lit a candle for poor William.

On a warmish day in September, Kitty was sitting on the bench outside the house in Riverstown in the pleasant autumnal sunshine. Though mostly still green, some of the nearby trees were already losing their leaves. These lay in crinkly piles of yellow and bronze, the first heralds of autumn's approach.

Kitty closed her eyes enjoying the sun on her face, and thinking to herself, "Might as well make the most of it, I reckon my summers are numbered." Then she stretched out her legs, recently affected by painful bouts of rheumatism, so they too could enjoy the luxury of the warmth. However her reverie was interrupted as she became aware of footsteps approaching, and the sound of voices whispering. "Sh. I think she's asleep," then, "No, I think she's waking."

On rousing herself Kitty couldn't believe her eyes. Standing near the garden gate, all smiles, were Granddaughters Anne and Edna. Both were holding a young child in their arms. Beside them, grinning broadly was Denis who remarked casually, "Just saw these two pretty colleens passing by with their little ones and gave them a lift on my cart. Thought ye'd maybe know them."

Aches and pains in her knees forgotten, Kitty was up and moving forward to greet her Granddaughters and their little ones. Soon all three adults were hugging each other closely. The babies were 'squashed' in the middle of this 'triangle of love.'

Once inside the cottage, Kitty learned how this amazing event had been able to take place. It seemed that Kathleen's 'train companion', Mr Hatcher, was not the 'Railway Romeo' which Kitty had thought him to be. Not only was he single, but also very much in love with her daughter. Edna described the speedy developments between her mother and Alfred Hatcher.

"Well, soon after their meeting, Alfred posted Mam the rail ticket he'd promised her, so of course she was able to see us and baby Kenneth again. And after a week with us, he invited Mam to stay at his big house for a few days."

Sister Anne was eager to continue the tale, "So when Mam came to see me soon after Norman was born, she was full of praise for Alfred. Me and Joe were both struck by the lovely new clothes he'd bought her. Joe reckoned it must have cost a bob or two. Of course, me and Edna wondered how long it would all last!"

Anne continued after a short pause, "Only a few months later she'd moved in with him and he asked her to marry him." Anne looked at Kitty, then said, "But of course she couldn't, could she Mam? She never got divorced from Dad! Anyway, me and Edna are happy for her!"

Edna nodded in agreement. "Yes. And they've been together for over a year now. Alfred's been generous with me and Anne as well as Mam. When he heard us saying we hadn't seen you for thirteen years, he said he'd pay our fare to come over to see you, Granny. Of course we had to write to your friend Denis here, and tell him about our plan. and to keep it a secret." She looked at Denis, ending, "And he did. And here we are!"

For Kitty, this was a most amazing surprise. Here were the Granddaughters she'd never expected to see again. And with them were Great Grandchildren she'd only heard of in letters! Now she *had* to admit Alfred seemed to be a genuinely generous and kind man, one who was making her daughter happy. Hopefully, their relationship would stand the test of time. But for now she was thankful to him and the Good Lord for making the visit possible. She was also grateful to Denis for his part in the 'plot'.

Their stay lasted only three days, since both Anne and Edna didn't want to be away from their families for too long. They were sleeping in the two bed-roomed council house which Sean and Elizabeth had managed to obtain when they'd married earlier that year. So during the visit, they were able to see their Grandma each day.

Although Denis and the Dowd children were at work most of their stay, Denis' wife and daughter, Mary, were only too happy to 'entertain' eight months old Edna (Anne's fourth child) and Kenneth, (Edna's first child) aged eleven months. But it was their doting Great Grandma who took them out to watch the hens being fed, and loved it when Edna and Kenneth tried to imitate their clucking sounds. And there was still time for Kitty and her Granddaughters to enjoy each other's company.

On the evening before their English guests' departure, Denis and Mary had arranged a ceilidh for them. Anne and Kitty were thrilled at the thought of actually being in Ireland to experience a real Irish party. Denis had invited some of the neighbours, including old Mickey, one of his Dad's friends. People said he could almost make his fiddle talk. Of course, Denis and Sean, had their tin whistles at the ready for the evening's entertainment Meanwhile, Mary, young Mary, and neighbours had prepared the usual mountains of sandwiches.

Indeed, it turned out to be a great evening, with Kitty happily sitting next to her Granddaughters. She loved seeing their faces as they watched the intricate footwork of dancers responding to the irresistible music of the jigs, expertly supplied by tin whistles and violin. Soon Anne's and Edna's feet were tapping in time with the dancers, and it wasn't long before Edna, beckoned by young Mary, was up and trying to follow the jig patterns herself.

It was then that Kitty asked her Granddaughters, "Would the two of ye like to show us one of your English dances?"

Anne shook her head, saying she'd never done much dancing. However Edna, ever ready to show off, and having been impressed by the new dance she'd seen in her local picture-house, replied, "Well it's not an English dance, but it's all the rage at the moment. It's called the 'Charleston' and it's from America. I'll show you some of the moves if you like, but I'll hum the tune - I doubt if it goes with whistles and violins!"

Though not keen on American music, Kitty clapped her hands for silence, and announced the next dance. She made a point of stressing it was American in origin. Then Edna took the floor and began the lively dance with its gawky characteristic moves, at the same time humming 'Yes sir, that's my baby'. The dance involved turning her feet out then in whilst keeping the knees together, and using the hands to criss-cross over the knees, it also included kicking up her legs to touch her posterior.

The Irish audience watched in bewildered silence for about ten seconds, clearly not expecting a dance which seemed so bizarre. But gradually, led by Kitty and Anne, they responded to Edna's enthusiasm and energy and began clapping in time to the rhythm. At the end there was loud applause and shouts of "More, more!"

Kitty whispered to nearby Denis, "Dear God! I don't know what anyone sees in all that graceless nonsense. Though I dare say it seems good to those Yankees!"

However, most of the rest of the evening was more to Kitty's taste as it included many of her favourite Irish songs.

Next day, when the time came for Anne and Edna to return home, there were, of course, sad farewells. As they were leaving the house, Anne turned and called to her Grandma, "Remember what we talked about Granny. If you feel you could make the journey to England, you'll make all your family very happy."

And blowing their last kisses, the two women and their babies joined Denis with his pony and cart.

Chapter 69

Surprising News From Anne

It wasn't long after her Granddaughter's visit that Kitty received news from her daughter, Anne. She was now forty-four and had not felt well for a while due to what she considered to be the onset of the menopause. After visiting her doctor, Anne was diagnosed with an ovarian cyst which was to be removed surgically that November. It caused Kitty some worry since surgery was not always successful.

However Anne's next letter contained different and surprising news. Apparently, after her rather long pre-operation examination, the consultant had said, "Mrs Holt, I won't be removing a cyst. I advise you and Mr Holt to buy some baby clothes as you are approximately seven months pregnant."

It had certainly been a shock for Anne and she wondered how Harry would take the news. In fact, he was proud and delighted. Young Harry, Nancy and Edna, now in their late teens, certainly hadn't expected another sibling to be joining them.

It was January 30th 1934 when Kitty received Nancy's letter saying her Mum had given birth two days earlier to a baby girl. She added that both were well, though her Dad, who'd always pronounced 'cyst' as 'swiss', referred to the baby as, 'Big Swiss'. He boasted, "Big Swiss weighed nearly nine pounds! Big but bonny!"

Of course, Kitty was relieved to hear the news. And it occurred to her that now might be the time to make that trip back to England. As she had often reminded herself, "You're getting no younger, Kitty. It's the knacker's yard for ye before long!"

In a couple of months, with Denis' help, tickets had been bought for her travel back to Bolton. Here she would stay with Anne and her family for a week. Nancy had written that for some time their mother had felt much more able to 'stand up' to her husband. She had, in fact, already warned Harry that he must be on his best behaviour during her mother's stay.

Kitty muttered "About time Anne spoke up to that gobshite!"

After a long journey which included a rather rough crossing from Dublin to Liverpool, Kitty finally arrived at Trinity Street Station about ten o'clock on a Sunday morning in late March. Here, her weariness disappeared in a trice when she saw Anne standing with a handsome, blonde, young man. Both waved excitedly as she alighted from the train. Anne soon had her arms round Kitty, tears of joy running down her face, whilst the smiling young man picked up her travelling bag. Kitty turned to him, smiling in return, observing, "And you must be young Harry? It's a fine figure of a man ye've grown into!"

The 'fine figure' put down the bag and embraced his Grandma. It was only then that Kitty realised there were two young women just behind Anne and Harry. One with auburn hair and green eyes held a sleeping baby, the second, slightly plump, had light brown hair and a lovely complexion. Introductions were then made.

"Right Mam, you've met Harry. Now here's Nancy - you knew her as Anne, and here's 'miracle baby' Edna. And this is our latest model, Norma."

Kitty hugged her Granddaughters in turn, then she took the sleeping baby from Nancy and gently kissed the child saying, "May the Good Lord bless ye and keep ye safe all the days of your life." Norma opened her eyes, screwing up her face to look briefly at the person who had disturbed her. Then promptly she went back to sleep.

"I can see you've made a big impression on our 'Big Swiss', Gran!" a laughing Harry observed. "Anyway I think we should all make a move. A Tonge Moor tram's due soon." Picking up Kitty's bag, he ushered everyone out of the station.

Once on board the tram, they were soon moving through Bolton's town, down Church Bank Street, and then on to Turner Brow and along

Tonge Moor Road. Finally, they reached the point where the road met Crompton Way. Here, the group alighted and walked the last half-mile, passing under the ever-windy railway bridge to reach the first slope of the terrace where the new corporation houses stood.

There was a brief walk along the terrace passing houses built in mock Tudor style, many were painted in black and white. When they reached the gate of Anne's house, Kitty paused and looked down at the road below where a few carts and cars were travelling. Next she looked over to the fields across from the house, saying, "Ye certainly have a grand house Anne, and it's a fine view ye have too."

A voice from the open doorway asked, "Is that thee, Kitty? 'Ere to see t' new babby? Well get thasel in! Th'ouse is gettin' cowd wi' t' door oppen!" Kitty turned to see Harry standing in the doorway in his slippers. He viewed her over the top of his spectacles then impatiently beckoned everyone to 'get in'. As Kitty walked in, she couldn't resist remarking, "Well Harry, it's some years since I was last here, but I must say ye haven't lost any of your charm!"

Harry ignored the remark and concentrated on getting the door closed.

From the kitchen came the welcome aroma of beef roasting. The Sunday dinner had been prepared and cooked by Harry Senior. Kitty had forgotten what a good savoury cook her son-in-law was - one of his better attributes.

Of course the chatter was non-stop whilst they ate, and also throughout the afternoon. Anne told her mother she would be seeing both Bob and Billy and their families during her stay. Bob would travel by train from Wigan, whilst Billy, now living in Bolton, was only a tram-ride away. Moreover, Kathleen would also be travelling up all the way from Brentford during her mother's stay in Bolton.

That evening, Kitty was more than ready for an early night's sleep and so by eight o'clock she made her way upstairs to sleep in the smaller bedroom vacated by young Harry. He was spending the night in the home of one of his 'boxing' friends.

To Kitty, the 'small' room seemed quite luxurious with its chest of drawers and wardrobe. Also, right next door was the combined lavatory and bathroom. Once in the comfortable bed with its warm eiderdown, sleep embraced her.

❧ ❧ ❧

Over the next few days, Anne and Harry's house was teeming with visitors.

Firstly came Bob and Ellen with their five daughters and son. Ethel, Mabel, Beatrice and Elsie were all now married. The younger twins, Joan and Robert, now aged thirteen, still attended school but were delighted to have the day off to see their Irish Grandma for the first time.

Next day everyone went over to Halliwell Road to see Billy, Jane and their three sons. William, the eldest was a good-looking young man, but as Jane had written, living very much in his own world. He greeted Kitty warmly but showed no signs of recognition. Bob, serving his apprenticeship as a master joiner, arrived after work. On seeing his Grandma he went over to embrace her. He said with a grin, "It's grand to see thee, Gran. I just hope tha's got some 'Uncle Joe's Mint-balls' for me - just like tha used to bring me in Wigan!"

Delighted at the welcome, Kitty laughed, replying, "Well, me lad, I'm afraid Riverstown isn't too familiar with your Uncle Joe!"

Eleven year-old Ronnie was the next to meet Kitty. He was more reserved in his greeting since it was the first time he'd seen her. According to Bob, he was quite a studious and shy boy.

The evening concluded with a variety of sandwiches: boiled ham, tongue, and egg, followed by trifle and an assortment of cakes baked by Jane.

❧ ❧ ❧

On Kitty's last day in Bolton, there was quite a lot of speculation regarding the visitors expected from Brentford. Kathleen was bringing the 'mystery' man, Alfred Hatcher with whom she'd now been living for two years.

"Do you think he'll be tall, dark and handsome, Mam?" Nancy asked.

But small, fair, pugnacious Harry spoke before his wife could reply, "There's nowt special about bein' tall, dark an' 'ansome! It's wot tha's made of wot counts. Southerners are usually mardy buggers who talk posh."

"That'll do Harry!" snapped Anne. "Nobody asked your opinion!"

Nevertheless, Nancy was determined to make a good impression on Alfred Hatcher. She pictured him to be something like the dashing film star, Clark Gable. Accordingly, she put on her favourite deep-pink and white striped dress with its fitted waist. It had a flared hemline which ended just below the knee. When ready, she twirled round and asked Anne, "Well, Mum, how do I look?"

Again, it was Harry who chipped in. He'd been reading the newspaper. Now looking over his spectacles at the hemline in disapproval, he declared, "Its too short! It's showin' tha bloody drawers and backside." Snorting, he returned to his paper.

Anne mouthed, "Take no notice!" but aloud said," You look lovely!"

Edna's contribution to impressing Mr Hatcher was via her cooking. The housewifery lessons at Castle-Hill Secondary School had proved very beneficial, so she was in the kitchen baking vanilla slices.

It was nearly midday when Kathleen and Alfred arrived. They were greeted warmly by everyone and whilst embracing, tears welled in Kitty's and Kathleen's eyes.

A very disappointed Nancy observed that her 'film star' was of medium height, had a fairish complexion, and wore rimless glasses. The only resemblance to Clark Gable was his moustache. In fact, it was Aunt Kathleen who impressed Nancy. She looked years younger than her forty-seven years, and wore a mid-green, plaid skirt which fell just below her knees, she also had on a matching jacket. Her light-green beret was placed at a jaunty angle. Nancy couldn't take her eyes of this attractive, stylish woman.

Edna returned to the kitchen to put the crust on a huge meat and potato pie. And soon the meal was soon ready to eat - and appreciated by everyone. Alfred was full of praise for Edna's cooking. She blushed with pleasure. Harry fixed Alfred with a 'look', remarking, "Aye. I don't suppose tha gets food like that in t' south!"

Chatter and laughter followed the meal as everyone continued exchanging recollections of past events. At seven o'clock young Harry returned from his boxing practice, so Anne announced they could now start the farewell 'party' they'd planned. It was young Harry who started the entertainment with the Irish comedy song, 'Paddy McGinty's Goat' which told of the billy-goat's exploits as well as those of the naughty ladies of the town. Everyone joined in the last lines of each verse - except Harry Senior who considered the only good songs were from the old Music Halls.

Next it was the turn of Nancy and Edna to sing, 'April Showers' which had become a big hit after Al Jolson had sung it at the cinema. There were calls for an encore, though on the second occasion Edna sang solo whilst Nancy danced to the music. Suddenly Kathleen nodded to sister, Anne. Both joined Nancy in the dance.

There was great applause from the onlookers. Even Harry Senior joined in, but then announced, "I'll gi' thee all a song now." And getting up from his favourite armchair by the fire, he began one of his music-hall songs.

'What a mouth, what a mouth, what a north and south!

Blimey, what a mouth he's got!...'

As Harry concluded his contribution, Anne declared firmly,

"Well, I think with *that* song, we can call a halt to proceedings. Kathleen and Alfred have to leave soon to catch the nine o'clock train from Bolton, and Mam wants to end the night with us all singing 'Auld Lang Syne'. It's fitting for this occasion, and it reminds her of her own Scottish mother.

So the 'farewell' song was sung. Embraces and some tears followed. Kitty's 'party' was at an end.

Chapter 70

Kitty's Final Journey

Once safely back in Ireland, Kitty settled down to life with her family there. Denis was eager to know details of her stay in England and was pleased she had been able to see all her four children as well as her grandchildren.

But as the months went by Kitty's health began to deteriorate quite rapidly.

Moving became both painful and slow and she often found difficulties in breathing. She wondered if the two long journeys, plus days filled with excitement, had all been too much for her. At the same time, she realised that the years spent scrubbing and cleaning in God's house might have played its part too.

With the advent of 1935, Kitty was spending much of her time confined to Bed. The pain in all her limbs had increased, and during coughing bouts she was producing a considerable amount of phlegm. At these times Mary proved to be a caring and considerate nurse.

Letters from England helped to take Kitty's mind off her ailments, especially the recent one from Anne. She'd written that though people were aware of increasing threats from Hitler, who now called himself 'The Fuhrer', the effects of the Depression were reducing.

Harry, realising the government's preparations for a possible war were causing the British economy to improve, began to plan for the future. He considered it would be a good time to start his own business in Bolton's indoor market - something he'd wanted for a while. He'd heard of a firm in town who were giving free knitting lessons on their machines. Of course, tuition was dependent on the learner purchasing one of the machines.

The next letter informed Kitty that Harry had had lessons, purchased a machine, and had his name down to buy a hosiery stall in the indoor market! Of course Anne was happy about the new venture. She wrote that Harry had been a quick learner since he'd had plenty of experience of working with machines at the mill.

Kitty was delighted. Both for Anne, and the UK's improving economy.

It was mid- March when Mary went to see if Kitty was ready for some porridge, or if she preferred to sleep after a restless night spent in coughing. But as she neared the bed she was alarmed to hear the painful sound which came from Kitty's throat as she breathed. Worse still, as Mary bent over to speak to her, she could feel the raging heat emanating from Kitty's entire body.

She whispered to her whilst gently feeling her red-hot forehead, "It's alright, Ma, I'll sponge ye down and ye'll feel better."

Kitty's lips moved, but no sound came. Her eyes fluttered open, then shut.

Immediately, Mary ran for Denis. Later that morning Kitty was transferred to the hospital in Sligo Town.

Soon after Kitty's arrival, she was placed in an oxygen tent. For three days, she alternated between fitful sleep and wakefulness. During the latter periods she spoke quite coherently for a while, recognising visitors Denis, Mary and young Mary. Suddenly she would imagine she was a child again, feeding the hens with her mother.

The next day, Kitty woke up early, even before the nurse had come to check on her. She felt better than she'd done for months and, as she lay back on her pillow, more images from her past and eventful life came drifting through her mind.

Now she was holding Sarah's hand as they stood with Mam counting the newly- born lambs in the fields near her home. Both were laughing as they all gave the lambs silly names. But where was Sarah now? She hadn't seen her for such a long time…

Then she heard her father's laugh as he patted her head saying, "Don't worry yourself, my ray of sunshine, sure ye 'll be fine." Reassured by his words, Kitty allowed sleep to take over again for a while. She awoke to find herself sitting in school again next to Mary Mahon. Her friend with the dark hair in its single long plait. Both were excited at the thought of being allowed to help the binders at harvest-time. Then, as suddenly as she'd appeared, Mary became enveloped by a greyish mist - and Kitty was left alone. Patting the spot where her visitor had been, she said wistfully, - "Aye Mary, ye were a good and dear friend to me, such lovely times we had."

Before she could drowse off again, the harsh sound of 'Kaa, Kaa, Kaa' roused Kitty and there on the end of her bed, perched a huge rook with its glossy black feathers and whitish face. At the same time, a young boy's voice called, "Shall we sit here Miss Kitty? It seems a good place for drawing."

"Oh Master Thomas, how grand to see ye again! And I see ye have your book and crayons with ye." As Kitty watched him, she became aware of the figure of a man standing behind the boy. He was smiling at her. As recognition of the 'stranger' slowly dawned upon her, tears came to her eyes, and she struggled to sit up, arms outstretched, murmuring, "Pat, Pat my love! Ye shouldn't be here. But oh how I've missed ye during all the long years!" Pat drew closer to Kitty, saying reproachfully,

"But Kitty darlin', are ye forgetting what I promised ye the day ye left for England? I said we'd be together somehow. And we soon will be. We'll..." Then the grey mist again swirled round the room and gradually disappeared from sight taking Pat with it.

Gazing sadly at the spot where Pat had appeared, Kitty softly spoke, "Our love gave me a fine son. One who's forgiven me despite my wrong doings. But what about my brothers and sisters? Will they ever forgive the shame I brought upon them?" At last blessed sleep overcame her again. And in that sleep, Kitty had a dream.

Around the bed stood her parents and siblings, all smiling. Then her sister, Mary Anne spoke, "Ach! What eejit thoughts! Sure none of us ever stopped loving ye!" And one by one, everyone in turn planted a kiss on her brow, then left. Immediately, all her children entered the room, including Lizzie, and all her grandchildren. Like the Tooeys, they gently and lovingly kissed her brow. Last of all she saw Robert. Wistfully, he blew her a kiss.

❧ ❧ ❧

It was about an hour later that the nurse went in to tend to Kitty. At once, she brought in the doctor and also Denis. The latter had waited outside his mother's room all night. The doctor spoke quietly to her 'son'. "I'm sorry Mr Dowd, your mother is unconscious and won't last much longer. It's possible she may be able to hear ye if ye'd like to have your last words with her.

The priest had also been sent for and gave her the last rites. A tearful Dennis said his 'Good byes' to his much loved mother.

The death certificate referred to Denis as Kitty's 'son-in-law'. He had deemed it the most diplomatic way of referring to himself. Kitty was buried in the 'Dowd' grave. Reunited at last with her first love, and in the land of her birth, she was at last able to sleep in peace.

It had indeed been a long way home for Kitty.

Sources of Reference

Adelman, P., & Pearce, R. (2001, second edition), *Great Britain and the Irish Question, 1800-1922*, Hodder & Stoughton

Ashton, J. (2021), First -hand information regarding his Grandfather, James Carr.

Bagley, J.J. (1967, fourth edition) *A History of Lancashire*, Darwen Finlayson Ltd.

Bunting, K (2020) Information on new industries at the turn of the century.

Bunting, R. A. (2020-21) Research and certificates regarding English and New Zealand descendants of Edward & Margaret Wyllie. Robert Gibbs and Catherine (Kitty) are her Great Grandparents.

Clear, C.(2007) *Social change and everyday life in Ireland,1850-1922*, Manchester University Press.

Cruse, L. (2001) Research and documents regarding her Great Grandmother, Catherine/Kathleen Carr and also Catherine's daughters, Anne and Edna.

Feiling, K. (1972) *A History of England*, Book Club Associates.

Frith, F.(2000) *Around Southport*, Frith Book Co. Ltd.

Gascoigne, B. (1994) *Encyclopedia of Britain*, Macmillan Press.

Gailey, A. (1983) *Rural Houses of the North of Ireland*, John Donald Publishers Ltd.

Gibbs, N. (2019) Information regarding his parents, William (son of Catherine/'Kitty') and Jane Gibbs.

Gibbs, P. (2020) Information regarding his Grandfather, Robert Gibbs Jnr.

Hannovy, J.(1990) *Historic Wigan: Two Thousand Years of History*. Carnegie Publishing.

Hannovy, J. (2003) *History & Guide: Wigan*. Tempus Publishing Ltd.

Holt, A.(1944-61) First-hand recollections of her mother, Catherine/Kitty.

Holt, P. (2019-21) Newspaper cuttings from Wigan newspapers regarding his Great Grandparents, Robert and Catherine/'Kitty' Gibbs during the late 19th century.

Jelley, A. (2020) Information regarding his Grandma, Sarah, sister of Catherine/'Kitty. Sarah emigrated to New Zealand in 1883.

Keating, D. (Ceitinn, D. County Mayo, 2018-22) Extensive research and certificates regarding County Sligo, the Wyllie family and the Dowd family.

Lowe, W.J. (2005) *Irish Constabulary Officers 1837-1922: profile of a professional elite,* I.E.S.H., vol.32, pp 19-36

Makin, L.(2022),Wigan Heritage Services. Helping with my research on Wigan in the late 19th century.

Marsh, E. (2021) First-hand information regarding her father, Richard Holden, son of Alice and Dick Holden.

Marsh, S. (2012) Information regarding Bolton Market in its early days.

Mills, F. (2020) Information on the work of a roof slater.

Mudd, D.J. (2020) Information on the life of sea-men in the nineteenth century. Robert Gibbs and Catherine/Kitty are his Great Grandparents.

Orwell, G. (1937) *The Road to Wigan Pier,* Penguin Books.

Taylor, A.J.P. (1966) *The First World War,* Penguin Books.

AUTHOR'S NOTES

My book is based on information which I have obtained regarding my maternal Grandmother, Catherine Tooey (ie Kitty) and also my imagination.

Born in County Sligo, Kitty emigrated to England about 1878, married Robert Gibbs in 1884 and returned to Ireland a few years after his death in about 1920. She died in Riverstown, Co Sligo in 1935. Denis Dowd was present at her death (on the death certificate, he referred to himself as 'son-in-law').

Kitty's story is also based on certificates, press cuttings and first-hand information from several relatives. Throughout my story of Grandma, I considered it important to include some of the historical and political events of her life-time.

My DNA test resulted in me discovering 'new' relations with connections to the Tooey family, ie. Arch Jelley in New Zealand (Grandson of Kitty's sister, Sarah). I have also met in person his son, Martin Jelley. Other new 'cousins' that I have met are Philip and Richard Gibbs as well as Jimmy Ashton and Lesley Cruse. Lesley and I have become good friends.

For readers interested in the family, I have included the names of the ten Tooey children (in likely order of birth). Mary Anne, Edward, Margery, Sarah, Catherine, Anne, Margaret (Madge), Alexander, David, William.

Also, I have included the names of those who emigrated:

Catherine /Kitty - Wigan, England - 1878

Mary Anne	- Wigtown, Scotland - 1880
Sarah	- Otago, South Island, New Zealand - 1883
Anne	- New York, America - 1891
Margery	- One of her children, May, went to live with her Aunt Anne in New York - date unknown
Alexander	- served in the Irish Army and later joined the American Army - date unknown

Edward had worked on Sligo Cargo ships since his early teens. When aged 29 years he drowned at sea in 1886, place unknown.